College Teaching:
Its Practice and Its Potential

BY

JOSEPH JUSTMAN
PROFESSOR OF EDUCATION, BROOKLYN COLLEGE

AND

WALTER H. MAIS
PROFESSOR OF PHYSICS, BROOKLYN COLLEGE

HARPER & BROTHERS: PUBLISHERS: NEW YORK

Library of Congress catalog card number: 56–6439

LB
2331
J8

CONTENTS

PREFACE

In writing this book we have been sensitive to the requirements which college teachers impose upon colleagues bearing gifts of professional advice and assistance. We do not presume to tell college teachers how to teach. Our aim is to help the college teacher or prospective college teacher toward a better vision and accomplishment of his professional undertaking without, however, disputing his privilege to decide for himself what constitutes good theory and practice. Accordingly the substance of this book represents a considered mean between a discussion of educational principles and a compendium of specific practices. Our hope is to contribute to an imaginative and forward-looking conception of the college teacher's job as a whole, yet realistically to assist him in the performance of his daily functions. That such a book is needed in these days of mounting college enrollments, augmented teaching staffs, and increased teachers' responsibilities we have no cause to question. That so ambitious a project may turn out to be beyond our capabilities is possible, though we remain hopeful.

The exposition of principles and practices in college teaching has too often been separated from the discussion of aims and purposes of higher education. Such separation of naturally allied ends and means seems to us regrettable, although we recognize its necessity at times. In this book we have endeavored to relate instructional practice to its underlying rationale in educational purpose: beginning with a statement of goals in college teaching, we develop in succeeding chapters various special aspects of the teacher's responsibility which stem from this general commitment. The reader will note this consistency in thought even if he disagrees with one or another of its postulates. For an acceptable formulation of objectives or goals in higher education we have drawn upon the main currents of contemporary thought and practice, avoiding entanglement with any special cult or "school of thought" as strenuously as we have re-

frained from riding our personal hobbies. Although it is not our
intention that the college teacher should be a conformist, we are not
trying to produce professional dissidents either.

The literature of higher education is still in the making. On some
aspects of college teaching substantial information is available, while
on others the volume of publication is meager. No amount of personal experience in teaching can adequately cover the gaps in our
knowledge concerning, for example, the nature of the learning
process or experimentally validated teaching methods. The problem
is one which concerns the entire profession even more than the occasional author. We have made no effort to conceal these shortcomings, our own and those which we share with our colleagues. Rather,
by drawing attention to unexplored problems in college teaching we
hope to stimulate further thought and investigation by others.

Our qualifications for writing this book are based as much on
consuming interest in the subject as on any demonstrable credentials
of competence. The larger part of two professional lifetimes has been
spent in teaching college students, and in study of and practical
experience with related professional functions including the supervision of instruction and curriculum planning and development.
Notwithstanding, we feel our limitations keenly. For what we have
learned we are indebted, first, to the many classes of students we
have instructed in our two distinct disciplines and, second, to the
colleagues within our institution and outside of it with whom we
have worked on common tasks. We have made use of the recent
literature of higher education to a greater extent than we can
specifically acknowledge.

JOSEPH JUSTMAN

WALTER H. MAIS

COLLEGE TEACHING:

ITS PRACTICE AND ITS POTENTIAL

I. *Goals of College Teaching*

Since discussion of the college teacher's activities requires a frame of reference, the logical way to begin is with a statement of the goals of instruction. Actually few matters pertaining to college teaching are more difficult to state. Professional experience may qualify a teacher to speak with authority on specific aspects of instruction, but what gives him the same right to determine goals? What *are* the right goals of teaching? Few questions produce a greater diversity of answers, and originality here is not a criterion of worth. Yet if education is to be conducted with any measure of consistency there should be common effort at understanding and agreeing upon objectives.

The goals of college teaching proposed here are not presumed to be the sole, true, or "right" goals. All that is claimed on their behalf is that they are reasonable and that they could be right, and even this the reader must judge for himself. The following criteria may assist in making such judgment:

1. Are the proposed goals important and feasible? Do they seem justified by the arguments offered in their support?
2. Are they mutually consistent and do they contribute to an organized conception of college teaching?
3. Are they sufficiently clear and definite to serve as a practical guide to teaching and learning?

There is no feeling of assurance that the goals will be accepted as offered nor any wish that they should be. Educational progress results not from ready concurrence but from giving hard thought to important issues. Independent exploration and assent are necessary conditions of consensus regardless of how we may strain for the latter. If the proposed goals are unacceptable to the reader, it is hoped that he will formulate or review his own, subjecting them to equally strict examination.

Lack of Clarity Regarding Ulterior Goals. Most college teachers would agree that instruction has aims broader than the simple mastery of subject matter. The test of successful teaching is in how the student has learned to live. Every teacher of liberal or applied studies sees in his subject a contribution to an educated way of living; unless a subject of study holds such promise it is not an educational discipline. Education deals with human growth—in mind, spirit, character, and effective behavior—and every subject of instruction is a tool employable toward this end. Important as is the student's immediate mastery of a subject, advancement toward the less patent ulterior goals of instruction is of greater moment. A portion of what is learned today is forgotten tomorrow. What remains and becomes the base for further growth is that which enters into a person's make-up, changes his habits and attitudes, reconstitutes his ideals, and enlarges his interests. Every teacher knows this and shapes his teaching accordingly. Which science teacher is not aware that through biology, chemistry, geology, or physics he is seeking to instil not inert information but insights into laws and processes of nature, ways of acquiring knowledge and truth about the material world, appreciation of how others have worked and learned, and interests that will challenge the students' imagination and effort?

In varying extent teachers understand what they hope ultimately to accomplish. But this understanding is not sufficiently defined and commonly shared to assure the best results in teaching. Teaching is not an individualistic process in which teachers may proceed in separate directions. Indefiniteness of purpose, conflict or inconsistency, duplication, or collective neglect or omission operate to the disadvantage of students. Not even a believer in *laissez faire* would maintain that liberal education can be accomplished without some common recognition of aims and some coordinated effort. Current shortcomings of college teaching need not be accentuated in order to drive home the point. It is not true that we drift in seas of learning without chart, compass, or rudder; it is probably true that outcomes and conduct of instruction could be improved were we inspired with clearer mutual realization of purposes.

To say that we aim at "liberal" or "general" education is not enough.

The term "general education" [writes Clarence H. Faust] like the term "liberty" and "equality" has acquired a wide range of meanings, including some irreconcilable ones. It cannot be defined by the simple expedient of pointing to examples. . . . Almost every college in the country, if presidents, deans, and catalogues are to be believed, provides a general or liberal education for its undergraduates, but it is impossible to discover any substantial common element in the educational program of our colleges.[1]

Not that college programs should necessarily have a large common element: as instruments of education they may vary widely. But the ends for which they are being used should have strong elements of identity, else we are not educating for the same purposes or do not clearly know what we are educating for.

It is not for want of effort that the goals of college teaching have not been clearly established. A sizeable literature on the subject exists, but for various reasons much of it has not been practically influential. Sometimes the language of discourse, though literate and urbane, is not readily translatable into teaching and learning experience. What sounds uplifting in a commencement address or witty and wise in an informal essay may not be usable in planning a course of instruction.[2] Some of the literature has been too forensic, bent on out-arguing the other fellow rather than stating the case fairly for both sides, thus diminishing its effect on many in the profession who

[1] *The Idea and Practice of General Education* (Chicago: University of Chicago Press, 1950), pp. 4–5.

[2] On the other hand, there have been practical and realistic attempts to come to grips with the problem. See for example *The Idea and Practice of General Education*, cited above; Huston Smith's *The Purposes of Higher Education* (New York: Harper & Brothers, 1955); the two Harvard publications, *General Education in a Free Society* (1945), and *General Education in School and College* (1952); *A Handbook for College Teachers*, B. B. Cronkhite, ed. (Cambridge: Harvard University Press, 1950); Ordway Tead's *College Teaching and College Learning* (New Haven: Yale University Press, 1949), and *Character Building and Higher Education* (New York: The Macmillan Company, 1953); and Harry D. Gideonse's "On Re-Thinking Liberal Education" in *Strengthening Education at All Levels,* Report of Eighteenth Educational Conference (Washington: American Council on Education, 1953).

have remained open-minded and accessible to reasonable argument. We spend much of our substance driving out "demons" who aren't there or who are possibly, after all, not demons—the elective system, specialization, emphasis on science, vocationalism, progressivism, and the like.[3] Added to the inherent difficulty of dealing with a subject so abstract, these tendencies may help to explain why we have fallen short of clarifying instructional objectives.

We need an affirmative statement of teaching goals almost as definite as the Ten Commandments, almost as compelling in their conviction. This we shall never get, and even as an ideal it is too remote. What we can have is clarification of what we are attempting in our effort to further the student's education. The goals should be sound in terms of society's needs and the learning behavior of the student; clear and definite so that they can be understood and their acceptability determined; formulated in terms which make evaluation of outcomes possible; and applicable in such a way as to stimulate creative effort in teaching. This is a tall order.

Misconceptions Concerning the Goals of College Teaching. 1. *That they are universal and absolute.* There is a tendency to assume that the goals of higher education are universal in range and immutable in character. If only they could be identified! It is true that some of our stated ideals have not changed much through the ages: love of God, the brotherhood of man, ideals of truth, integrity, courage, and justice are part of a universal tradition transcending the limits of time, place, and order of society. Not all ideals, however, are of equal universality and permanence. The values of religion are not conceived by us precisely as they were in the Middle Ages, and the concept of justice has changed by historical evolution. No civilization can evade the task of examining universal values and translating them into working principles consistent with the demands of its own age. For education to base its goals on universal ideals as abstractions would be to attempt to build a sound structure of human character on a foundation of words: the result might be ornamental but is sure to be substantively defective.

Even granting the existence of truly universal ideals, the goals of

[3] See, for example, citations from discussion of the elective system, in Freeman Butts' *The College Charts Its Course* (New York: McGraw-Hill Book Company, 1939), Chapter XV.

teaching cannot be limited to such. Other values claiming the allegiance not of the whole but of only a fraction of mankind may have equal or greater significance, viz., Christianity, democracy, the Anglo-Saxon concept of jurisprudence. The Christian religion is not universal in the sense that it is not accepted by a majority of the world's population; the ideal of democracy is alien to some of the world's largest nations; democratic England and democratic France follow different systems of legal justice. Yet it would be unthinkable to fail to include among goals of instruction the ideals of Christianity, democracy, and our inherited legal tradition. Furthermore, new ideals are constantly in the making: in their emergent stages they may be understood by and acceptable to a relative few. Yet they cannot be neglected in college teaching.

In formulating goals of instruction it is not sufficient to assume that we can adopt without reservation ready-made ideals culturally transmitted to us. We must fashion our own goals by analyzing both our traditional inheritance and the more recent and emerging principles by which our way of life is being ordered. Each generation has an obligation to do this for itself.

2. *That they are epitomized in the term "training the mind."* For many teachers a statement of goals in such terms as "clear and disciplined thinking, sound reasoning, knowledge and intellectual power" carries conviction. These are important goals, but two things must be considered with reference to them. First, they are not as attainable as their facile expression might lead us to believe. It takes more than a daily diet of grammar, rhetoric, logic, mathematics, or any prescribed study successfully to train the mind. We have long experimented with this sort of training in one form or another, and though we have succeeded in educating some students, we have failed lamentably with others. It is not intelligent to propose, as some have, to keep this method of training and discard the unsuccessful students. We need other forms of training as well, concerning some of which our knowledge may still be scanty. Possibly the ends of formal discipline are more attainable indirectly, by nourishing the mind with a variety of studies rich in substantive experience rather than through a few specified formal subjects. Intellectual discipline is a creditable goal but its difficulty of attainment should not be un-

derestimated nor experimentation with more productive ways of achieving it abated.

Second, training the mind is not enough. Man is not all mind: he has feelings, emotions, physical needs, and a corporeal existence. Mind itself needs to be not only trained but also equipped with ideals to guide its reasoning, interests to challenge its imagination, and something "to think about." A moral character and an exemplary way of life are not inevitably the outgrowth of good mental processes. The effective thinker may be a scoundrel or a decent person, an atheist or a devout believer, a democratic person or an authoritarian, a demagogue or a statesman. Without a rich substance of knowledge a disciplined thinker may be an arid person; without positive faith and ideals, a lost and unhappy one.

To an extent the intelligent person creates his own world of knowledge and belief, and so forms his own character and way of life. But not entirely; and in any event he must have a foundation from which to proceed. The creative intellectual life is mainly that of reconstructing one's ideas and beliefs, not of building them *de novo*. The resultant philosophy of life must to a degree be common with that held by others in the same cultural setting. It is given to few gifted individuals to formulate a unique philosophy of life and hold it against the onslaughts of shared experience. Education is not a game of chance played with the lives of individual youth, but an organized attempt by society to perpetuate and improve itself by influencing young people to follow in its footsteps, adopting what is best around them and carrying it toward higher levels of achievement.

3. *That there is inherent conflict between liberal and practical values.* It would be good for education if the ghost of this ancient argument were finally laid to rest. On this issue practice has outdistanced theory: while the historic debate is continued, there are few liberal colleges which do not include among their offerings preprofessional or utilitarian courses, and almost half the youth in higher education are enrolled in colleges of agriculture, business, education, engineering, journalism, technology and other applied arts and sciences. Is it right to conclude that colleges have become illiberal to the extent that they have admitted courses in business administration, personnel management, labor economics, industrial

psychology, and social work, or that youth in specialized colleges are being largely denied a liberal education? A fairer conclusion would be that a redefinition of liberal education is taking place which, avoiding the old dichotomy between liberal and practical learning, seeks to synthesize elements of both into a new compound serving practical as well as cultural needs.

There might have been a time when utilitarian demands on living did not exact so heavy a tribute on intelligence. One could earn a livelihood, attend to family and social wants, and use his leisure time for intellectual and creative pursuits challenging his talent and imagination. (It is doubtful that the time ever existed when problems of economic survival, statecraft, social organization, and achievement in higher occupations did not drain off a large portion of human intellectual energy: the difference between formerly and now may be one of degree.) Contemporary living, however, commands all the intelligence of which one is capable. Well-trained minds are engaged not only in cultivating the arts of scholarship but also in directing business and industrial enterprises, solving engineering problems, inventing machines and ways of using them, developing mass media of communication, administering public affairs, and other tasks both difficult and critically important. Many of these tasks call not only for a staunch mind in an almost indestructible body, but for a great deal of specialized "know-how" which cannot be gained without specific training. The self-made engineer is virtually nonexistent and the self-trained industrialist is becoming increasingly rare. Yet these people most require the values which liberal education can afford.

The majority of college graduates will not be captains of industry or leaders in public affairs. They will be men and women engaged in a middle-income occupation who aspire to be effective citizens, parents, friends and neighbors, and private individuals. They also require an education which goes beyond the abstractions of the historic disciplines and comes to grips with the real problems of living. Their education should be liberal enough to encompass those personal, social, political, economic, and even vocational problems with which they need help. An education so general that it lacks the capacity to explore these problems is not adequate.

There is small danger that, in affording such education, colleges will be diverted from their mission of liberalizing students into one of providing narrow forms of training. That *could* happen if the colleges were not alert to their task of using the substance of studies not as an end in itself but as a means of fostering breadth and depth of understanding, the power to use knowledge, and the character to use it properly. Things have not come to such a pass. The problem before us is to establish and maintain for each student the appropriate balance of cultural and functional learning experience which will fit him for the pursuits of living.

The same argument applies to specialized colleges which have emphasized training for specific occupational endeavors. An exclusive training of this sort does not prepare a person for comprehensive living, and may not even be the best sort of vocational preparation. It is men of creative imagination and disciplined thought who make advances in professional discovery or invention. A trained specialist in business, engineering, or medicine may be nonetheless a poor citizen and inadequate human being. These institutions need to liberalize their goals, reducing but not eliminating their distinctive emphasis. The object should not be to imitate liberal institutions of learning but to widen students' educational horizon so that they gain in effectiveness as cultivated persons and members of society.

Elements of Permanence in College Education.[4] Much in college instruction is in continuation of a tradition extending from the beginning of civilization. In the course of its history mankind has accumulated learnings essential to survival, social stability and development, and individual growth; tempered and refined by experience, these learnings have become embodied in the tradition transmitted from one generation to the next. The continuing refinement of tradition and its perpetuation are an important function of college teaching.

Conflict has developed concerning the role of tradition in education. Actually traditional learnings are an indispensable tool in human development, and we could use more of them than we possess. Only a fraction of the knowledge that mankind has acquired has been preserved and transmitted. A person in his lifetime learns more than he can convey to another; a culture remote from us in time or

[4] See also Sidney Hook, "Perennial and Temporal Goals in Education," *Journal of Higher Education,* 23:1–12 (January 1952).

place may have mastered the art of peaceful living to an extent unknown to us today, but we are dependent for knowledge of that culture upon the piecemeal and partial discoveries of the research worker. Each generation makes some contribution to living which it never can transmit in full to its successors. All the more reason for cherishing what we have, and trying to recover more. But it is wrong to assume that the essence of traditional learnings has been carefully distilled and placed within convenient reach—that it is available, for example, in certain books, disciplines, or religious or secular institutions. Our tradition is in unorganized as well as organized learnings discoverable wherever men gather and in whatever they do. Not being neatly classified, they must be dug out, sorted, and evaluated. Reliance upon tradition calls for discriminating selection and use of learnings. To affirm that education must be rooted in tradition is not to waive responsibility for identifying the traditional elements valid for present purposes.

The most enduring traditional elements in a world of material change are ethical and moral concepts governing relations of people, and esthetic standards guiding their tastes. A teacher can impart few things of greater worth than the inherited ideals, beliefs, attitudes, and principles of right and graceful living and their application to contemporary experience. But even fundamental ethical, moral, and esthetic learnings do not always come forward and identify themselves, and they do not teach themselves. Responsibility for presenting them to students must be assumed by every teacher on all educational levels, and teaching them calls for subtle skill.

To this portion of the traditional heritage should be added the intellectual: tools of thought and of expression, ways of learning and of assessing knowledge, and a large storehouse of ideas and information on almost every conceivable subject. It is manifestly impossible to convey all or most of the intellectual heritage; it is essential to convey that portion of it which has close relevance to present and future living. A college education which chose to turn its back on the intellectual tradition would be no education at all, while one which sought mainly to recapitulate past learning would be equally misguided. The problem is to choose carefully from the past that which can light the way toward the future. Study of Aristotelian philosophy is justifiable even in a crowded college curriculum, but as much cannot be said of Aristotelian science or psychology. Wholesome respect for the intellectual tradition need not blind us to its limitations: it constitutes a foundation for education, not the whole structure.

Some of the most important intellectual learnings are in the form of ideals to the development of which mankind, past and present, has collectively contributed: intellectual honesty, objectivity in assessment of knowledge and in forming conclusions, the practice of thinking logically, brushing away irrelevancies, of organizing ideas clearly, validating sources of information, checking references, questioning authority, thinking experimentally, and pursuing the truth wherever it leads. It is on this element of our tradition, rather than on obsolete theories or information, that emphasis in instruction should be placed. The danger is that we may take these outcomes for granted, without assuming explicit obligation for them. Ideals and values are formed only as opportunity is afforded for using them in meaningful experience.

Tradition has given us the ideal of the balanced person—balanced in qualities of mind, character, and body, with respect to personal aims and social obligations, between a yearning for freedom and a respect for order, between individuality and conformity. We should not abandon this ideal through improper emphasis on the intellectual or the spiritual or the materialistic. Liberal education is itself a great historic concept which though re-examined and adapted to a changed world, should remain our steady objective.

—**And of Change.** There are aspects of college teaching for which no precedents exist. It is unnecessary here to review the major developments in our time which have created unique problems in education. Mention of a few patent facts should suffice. One is the size and constituency of the college population.[5] There has never been a time when so large and varied a student body was engaged in pursuit of higher education. The consequence has been not only an increase and enlargement of institutions of learning, but a fundamental change in the meaning of college education. To the new problems confronting us the old familiar answers do not apply. Educating two and a half million students is a different task from ed-

[5] This subject is more fully treated in Chapter IV.

ucating one quarter of a million.[6] Basic matters must be reconsidered including goals of instruction, courses of study, teaching methods, and even educational standards. To a growing extent changes along these lines are being effected. One may not like the changes, but realistically one has to admit the need for new thinking on the intent and method of higher education.

Another factor of educational change lies in the increased complexities of living in the modern world. With due respect to past ages, there was never a time when "life, liberty, and the pursuit of happiness" presented so much of a challenge to the capacities of the human intellect. The need for understanding and living intelligently in the world is matched only by the difficulty of so doing: only the simple-minded nowadays feel confident that they know what is happening. In a relatively short time our social world has undergone revolutionary changes, and the revolution still proceeds. In a material sense fundamental ways of life have probably been altered more within the last century than in all the previous period since Europe's emergence from the Dark Ages. Social scientists have been kept busy cataloguing the changes and noting their effects, but even they tend to be left behind by the sweep of events.

Not every aspect of living has been thus affected, nor has it been equally difficult to accommodate to all changes. Many problems of material existence have been simplified. Though the extent of knowledge is greater, our access to it is easier, and there is no reason to assume that in time even the most perplexing of our social problems cannot be understood and resolved with hard and patient work. But we should not underestimate the task of educating students in an understanding of society and the art of good citizenship. It is improper to assume that, because in the past persons with general liberal training acquitted themselves creditably in the exercise of social and civic responsibilities without specific directive instruction, students can be relied upon to continue to do so in the future. It is safer to take steps to assure that a college education, in addition to its scholastic values, should also help young people to become alert, sensitive, and contributing members of society.

The college teacher is faced with a task which, though not novel,

[6] In 1900 the college enrollment was approximately 240,000.

is more difficult than formerly—the making of citizens. *How* this is to be done constitutes a problem, considering the size and diversity of the student population and the number and potency of conditioning influences outside the school. It cannot be done through any one prescribed course of study, specific allotment of course credits, or examination. Training in citizenship is a function shared by teachers in all courses of instruction, and by the program of informally guided extracurricular experience. How the student is directed in use of social and leisure-time campus activity may have as much bearing on training in citizenship as any courses of formal instruction.

The size and composition of the student population and the greater challenge in educating for citizenship are two factors contributing toward change in higher education. There are others, each involving instructional obligations differing in degree and kind from those of the past: more general need for systematic occupational orientation, for fostering mental and emotional well-being in times characterized by hurry and tension, for productive use of leisure in an urbanized environment featured by mechanical "labor-saving" devices, for spiritual stability and a humanistic sense of values in a world adrift. In sum, as college teaching looks toward preserving what is best in our past, so should it address itself, less confidently perhaps, toward meeting the new demands of the present and the future.

Goals of Instruction

By indirection some important goals of college teaching have already been suggested. The following summary offers not a comprehensive listing of all major goals of instruction but rather a selection of those toward which common instructional effort should be directed. If any slight has been incurred, it is with respect to special values which may accrue from the study of a specific subject. Such neglect is tantamount to admission that in imparting to able and interested students the distinctive values of its respective disciplines, college teaching does well. Instruction in mathematics succeeds in turning out able young mathematicians, and the study of history fine future historians. College teachers should continue to emphasize their specialized aims in instruction but pursue also the common general goals involving all students.

1. *Physical and mental health.* Higher education cannot be occupied with cultivation of the intellect to the neglect of other forms of development. Its business is the cultivation of the whole person in all the respects essential for competent living. While its responsibilities do not extend to such learnings as the student can attain for himself or as other educative agencies can provide better, it has an obligation to assess progress toward balanced attainment and furnish help whenever needed. The development of physical and mental health falls partly in this category.

Modern living places great strain on the human biological system. Medicine has performed wonders in conquering disease, setting up health safeguards, and extending the span of life but has not been notably successful in reducing disabling nervous and mental disorders. To reach old age is not unusual, but to live one's life with serenity and mental composure seems more difficult. A person's constitution is part of his native endowment and there is a limit to what environmental influences and formal training agencies can do toward fortifying it. But to the extent that education can foster good health through instillation of knowledge, habits, attitudes, and interests, it has an obligation to do so.

By the time the student reaches college his basic patterns of healthful living have been formed. It is the college's function to induce intelligent self-examination of these patterns, their reconstruction where necessary, and the cultivation of additional healthful pursuits and interests designed to carry a person successfully through a lifetime. A fact deserving of greater attention than it receives is that college graduates in the main lead an existence requiring less than average muscular activity and greater "wear and tear" of the vascular and nervous systems. More appropriate propaedeutic health programs could be devised than are now in use.

Health and physical education are important, but the goal of healthful living requires more than this. Physical well-being is not enough to insure mental health unless a person is fortified with strength and breadth of spirit to which liberal-arts study contributes more than calisthenics. In a sense the entire college course is a program in health education, and every teacher a contributor to health development to the extent that his instruction promotes a sense of values and a constructive philosophy of life.

2. *Ethical and moral quality.* The college has wonderful material to work with, and exceptional opportunity to train outstanding men and women. Without reflecting on the college-trained product, it is questionable whether this is achieved to the extent possible. We tend to honor in the abstract the principle of ethical and moral education, but to practice it incidentally, only as occasions offer cause for commendation or reproach. That we are successful is more of a tribute to the quality of our students than the result of conscious, persistent effort to make character training a central goal of instruction. If teachers undertook to cultivate ethical and moral ideals as resolutely as they cultivate knowledge, society would profit greatly. There are never enough men and women of outstanding integrity, moral courage, and independence of spirit to discharge the exacting responsibilities of leadership and to stimulate others by their example.

In a sense befitting the college, the aim of character education is to produce responsible people who "stand on their own feet"; who apply with sensitive and honest discrimination standards of right and wrong and do not fear to stand by their judgment; whose pattern of conforming or nonconforming behavior is dictated by decency, good sense, and regard for truth, not by convention, expediency, laziness, or desire to be "different."

Character [writes Tead][7] is manifested in a certain personal resolution and determination to adhere persistently to the best the person knows and can discover in his choices of activity and commitment. Character denotes a capacity to stand and having done all to stand with courage and perseverance, with willingness and with ability to face up to and pay the price of consequences of decisions personally arrived at as wise or sound . . . Fidelity to rational and defensible standards is a hallmark of the person of character. The care which the individual exercises in establishing, evaluating, and revising the standards used to shape his decisions is itself a further index to his fidelity. Ability to criticize, revalue, and bring into a more comprehensive system of values one's always extending body of experience is a character attribute no less than an intellectual one.

[7] Ordway Tead, *Character Building and Higher Education* (New York: The Macmillan Company, 1953), p. 19.

Considering the diversity of forces at play, college education is not among the most formative influences in character development. The student's character has been shaped by heredity, family training, environmental associations, the church, and earlier school experience. What the college can do is to serve as an intellectualizing, coordinating, and when necessary corrective influence, helping the student to transform precepts into principles and to organize principles into a personal philosophy, to know and improve himself as a person, and to be more resolute in the exercise of rationally justified conviction.

3. *Intellectual independence.* There is no adequate substitute for the old disciplinary ideal of the trained mind. Knowledge is unavailing without the power to use it, and ethical values need intelligence to guide their application. Disagreement with the theory of formal discipline does not imply rejection of its ideal; such disagreement centers on the exclusiveness of the ideal, and the narrow and questionable means used in furthering it. Modern educational thought is more inclined to the assumption that any intellectual pursuit rich in substance and comprehensible in terms of the student's experience can be an instrument of mental training, provided the mind is exercised thereby. Mastery of content is important, but a more permanent goal should be that of developing the powers and habits of mind requisite to independent acquisition of knowledge, evaluation, and application in use. Intellectual independence is at a premium in both individual or collective pursuits. "Our goal in education is to help students to help themselves, each with his own set of qualities, his own background of family and neighborhood, his own inherited and acquired philosophy, and whatever particular future may be his." [8]

The problem is how to do it. If sampled observation may be trusted, much of current teaching practice reflects the assumption that by engaging in study of a powerful subject the student is concomitantly learning to think well. Creditable independent achievement is recognized and rewarded, but not nearly enough is done to stimulate and train the student in the exercise of independent effort reaching toward progressively higher levels of achievement. We tend

[8] Max S. Marshall, *Two Sides to a Teacher's Desk* (New York: The Macmillan Company, 1953), p. 11.

to forget that only to a limited degree is growth in independent power automatic. Instructional emphasis on factual attainment will produce the informed person, emphasis on techniques the technician. To foster creative and critical thought instruction must elicit a quality of learning which stimulates initiative, imagination, and the exercise of mind in rigorous and productive operation.

The nub of the problem is in the conception of what constitutes teaching and learning. If teaching means imparting subject matter, and learning a process by which the student assimilates his own respectable share, this is one thing; if teaching is conceived as enhancing the student's realization of the values of a subject, helping him to bring to bear his own resources in formulating and pursuing a method of attack, and guiding him in the process, that is another. The college curriculum is not perfect, but with the exception of disputable fringe courses, offerings as currently constituted are potential disciplinary tools. There is enough in the college program to provide every student with a lasting intellectually-formative experience without returning to older discarded studies. It remains to teach them as they should be taught.

4. *Deep intellectual interests.* It is not possible to encompass within the years of schooling all the education a person needs to carry him through life. When the compulsions of formal study have ceased, a person assumes his own obligation to continued self-education. While the urgency of practical need provides incentive for some self-education, self-impelling intellectual interests must account for the rest. A person continues to grow as his interests inspire him to sustained quest for knowledge and its improved use.

Continuance of self-education in adulthood is too important to be left to chance opportunity and experience. Our accomplishment on this score is not good. Too many college-trained people, once they leave college, slough off serious intellectual pursuits other than those related to professional and economic demands, settling down to a routine of social and avocational living offering little exercise to talent and imagination. Tastes become conventionalized and distinctive capacities stunted through disuse. Able people "relax" in their evenings reading detective stories or picture magazines and watching television shows. In time such habitual relaxation draws them away from the main streams of intellectual and artistic life in which they are competent to participate, leaving them subject to the common inanities of leisure-time "enjoyment." Strong interests may not assure a flourishing intellectual existence but they are a potent force in this direction.

Instruction in any subject should include among its goals the cultivation of interests looking beyond the immediate requirements of study. No great problem presents itself with those students who early reveal a special inclination for the subject; it takes poor teaching to discourage students with, for example, a strong bent for mathematics or art or literature. The problem is greater with students who show no special preference for a field of study. The situation then provides a test of teaching skill, and though it may be unrealistic to expect to engage every student's interest, some students should be reached. There is room for differences in intellectual tastes, and students should be free to choose as their special interests subjects toward which they feel most congenial. A person need not distribute his interests widely over the cultural landscape, but each should cultivate *some* beyond those serving immediate utilitarian needs. Interests productive of growth through avocational activity should be particularly encouraged.

In the final analysis each teacher must determine for himself how this may be accomplished. Some general principles hold true: interests are generated through challenging but satisfying learning experience, when students become convinced that they can make a contribution to a subject which they hold in high esteem, when they are so deeply drawn into the subject that they become captive to its inherent demand for mastery. The approach to instruction cannot be lackadaisical or impersonal ("those who can will learn") or from the viewpoint "for specialists only." The teacher must present his subject so as to make it appealing to students, try to involve each student personally, elicit from him an ever-increasing contribution of effort, and help him to realize as much as possible from his intellectual investment.

5. *Enlightened citizenship.* While the obligation to educate for citizenship requires no justification, it may be necessary to explain why it is incumbent upon the college, following twelve years of earlier schooling, to assume this as a specific function. All organized instruction concerns itself with the training of citizens, and to the

extent that the learner's capacity permits, instils understanding, ideals, attitudes, and habits of approved civic conduct. The secondary school does an earnest and, on the whole, effective job with teen-age students representing an intellectual cross section of the American public. But its effort is accommodated to the lower intellectual level and lesser maturity of its students. Large as the college population has grown, it is still relatively select, intellectually and socially: out of it will come not only the leadership of society but also a large private citizenry capable of molding its opinion and influencing its action. Such a citizenry needs training in social and civic responsibility far beyond the limits attainable through earlier schooling.

Citizenship training in the college is of a different order from that offered on lower educational levels.[9] Without discrediting the ideals and principles cherished by society, instruction in the college must submit them to the students' critical examination. How were they achieved, what alternatives to them exist, what are their relative merits and shortcomings, what strengths and weaknesses are displayed by our social principles in action, how may social improvement be effected without sacrifice of basic ideals? What, then, are the civic responsibilities of educated men and women, and how are they discharged? The college postulates no single answer, but helps students arrive at a rational affirmation of their faith in the ends and processes of democracy and affords them opportunity for testing these beliefs in practice. In the final analysis the student decides for himself; the college can help him toward critical assessment of beliefs and more responsible use of the civic franchise.

The process of general education is itself conducive to the training of citizens: whatever aids in building mind and character contributes toward citizenship. Instruction in the social studies is an important contributing factor. Every classroom is a citizenship center, and every discipline a medium of training. The teacher needs to alert himself to opportunities which exist or can be created for the development of civic ideals, attitudes, and habits later to be exercised in a larger social sphere. In its organized life the college should constitute a citizenship laboratory, offering the chance not only to

⁹ See also *The Idea and Practice of General Education, op. cit.,* p. 6.

practice established principles of democratic behavior but also to experiment with new ways of implementing democratic ideals. Outcomes should be assessed, and resultant learnings clarified for the student. Terminating his college course a student should feel that he has had an experience in civic living which will benefit him in the future.

6. *Economic competence.* It is not an assault on the ideal of liberal education to suggest that college instruction has a special responsibility to prepare the student for his economic role in society as worker or producer, consumer, planner, and social critic. The economic phase of existence is critical in its influence on general well-being, and most people either require or strongly benefit from direct educational preparation for difficult economic responsibilities. To argue that the business of the college is general education and that a person's economic future is his private concern is a refusal to face reality.

There is more to economic competence than ability to earn a livelihood. A person must be prepared to take his place in the economic partnership of society and address himself to the solution of its problems as well as his own. He is not only a consumer of goods and services, investor, property owner, and tax payer but may be called upon to direct or participate in public undertakings as councilman, school board member, or arbitrator in labor disputes. He needs training in the conduct of larger social responsibilities and of his own economic affairs. This training the college willingly provides through its general educational process, including courses specifically pointed toward growth in economic understanding. Where the profession commonly balks is in admitting that vocational orientation is an essential element in preparation for the economic needs of living. This is considered outside the sphere of general education, obtainable by the person in his own way or through other training facilities.

Orienting a student toward a vocation does not necessarily involve specialized vocational training. The college program cannot reasonably be fractured into the hundreds of vocational splinters leading off into students' later pursuits. Responsible leaders of industry agree with educators that a liberal training fostering moral and intellectual development and acquisition of important knowledge is fundamental to success in the type of occupations in which college graduates commonly engage; and that specialized occupational skills can be acquired later through formal study or in the course of job experience. Acting on this belief, specialized colleges have been for some years broadening their base of general education, seeking to establish a proper balance with technical studies. The liberal college has a different problem: most of its graduates do not enter the technical occupations but those placing greater premium on intelligence, initiative, industry, leadership, and ability to get along with people than on preparatory specialized skill. The solution of this problem lies not so much in balancing general and vocational studies—although some representation of the latter is necessary—as in *using the resources of general education* to help the student explore career possibilities, ascertain his interests and aptitudes in relation to possible vocational choices, make an intelligent selection, and develop a suitable plan of preparation.

The scope of the existing program of general education is adequate to afford many students at least a good start toward preparation for a career. By definition liberal studies embody and in turn show the way to many fields of human endeavor. The student needs to be guided toward what is for him the right field. Sometimes, in recognition of widespread interests or needs among students, the college will expand its offerings to admit additional professionally oriented courses, shaping them so as to enhance their liberal values. Often the student will have to decide that, in the interests of a career, he must continue specialized study in an institution beyond the graduate level. The point is that a college graduate should not be taken by surprise at the need to establish himself in a proper calling but should be ready for it. Such readiness may consist of knowing what he wants to do and being prepared with general knowledge and understanding of the job. Approaching the point of entry, the student will discover for himself whether he needs specialized preparation and how it may be obtained. After all we are educating the student further to educate himself.

The career values inherent in general college studies should be pointed up and extended.[10] The value of an instrument of liberal learning is not impaired when its vocational possibilities are made

[10] For further illustration, see Harry D. Gideonse's "On Re-Thinking Liberal Education," *op. cit.*

explicit and opportunities afforded for student self-exploration. The limit in scope and diversity of liberal offerings has not been reached; more courses will be admitted, even under vocational pressure, which will be found to possess liberal value. Some of the most respected current offerings were professional in origin; perhaps some day courses now on the vocational fringe may be regarded as bulwarks of liberal learning.

The Educated Person. The foregoing suggests a conception of the educated person different in some respects from that which has traditionally guided the college. The conception may be unaccepta-ble to some: it is not primarily one of a humanist or scholar. Yet the attributes are there, although their emphasis is on producing not the studious, contemplative man but the effective one. Some of our graduates become scholars, teachers, research workers, men of let-ters and of the arts. But not all or most. How shall these be certi-fied? Do we call them near-scholars or near-men-of-letters, like the young man whose calling-card was inscribed "Failed A.B."? These are young men and women whose education was not meant to fit them for a life of study but for less dedicated but equally useful pur-suits. Are they not entitled to be called educated or, conversely, should not education seek to make them better, more enlightened, and more effective in the things they are called upon to do? The college must continue to produce scholars, but should not mold its pattern of education on the scholarly life alone.

Society needs educated people—highminded, thoughtful, in-formed, and competent. The qualities which bring distinction in the world of the arts and science are much the same as those needed in the conduct of prosaic life activities. Business and politics, indus-try and domestic pursuits require high levels of intellectual honesty, respect for truth and accuracy, quest for knowledge, bold and imag-inative thinking, and patient persistence. The moral and intellectual virtues which once distinguished the rare, cultivated person need to be extended to as many people as possible.

The educated person today needs powers surpassing those of any previous age. There is more to be learned, yet to be a learned person is not enough: one must be right thinking, right feeling, right doing. If our educated person lacks the erudition of the Renaissance scholar or the urbanity of the Victorian gentleman, that is no cause for discouragement. He is probably better balanced, and balance is what we urgently require. We are educating so many that among them are bound to be distinguished artists, scholars, and spiritual leaders who will advance mankind's highest achievement. The potential "remakers of mankind" should not be neglected, but education should not be conceived in their terms alone. They are also educated who with kindness and intelligent skill fulfill their obligations to themselves and to society as citizens, workers, neighbors, family men and women, and human beings.

SELECTED BIBLIOGRAPHY

Carmichael, Oliver C., *The Changing Role of Higher Education*. New York: The Macmillan Company, 1949. 102 pp.

Cole, Stewart G., *Liberal Education in a Democracy*. New York: Harper & Brothers, 1940. 309 pp.

Conant, James B., *Education in a Divided World*. Cambridge: Harvard University Press, 1948. 249 pp.

Donham, Wallace B., *Education for Responsible Living*. Cambridge: Harvard University Press, 1944. 309 pp.

General Education in a Free Society, Report of the Harvard Committee. Cambridge: Harvard University Press, 1945. 267 pp.

Gideonse, Harry D., "On Re-Thinking Liberal Education," pp. 30–52 in *Strengthening Education at All Levels*, Report of the Eighteenth Educational Conference Held under the Auspices of the Educational Records Bureau and American Council on Education. Washington: American Council on Education, 1953.

Greene, Theodore M., *Liberal Education Reconsidered*. Cambridge: Harvard University Press, 1953. 46 pp.

Henderson, Algo D., *Vitalizing Liberal Education*. New York: Harper & Brothers, 1944. 202 pp.

Jones, Howard Mumford, *Education and World Tragedy*. Cambridge: Harvard University Press, 1946. 178 pp.

Kallen, Horace M., *The Education of Free Men*. New York: Farrar, Straus and Company, 1949. 332 pp.

Livingstone, Sir Richard W., *On Education*. New York: The Macmillan Company, 1944. 290 pp.

Russell, Bertrand, *Education and the Good Life*. New York: Boni and Liveright, 1926. 319 pp.

Smith, Huston, *The Purposes of Higher Education*. New York: Harper
& Brothers, 1955. 218 pp.
Taylor, Harold, ed., *Essays in Teaching*, Chapter I, "The Idea of a
College." New York: Harper & Brothers, 1950. 239 pp.
Tead, Ordway, *Character Building and Higher Education*. New York:
The Macmillan Company, 1953. 129 pp.
Ward, F. Champion, Faust, Clarence H. *et al.*, *The Idea and Practice
of General Education*, Chapter I, "The Problem of General Educa-
tion." Chicago: University of Chicago Press, 1950. 333 pp.
Whitehead, Alfred N., *Aims of Education and Other Essays*. New
York: The Macmillan Company, 1929. 247 pp.
Woody, Thomas, *Liberal Education of Free Men*. Philadelphia: Uni-
versity of Pennsylvania Press, 1951. 296 pp.

II. *Responsibilities of the College Teacher*

The Idea and the Actuality. A newcomer to college teaching has a surprise in store. Fresh from the university or a less academic setting of private or public business, he looks forward to an uninterrupted career of scholarship—teaching favored courses to favored students, study, research, and publication. Soon the pleasant preliminaries of induction are over, he settles down to his work, and unexpected facets of the job begin to reveal themselves. A trained specialist, he is "invited" to teach one or more general courses with only a tangential relation to his field of interest to students whose special interests may be even more remote. Gaining in familiarity with the institution and in professional standing with colleagues, he finds himself drawn into an increasing miscellany of non-teaching activities—student counseling, administration, policy deliberation, curriculum revision, supervision of special projects, and extracurricular activity. A portion of his time and energy is absorbed by these activities, and opportunity for scholarly pursuit correspondingly diminished. Evenings, when he is not too tired, week-ends, and during vacation periods he can work on research and publication: the output is seldom as large as anticipated. Occasionally he pauses to reflect on how relatively unprepared he was—psychologically and technically—for some of the duties in which he is now involved.

The result is not usually shattering: one soon learn to effect a compromise with former beliefs. Most teachers succeed in developing a realistic concept of their responsibilities, strengthening their

competencies to meet new requirements, apportioning their tasks so
as to leave room for private pursuits. Some accept the compromise
grudgingly, being reluctant to submit themselves to any assignment
which distracts from teaching and learning. Others "adjust" too
well, assuming readily their institutional responsibilities but gradually shedding those more onerous obligations which they owe to
scholarship—and to themselves. While the situation is not critical,
it would be better if college teachers received a more realistic orientation to their job and a more representative preparation. There is
little danger that the profession will thereby become routinized, since
functions are no sooner catalogued than alterations or additions
emerge.

This chapter speaks in some detail of the college teacher's functions, not perhaps as they should be but as they are. The extent of
discussion devoted to each of the teacher's several responsibilities is
not a criterion of its value: one must not become so befuddled by
the complexity of the job as to lose sight of its principal purpose,
which is teaching students. Prerequisite to college-level teaching is
self-absorption in scholarship—helping to advance knowledge by un-
covering, organizing, or sharing it with others. These then are the
two fundamental responsibilities—to teach and to study. But others,
though in a subordinate position, are important. The process of education involves auxiliary enterprises the purpose of which is to enhance the effectiveness of teaching and learning, and in some of
these enterprises the teacher is a leading agent.

The College Teacher's Job. By nature, a profession cannot be
defined with precision: its limits are not fixed, its constituent processes not analyzable to the last detail. It is a calling which values
talent more than technical proficiency, creative originality more than
orthodoxy, responsibility to self more than subservience to the will of
others. Its rewards derive from satisfaction in service rendered as
much as from material return. The practice of a profession varies with each practitioner and the circumstances under which he
works. A profession is never finally mastered: its foundations of
knowledge keep growing, and new demands and responsibilities are
constantly being added. So with college teaching. There is danger
in trying to crystallize functions which are and must remain fluid.
There is danger also in attempting to single out specific elements of

an interrelated whole: the organic or unifying principle may be lost from view. Despite the risks, an attempt should be made to reach a clearer understanding of what the job of college teaching entails.

We try to avoid oversimplification, but it is necessary also to take issue with an opposing tendency—to protect college teaching against exposure to rational analysis and criticism. There are those who view college teaching as a mystery, to be approached in a spirit of veneration rather than searching inquiry. "Good teachers are born, not made" is their cry, as if that settled the argument. The venerable slogan is a mischievous half-truth which long ago earned its retirement. Good teachers are no more "born, not made" than good engineers, concert pianists, or baseball players: in each case a gift of inheritance is combined with sound training, long practice, and a sturdy will to succeed. So narrow a concept of college teaching leaves little hope of professional improvement except via eugenics. The urgent task of the profession is to improve teaching competence here and now. Selection of new teachers should aim at disclosing those possessing real teaching accomplishment, however acquired, and promise of further development. One of the most encouraging features of recent professional education has been the growth in pre-service and in-service training programs.

Central in the teacher's conception of his job must be acceptance of his mission as educator. This unifies his specific functions, influencing their quality and direction. It explains why a teacher must pursue scholarship yet not devote himself exclusively to research, and lends dignity to the administrative and semi-clerical chores he occasionally performs. As education changes, the teacher's tasks will change: in our own day the expansion of personnel services has necessitated the increasing use of teachers as counselors, requiring the addition of one more talent to their already substantial equipment.

Education is a way of doing things as well as an end result. All that a teacher does should be suffused with an "educated" quality. A dean or head of department administers in such a way as to enhance the confidence and self-respect of teachers and students and foster the purposes of education; a counselor recognizes the individuality of students, their need for exercise of initiative, freedom of choice, and progressive self-dependence; the teacher does not merely demonstrate, or inform but stimulates students to learn for themselves, and guides them in so doing. Since teachers work with people, whatever their other accomplishments they need special natural or acquired facility in this respect. In the teaching profession one needs to like, trust, and respect people. But normal affection should be combined with understanding people and how they operate by themselves and in groups. Every teacher is a practical psychologist, bringing to bear psychological insights and skills on all his endeavors, whether in faculty deliberations or in less momentous "grievance" interviews with students soliciting a change in grade. Whatever the result, the other person should be left with undiminished dignity and unimpaired self-respect.

Growth of the Teacher's Responsibilities. In the college's evolution from a "school" to an "institution," the teacher's job has been correspondingly extended. Although a teacher's schedule does not cover the wide range of subject matter it once did,[1] his courses are more intensive in depth and exacting in scholarship, requiring greater expenditure of effort to keep abreast of information. Classes, formerly organized on a tutorial or small-group basis with relatively few lectures, are now normally larger, with a range extending from great lecture assemblies to seminar or "individual" conference sections. Lecturing is no longer reserved for an institution's "distinguished professors," nor is the conduct of advanced seminars the privilege alone of senior faculty members. A teacher needs to be equally at ease before a "mike" in a large auditorium or sitting shirtsleeved in his study before an informally arranged group; he must know how to plan and teach a course on a mass basis, and how to organize study for one student. The apparatus of instruction—books, reading lists, laboratory and workshop equipment, audio-visual aids —has grown enormously. To correct the tendency toward overspecialized education, colleges have developed "integrated" courses

---

[1] "My 'chair' demanded classes in Zoology, Botany, Geology, Mineralogy, Chemistry, Physics, Political Economy, Paley's 'Evidences of Christianity,' and, incidentally, German and Spanish! I also had charge of the weekly 'literary exercises' consisting of orations and the reading of essays . . . with a class in Sunday School as a good measure." David Starr Jordan at Lombard College, Illinois, in 1872, quoted by W. H. Cowley, "A Century of College Teaching," *Improving College and University Teaching,* Vol. I, No. 3 (November 1953), p. 4.

organized on a broad base and sometimes offered jointly by several departments. The teacher may be called upon not only to acquire mastery of new subject matter but also to learn to teach cooperatively with colleagues of different training and orientation.

The college has always ministered to students' needs beyond the academic. Religious and moral training, discipline in its constructive as well as punitive aspects, and essentials of physical well-being have long been a concern with which teachers were charged. More recently the college, sensitive to individual differences among students, has undertaken better to fit its program to each student's needs. The concept of "needs" has been broadened to include not only those commonly acknowledged by society but also those which may be peculiar to the student and his individual adjustment. Personnel work with students has become an enlarged college function, and systematic counseling programs have been consuming an increasing share of attention. In addition to full-time workers in specialized services, colleges enlist the aid of teachers in "educational" counseling, with or without corresponding compensation in service credit. The teacher, already engaged in guidance incidental to course instruction, may also be called upon to serve in a more formal role, with special requirements of technical knowledge, sources of information, and interviewing skills.

Compared with an earlier generation the college has become a complex organization, extending into many spheres of activity and employing a large number of non-instructional specialists. But the operation of the educational program is the concern of the teaching faculty. The curriculum is under constant review and changes in course offerings are continually being effected. Financial grants from government and private agencies have stimulated experiments and projects of various sorts. Institutional self-evaluations are being conducted under the auspices of faculty members and students. With current student enrollments, problems of institutional government— formulation of policies and rules affecting admission, retention, accreditation, deportment and discipline, special awards—have become of considerable moment. As faculty member the teacher shares in these activities as policy maker and frequently as technician—for example, in curriculum evaluation or revision. The competencies he is called upon to exercise may have little correspondence to those in which he was originally trained, yet his professional influence extends much further than the limits of his classroom instruction.

However the teacher chooses to use his franchise as a citizen, his professional status marks him for a special role in society. Logically perhaps his civic and his professional position should be distinct, but it has repeatedly been demonstrated that a teacher cannot divest himself of his academic identity simply by omitting his title and institutional affiliation. The public insists on making the identification. This circumstance has advantages as well as limitations. While fostering circumspection in utterance and caution about becoming involved in public controversy,[2] it affords better than average opportunity for exerting beneficial influence. College teaching enjoys social prestige, and the public is inclined to be attentive even when the teacher dwells on matters outside his distinctive field of competence. This prestige, along with the intellectual capacity to be of service, should be capitalized for the public benefit more fully than it has been. The college teacher has technical qualifications to be of unique usefulness. Assuming such civic obligations may not be, in the strict sense, part of the college teacher's job but it is conducive to professional and personal enrichment.

This statement of the college teacher's responsibilities will now be analyzed in greater detail under these headings: the teacher as course instructor; the teacher as scholar; the teacher as counselor; the teacher as faculty member; the teacher as citizen.

THE TEACHER AS COURSE INSTRUCTOR

The ungraceful term "course instructor" must serve for want of a better mode of reference to the responsibilities involved in the direct conduct of classroom instruction—planning and organizing courses, teaching students, evaluating their accomplishment and one's own instruction. In the teacher's entire occupation, nothing is more important and nothing more enjoyable. A teacher exists to teach. This feeling prompts overworked college presidents and deans to teach at least a single course, and excites the ambition of non-

[2] No suggestion is intended that the college teacher refrain from taking sides in such controversy when his sense of duty impels otherwise. The implication is that he must be sure to take a responsible position.

teaching associates "eventually to do some teaching." It is by contact with students in the classroom that one gains and retains the franchise of teacher.

Responsibility in Teaching. The teacher's responsibility is not only to share with students the substance of a field of learning, but also to stimulate and guide growth in mind, character, and personality. One is instrumental to the other. Instruction is most effective when the teacher knows (1) the ends of growth to which his teaching is directed, (2) the learning qualities of his students, and (3) the ways in which the subject matter may be shaped in order to serve its function. Instruction is never without outcomes in growth beyond attainment of academic knowledge, but unless they are planned and controlled as far as possible, the outcomes may be fortuitous, undesirable, or inefficient. To realize the fullest educational potentials of teaching one must first assess the values and possibilities of a subject, then plan, organize, and conduct instruction accordingly.

A subject is a flexible instrument. It can be adjusted in level of difficulty and type or quality of emphasis, or refashioned to suit the needs of learners. The history of education gives abundant testimony of the way in which subjects have been altered leaving little resemblance to earlier forms. A teacher's allegiance to a subject is a creditable mark of personal investment in its scholarship, but such loyalty should not deter him from making changes needed for educating students. In most cases his alterations will not diminish students' mastery of content but enhance it.[3]

A subject is not the only medium of education: the teacher himself is another. It is impossible to teach without sharing one's person with students—one's attitudes, beliefs, standards of value, qualities of thought, even peculiarities. Knowing this the good teacher sets out to make conscious use of himself in instruction, being certain that what he imparts is consistent with the ideals he professes. Though this may occasionally "cramp his style" it also reinforces his effort and expands the opportunity to move beyond the limits of the subject in guiding students' development. Ethical, moral, and esthetic values are communicated better by people than by subject

[3] In this connection, see also Joseph Seidlin, "High Standards: Sacred and Profane," *Mathematics Magazine,* March–April 1950, pp. 189–92.

matter. For this reason a self-taught course is not as educative as one taught by a good teacher, and audio-visual self-teaching devices no substitute for the human presence.

Attitudes toward Courses. It is normal for a teacher to have favorite courses and to feel indifferently about others in the same general field. Preferred courses are apt to be those reflecting one's special competence, advanced-level courses, and those admitting a select student constituency; customarily less favored are introductory or "freshman" courses, general offerings of broad scope, and integrations of subject matter for which specialized competencies do not suffice. Seldom will a teacher voluntarily choose a course in which he feels himself less than expert or which is known to draw students of lesser capabilities and interests.

While this attitude is understandable and the teacher as a rule should teach courses in which he feels himself most competent and secure, there is value in periodically accepting assignment of a course outside one's orbit of assured mastery or for other reasons lacking in instructional appeal. This is not self-punishment, but an opportunity to extend one's scholarship and teaching skill. In his own interest a teacher should not restrict his teaching to a few familiar courses, no matter how expert in them he may have become. At his own initiative he should seek to add to and vary his offerings, withdrawing for a time from courses he has taught continuously for some years. Newly organized offerings and those deviating from the conventional structural pattern are particularly helpful toward retaining educational perspective, freshness of approach, and vitality of interest. Shortcomings in scholarship can be corrected prior to and during instruction provided one has good grounding in the subject and sufficient time for preparation. The mark of the scholarly teacher is in the continuous quest of knowledge that he brings to instruction; experienced teachers will admit that their earlier, more challenging experiences with a course were sometimes the best. The burden of work will not be excessive if a teacher's schedule includes but one new course at a time.

For that matter even familiar course offerings should be continually revised and, once in a while, completely revamped. The same course taught many times in the same way loses progressively in effectiveness as an educational instrument. Instructional goals, content, and methods change, as do students and the teacher himself. It is well to prepare and keep detailed notes of instruction as long as the teacher uses them primarily for renewed planning. One form of course organization may be better than another, but none is so preeminently superior that it compensates for the loss of enthusiasm produced by routine. The teacher is well-advised to examine his best courses to ascertain whether or not they have become too hardened and polished by use to retain their effectiveness without change.

Attitudes toward Students. One naturally likes students to have a preferential interest and inclination for his subject or at least exhibit a marked capacity to learn. This attitude tends to bring students and teacher closer together, foster higher attainment and greater mutual satisfaction. But normal liking for better students should not influence the teacher to give them better treatment, nor blind him to his equal obligation to other students. A teacher is not like the temperamental master artist who welcomes into his studio only the gifted pupils and rejects the rest. His responsibility is to try to educate all students, irrespective of strengths and infirmities, each according to his needs.

The large population of students now in the college is of mixed capacity, background, and attainment. Individual differences are bound to prevail in any group, and in so large a cross section of society as that represented by the current college enrollment the divergence is magnified. In all but select classes some students of ordinary caliber will be found. The teacher's obligation is also to these, though not to the extent of allowing them to preempt the bulk of instructional attention. Fortunately for the teacher's patience and capacity for tolerance, a self-selective process operates in the students' progression through college study, enabling the teacher in advanced courses to deal with students of greater ability and interest. It would be fine if this were true in all courses; but since it is not, the teacher should be prepared to take students as they come, begin at the point from which they can proceed to learn, and do his best to educate them.

Though the award of grades, honors, and special distinctions may be competitive, education is not. Students can be compared in particular respects and superficially as whole persons, but intrinsically each constitutes a unique composite of traits, capacities, and needs, requiring a distinctive kind of education. What is accomplished or proved by demeaning a student with no stomach for calculus through comparison with another with a larger appetite for the subject? Being unequal in capacity and interest, they are likely to be unequal in achievement. The teacher's job with the poor student is to help him overcome his distaste for the subject and attain a passable degree of competence. Perhaps in other subjects the student has more promise and inclination toward achievement. Teachers sometimes fail to understand how a student can approach their subject without a compelling urge to learn it: the incidence of such cases is high.

This is not a brief in support of mediocrity. The college has an obligation to the gifted student greater than it customarily discharges. Such a student should be encouraged and guided in his pursuit for education beyond the limits of attainment possible for others. But as the recipient of instructional benefits he is no more privileged than anyone else: all college students are entitled to learn provided they are willing to make the effort. As it is, abler students are apt to receive plaudits and awards out of proportion to the actual effort they expend. It would be better if such students enjoyed less outward prestige and an intrinsically more rewarding education.

Attitudes toward Self. Teaching is a profession in which incentive to excellence comes primarily from within, the teacher himself being the chief instigator of the accomplishment he attains. Even modest competence in teaching is not easy to come by: mastery is much harder. To teach is to build minds, mold character, instil knowledge and interests, working from sometimes unpromising beginnings; it is to help cultivate genius where the seeds of genius exist. Knowing this, the good teacher tries to prepare himself with knowledge of the subject and of the students, definite objectives, and procedures for making instruction effective. He plans instruction with the intentness of a military campaign. But no pressure or tension is reflected in his teaching. Work in the classroom proceeds unhurriedly, naturally, and agreeably; students enjoy learning even when standards are exacting. It is difficult for an outsider not to underestimate the skill which enters into good teaching; only the teacher knows how much thought and labor are involved.

From failure to understand how much persistent self-searching effort is required to reach a high level of teaching, many mistakes follow. The rudimentary skills may be acquired in a few years. It is then that so many teachers settle down on a comfortable plateau, expending their excess energies in collateral routines but advancing no further toward mastery of teaching. Yet instruction is their principal business, and there is no end of ways in which a teacher can enhance his contribution to students by improving his teaching. Is the course so good that it could not be better? Why are some students failing—is it only for want of capacity or industry? Are the abler being called upon to do their best? Can the course be enriched in substance, or shaped more closely to the ends it professes to serve? Such questions suggest themselves to the sensitive teacher and point the way to improvement of instruction.

The quest for mastery in teaching should be pursued without self-consciousness or self-deprecation. A teacher can learn to teach well if he sets out to do so: he has the requisite intellectual resources and the opportunity. With each passing semester, with every course begun and completed, he may become more adept in handling his responsibilities. Mishaps are bound to occur—a lecture does not come off, a misunderstanding develops with a student—but these should not put him off stride. What he needs to avoid is complacency, the feeling that he is doing "well enough" and can afford to turn to other things. If he employs for himself the same rigorous standards he is expected to apply to students, all will be well.

The Teacher as Scholar

No question exists regarding the indispensability of scholarship as an element of professional competence. The question concerns the kinds of scholarship desirable and the extent to which scholarly publication should be obligatory.[4]

What Is Scholarship? The conventional evidence of scholarship is absorption in specialized research culminating in publication. The

[4] See, for example, W. Hugh Stickler, "Improving College Instruction," *Improving College and University Teaching,* Vol. II, No. 2 (May 1954), pp. 25–34.

title and honors of scholarship are accorded to the experimental scientist, the linguistic, literary, historical and social research worker, the archaeologist or anthropologist, but not so in like degree to the creative artist or teacher. Rarely do we hear an able administrator or a talented counselor referred to as scholarly. This restricted concept of scholarship would be harmless except that it influences the common view of what constitutes worth in a college teacher. A Chaucer with an inclination to teach might have some difficulty in obtaining a first-rate college position, while the foremost authority on Chaucerian syntax could qualify for a "distinguished professorship." The conventional usage is especially unjust to the thorough-going teacher who, though he may abstain from publication, invests his teaching with a quality for which unremitting devotion to knowledge is necessary.

The test of scholarship is not in the pursuit of any specified activity: outlets for scholarship are many. Scholarship is a quality one brings to bear upon experience, a method of addressing and working one's way through problem situations. The mark of scholarship is in seeking to apply all pertinent knowledge to the conduct of an undertaking, and in using that knowledge with precision. Its attributes are compulsion to know and to do the right thing, to conform to standards for ascertaining and testing truth, to maintain the greatest possible objectivity in evaluation of results. Its common aversion is toward the spurious, pretentious, or slovenly. As such, scholarship may be manifest in whatever activity engages the intellect, academic or not.

A college should be a society of scholars. Scholarship in the college has as many forms of expression as its own varied activities. It is needed in teaching, counseling students, planning courses of study, administering the processes of institutional government, and transacting its practical business. Consider the educational effect if the college president, deans, and faculty members employed their scholarly talents for nothing but research in subject fields, according their other responsibilities only slip-shod attention.

In as varied a group as a large college faculty it is unrealistic to expect teachers to have the same types of scholarly interests. All should endeavor to perform with scholarly distinction their first and highest responsibility, which is teaching students; beyond this each may exercise his scholarly leaning in what interests him most and for which he has aptitude. A teacher will gain most in professional competence if he aspires to do what he naturally favors, provided this is germane to education. It is poor policy to convert a fine social adviser or athletic coach into a mediocre research worker. The modern college is so complex in its functions that it is advantageous to use the special capabilities of teachers in special ways.

Scholarship and Creativity. Though not identical, scholarship and creativity are cognate qualities, the highest forms of scholarly pursuits being those affording freest exercise of imagination and talent. Not all scholarly production, however, is equally conducive to creative development: counting verbs in the second aorist tense may be an absorbing pastime but how it benefits the performer is questionable. Research for its own sake and routine investigations whose sole purpose is to add to the sum of learning are better left to universities and specialized research centers. Although any scholarly preoccupation is better than none, given his choice the college teacher will do better to engage in activities which add to his personal and professional stature as well as to the domain of knowledge. The creative value of a research activity is one criterion of its worth.

Creativity is not limited to productive research. Most of what a teacher does benefits from a creative approach and the infusion of the creative spirit. Teaching can be a dull process of transmitting second-hand information or a creative experience in helping students find themselves and make their own advances in learning. Instructional method can be a repetition of past practice or an original attempt to meet learning requirements in new ways. The teacher's aim should be to imbue all of his work with a characteristic creative quality, shunning the trite and commonplace. The best place to begin is with oneself, with an examination of one's own thoughts regarding the opportunities and obligations of his profession. The creative spirit is infectious; a few teachers can make a difference in stimulating and vitalizing a faculty. For a profession which is undeniably a gathering place of superior minds, college teaching is surprisingly susceptible to old formulas and stereotypes, to hypotheses seldom challenged and never proved. If this seems an exaggeration, analyze carefully the next faculty discussion you hear on a portending change in the curriculum and decide for yourself.

Value of Research in Teaching. If earlier reference to research seemed in any manner slighting, such was far from the intention: few scholarly endeavors can be more enriching to the teacher, his institution, and society. All that prior discussion aimed to convey was that (1) research is not the only outlet for scholarship; (2) since not all are equally gifted with capacity for research, some teachers should be encouraged to pursue other forms of scholarship which suit them better; and (3) the best type of research is that which makes creative demands upon the person performing it.

Broadly defined, research activity concerns itself with discovery of knowledge, its organization and synthesis, and its orderly communication to a public competent to receive it. It may be conducted on the advance frontiers of learning or in the safer purlieus of the rear echelon. In either case it is an important collateral activity with teaching, and one which every teacher should try to cultivate. The personal and professional effect of involvement in research is more important to the college teacher than the intrinsic worth of his discoveries. For the teacher cannot with propriety always be a dealer—even if a good one—in handed-down information. To maintain his vigor and freshness in instruction he must from time to time make contributions to knowledge which are his own. To evoke originality from students one must manifest some originality himself. The teacher owes a duty to himself constantly to keep some research going: if findings are publishable and time is available to prepare them for publication, so much the better. But this is not as essential as his own refreshment at the well of learning.

As noted above, a teacher should not be expected to sacrifice a greater talent for one of lesser promise. There are those who will make research a major pursuit, others to whom it will remain a sideline. This is all right. Dedicated research calls for qualities of mind, temperament, and effort different from those, for example, of the successful social organizer or group catalyst. The college needs both types of talent. But some concern with research helps nurture the scholarship that every college teacher needs. Without any research interests whatever, one misses much that is fundamental to his professional well-being.

Possible subject matter for research offers so large and varied a choice that we would not attempt to be dogmatic about what is legitimate to the teacher's interest. However, it is fair to say that research should have some bearing on the instructional tasks with which the teacher is occupied, reducing the danger of unrewarding specialization and of impatience with teaching responsibilities which subtract from available research time. On the whole, subjects of research should be of broader significance and dimension than that typified by many doctoral exercises. At the present time major effort in research is in the substance of teaching; though such research should proceed, there is need also for intensified investigation of the educational process in its various aspects. Important information remains to be gathered and problems to be solved relating to attitudes, behavior patterns, and needs of later adolescence, the learning process on higher intellectual levels,[5] and methods in college teaching. More institutional studies focusing on specific student populations, programs, and educational practices are needed. College education as a whole is as important as the branches of knowledge which enter into it: specialists from every field of scholarship could make valuable contributions to the wider profession if they would extend their interest.

THE TEACHER AS COUNSELOR

The development of personnel services in recent years has called for the increasing use of specialists, but the classroom teacher may also be involved in a less specialized capacity. This discussion is addressed to the teacher whose primary responsibility is as instructor, but whose incidental or additional duties bring him into contact with counseling and personnel problems.[6]

Counseling and Education. College education has come to mean not solely intellectual training but the balanced development of the whole person. Providing the right cultural climate and organized civic, cultural, and recreational activity has become as important as offering proper courses of study. A concomitant development has been increased recognition of the distinctive needs of the student as

[5] Further discussion of this subject is offered in Chapter V.

[6] The large literature on personnel work in the college could be sampled with profit. A fine summary and bibliography appear in Esther Lloyd-Jones's "Personnel Work and General Education," Chapter X in *General Education,* Fifty-First Yearbook, Part I, of the National Society for the Study of Education (Chicago: University of Chicago Press, 1952).

person and member of a social group. To help insure the right kind of comprehensive education and maximum benefit from his experience for each student, a large group of educational services has been instituted which mark a departure from the past. The change has been in extending the area of concern, more clearly identifying its specific elements, and organizing and systematizing the process of educational service. The functions of personnel work are better defined, its procedures more carefully formulated and closely followed. This work is an intrinsic part of the college program: teachers and full-time personnel specialists work toward common objectives and share in many of the same responsibilities.

Institutional Responsibilities. There are more of these than any teacher is likely to notice. A recent monograph [7] of the American Council on Education lists twenty-six, including diagnostic testing, educational and vocational counseling, health supervision, housing and food service, extracurricular, social, and religious activities, financial aid and part-time employment, job placement, marriage counseling, and aid in adjustment of students from foreign lands. Contingent upon the type of institution (e.g., whether residential), the nature and needs of students, and available resources, a college will make the provisions considered essential to students' education and such other provisions as promise to make their experience more satisfying and rewarding. Some personnel services have become a practical necessity for all colleges: health services, personal and educational counseling, special preprofessional guidance, extracurricular, social, and recreational activities, and the like.

Institutions vary in their mode of organizing and staffing these services. In some direction is centralized in a department of specialists headed by a dean, working cooperatively with teachers and administrative officers; in others, administration is more widely dispersed with staff members situated in various departments coordinately charged with specified functions. However organized, the conduct of personnel services is necessarily shared by many people, in some instances by a large portion of the teaching staff. For those functions requiring special capacity and intensive training, specialists are employed: physicians, psychologists, religious advisers, voca-

[7] *The Student Personnel Point of View* (Washington: American Council on Education, 1949), cited by Lloyd-Jones, *op. cit.*, pp. 217–18.

tional placement counselors, and others. Some types of specialized personnel activity are vested in teachers not primarily career workers, but qualifying by virtue of aptitude, interest, or desire to be of service: class and extracurricular advisers, graduate and preprofessional counselors, scholarship fund trustees, and the like. A large share of less specialized activity is performed by teachers either as an additional duty or on special assignment for which deduction of teaching load is made. Commonly this activity represents some aspect of broader educational counseling—helping students to formulate a college plan of study, advising on courses and study objectives, assisting with problems of academic adjustment, or acting as institutional mentor for one or several students.

Counselor's Function. The objectives of educational counseling extend beyond the immediate situation for which counseling is required; the task is not only to help the student solve a problem but in the process also to move toward greater self-dependence. A person is rarely so self-sufficient that he does not at times lean on outside advice or support, especially in crises calling for specialized resources in knowledge and skill, but the educated person is characterized by the capacity to think and act for himself in matters within the normal compass of living. Educative counseling is directed toward this end: the process should be governed not by haste to reach a decision, but by the more important criterion of helping the student to make the right decision for himself. The proper solution of a counseling problem is not always that which is pragmatically effective or helpful in attainment of an immediate goal. The counselor should be concerned with the long-term effect of a problem situation on the mind and character of the student. Good counseling sometimes prompts the choice of a solution subordinating immediate gains to more remote but sounder and more enduring values. Emotional maturity, self-discipline, learning to take minor setbacks in stride, and ability to see things in a larger frame are necessary objectives of counseling. "Coddling" the student is a mark of unskilled counseling, and justifies the honest grievance that many teachers have against needlessly prolonging infancy.

The counseling process differs in some ways from instruction. One difference lies in the informality of the relationship between counselor and students. A more important difference is in the source of initiative: however informally instruction may be conducted, initiative centers in the teacher, else the result would be not an organized course but a series of improvised learning experiences. In counseling the initiative rests with the student; it is his experience which gives rise to the problem, and his solutions which are being considered. The counselor is an energizer and catalyst of ideas, a friendly and thoughtful critic. The forceful, effective classroom teacher, unable to hold his own ideas in check, can make a poor counselor. On the other hand, this does not mean that the counselor should be principally a listener or a weak and acquiescent accomplice. In view of the range of experience with which he may be confronted, the counselor is not infrequently on unfamiliar ground. Unlike the teacher at ease in his subject of instruction, the counselor must operate with caution, avoiding ready pronouncement. For a person accustomed to express himself with scholarly authority in the classroom this is not easy, yet the alternative of a possibly careless remark or hasty answer may launch the student on the wrong road.

The quality of counselor-student relationship should be such as to encourage self-exploration and free expression. A greater degree of personal rapport is needed than even that for effective teaching: as member of a class the student may be inhibited and still an effective learner; in counseling little advance can be made without adequate self-revelation. Without the assumed heartiness repugnant to a sensitive student, the counselor must be able to communicate his interest and desire to be of service. Students are not easily fooled and the counselor who simulates enthusiasm finds himself quickly rejected. Teachers who do not have a natural interest in the everyday problems of students will do well to excuse themselves from a counseling assignment.

A counselor works as part of a program and member of a team. He should be familiar with the educational program, work in harmony with its objectives, and use its resources of professional and technical advisers and assembled information. The limits of the teacher-counselor's competence are soon reached in matters involving technical advice, and he should not hesitate to call upon the assistance of more highly specialized colleagues. The best service a counselor can sometimes render is to help the student identify a problem and direct him to a proper source of further assistance.

Whatever material aids are available should be used, particularly student records. It is risky to counsel on any matter of importance without first reviewing the student's record, and counseling should not be considered complete until a summary report has been inserted in the record. A counselor feels foolish when, having "resolved a difficulty" by intuition and quick wit, he discovers in the records its complex history narrated and documented in very different terms. Conscientious use of records makes for good counseling. Acting on inspiration alone is for geniuses and amateurs.

The Teacher as Faculty Member

Personnel work is not untypical of the many services the teacher may be called upon to perform for which he has no ready competence. A beginner in curriculum planning will be impressed by the technical equipment needed over and above familiarity with subject content. To develop proficiency in the extra-instructional tasks requires willingness to learn by experience; not even a more thorough professional training would prepare the teacher for constantly evolving new responsibilities. Rather than resign himself to accept such "chores" as come his way, the teacher should cultivate the opportunity to engage in and master the jobs for which he has a special aptitude or inclination.

The Organized Faculty. A college, it has been remarked, is a "community of scholars." Implicit in "community" is not only the physical proximity of individuals but also a functional interrelationship based on shared concerns. The college faculty is a group of colleagues contributing their special accomplishments in a coordinated effort to educate students. However eminent in their own right, individual teachers do not make a good faculty unless their work together is characterized by a community of spirit and action. True, one can point to specific departments of instruction composed of talented nonconformists whose success seems in defiance of the principle of cooperation, but these are apt to be found in institutions sufficiently large to absorb them, exploit their assets, and compensate for their shortcomings; even then they are exceptional. It is good for a faculty to have individual variations in temperament, philosophy, and approach to educational problems, and even as much nonconformity in practice as the well-being of the institution will admit. But individual teachers should also have educational concerns broader than their scholarly specialties, be able and willing to reach accord on common problems, and lend their specialized capabilities to common tasks. Without surrendering their prerogatives as individuals they should be able to work together conceding as well as taking. A good faculty's strength is in its diversity, but also in its capacity to cohere when cohesion is necessary.

Without distracting from its primary obligation to instruction and the pursuit of scholarship, a faculty should be ready to assume related obligations designed to promote the educational welfare of students. It should receive hospitably proposals for new types of service, accept new duties resulting from their adoption, and be alert in reacting to new opportunities. The scope of faculty jurisdiction varies with institutions. Many are so organized as to leave teachers relatively free of burdens not inherent in teaching and study; others from choice or necessity enlist the faculty more fully in the conduct of extra-instructional affairs on both policy making and operating levels. No institution can afford to release the faculty entirely from non-instructional concerns: whatever of educational significance occurs in the college is the faculty's business. A responsible faculty should claim as its professional privilege the right to review all that bears upon the education of students, and take the initiative in proposing evaluation, innovation, or change.

A faculty "makes or breaks" a college through the caliber of its individual membership and the effectiveness of its operation as a group. An alert staff, sensitive to its responsibilities, open to new ideas, imaginative in approach to problems, experiment-minded, and reasonably happy in personal relationships can make a college a stimulating center of education. The test of a good faculty is not in how seldom it retracts but in what it attempts. The major problems of education have not been solved: old problems persist and new ones are continually added. If education is to go forward, teachers must incur the risk of making mistakes. There are no "authorities" from whom to seek infallible guidance; the best authorities are teachers themselves, getting and sharing ideas, and having the courage to try them out even at the cost of later being proved wrong.

Attitudes of the Faculty Member. There is no point in seeking to distinguish between the good faculty member and the good teacher; the term "educator" defines them both. A few personal and professional attributes especially deserve mention as contributing to success in extra-instructional faculty functions. Among them are interest in the larger domain of education, willingness to forego the comforts of established accomplishment and enter untried tasks, and the ability to free oneself of sectarian loyalties and biases. Working in a college-wide function the teacher promotes not his disciplinary interest but the good of the institution. He cooperates with new colleagues, comes into contact with points of view different from his own, and learns of students' needs other than those with which he is already familiar.

Engaged, for example, in institutional curriculum-making policy, the teacher perhaps for the first time realizes the ramifications of the college program, discovers the claims and aspirations of subjects heretofore remote from his interest, and sees his own discipline in a new perspective. He must try to address himself to each problem with equal zeal, viewing each subject entering the orbit of his activity as if it were his own and giving it the benefit of his best nonpartisan judgment. He is a creator more than a critic and, in relations with colleagues, a diplomat as well. Such qualities are not easily come by, particularly academic tolerance, impartiality, and sympathetic understanding of what different subjects aspire to do: more mistakes in curriculum making have resulted from the influence of uncontrolled and perhaps unconscious bias than from shortcomings in knowledge.

A similar approach is helpful in fostering success in other noninstructional faculty functions. The task is to undertake to learn whatever job is required, and perform it not in the narrow capacity of specialist but with a broader understanding of the complexity of education, the people who engage in it, and the students it serves. A teacher should not serve too long in the same extra-instructional function, lest his interest diminish and the work lose its challenging appeal. By changing assignments at intervals he can keep his enthusiasm refreshed, bring new insights to a job, and at the same time broaden his professional competence.

A teacher should be active in the proceedings of faculty meetings and conferences, regardless of personal disinclination to attract attention. Faculty deliberations should not be dominated by administrators, senior colleagues, or a few vocal staff members but shared by all responsible citizens of the college community. Every teacher has the obligation to conduct himself so as to make a substantive contribution to matters under discussion and also to group morale. Sound ideas forcefully expressed without regard to the feelings of others may have deleterious effects upon intra-group relations and even fail to accomplish their purpose. A teacher should honestly express his thought but do so with sensitivity toward colleagues, particularly those with whom he disagrees. Ours is an articulate profession, and articulateness unmixed with kindliness and unchecked by self-discipline can be a liability in cooperative effort. By exercise of dignity, temperateness, and good humor each teacher can enhance the well-being of the group without detracting from the intrinsic merit of his contribution.

The Teacher as Citizen

Society and the College. Recent trends have intensified the need for closer relationship between the college and society. Increased costs of education have impelled college officials to seek better and more assured public support at the same time that educational developments have brought the work of the classroom into closer contact with the world outside. In increasing measure society is recognizing in the college a social resource of scholarship and technical competence serviceable for its purposes. For many years the government has subsidized agricultural and special vocational training; financial grants from individuals and foundations have fostered research along lines which promise public benefit; recently government and industry have been sponsoring in the colleges numerous special study projects. College and university teachers are being called to responsible positions in government and industry on a consultative or full-time basis. Regionally there has long been maintained a close connection between some institutions of higher education and government or other agencies of public service.[8]

The public influence of the college is not, however, as great as it deserves to be. Many citizens still view the college as solely an academic establishment. By and large college teachers do not offer

[8] Notably exemplified in Wisconsin and other midwestern states.

themselves for public service: to be enterprising in this respect is regarded professionally immodest. Over and above the institutional facilities of assembled knowledge, cultural service, and organized experimentation and research, the college has in its faculty a pool of highly-trained talent, proficient in many of the services which the public needs. If more use is to be made of these resources all concerned, and especially the teachers, will have to show greater interest and initiative.

Public Status of the College Teacher. As a profession college teaching stands well with the public. Though subject to satirical reference as dreamer, intellectual, or more recently "egghead," and at times to rougher handling by a fringe of the public and the press as an irresponsible liberal or "leftist," the college teacher enjoys considerable esteem. In a culture where prestige is more often the prize of wealth and material power, this is a fortunate circumstance which could be capitalized to greater common advantage. The public is inclined to admit the college teacher's sincerity even when it is opposed to what he says, and except in moments of tension to afford him attentive hearing even on issues beyond the limits of his recognized authority. It devolves upon the teacher to use the opportunity responsibly.

In relation to society the teacher has a twofold responsibility. As educator and scholarly specialist, alone or in association with others, he can render such specialized public service as his resources permit and the public needs and will accept. As citizen he can exercise the same civic rights and obligations as do others by participation in the life of the community, setting a good example of conscientious performance of duty. In a democratic society leadership and followership are frequently interchanged roles, and for any given task experts may be at lesser premium than willing participants. The public respects a person who works well in any capacity allotted to him, and is apt to have less confidence in one claiming special distinctions to which he feels himself entitled.

Opportunities for Special Service. The college teacher is in position to render specialized public service. He can work on the school board or as consultant to schools or parents' organization; participate in community studies of health, housing, sanitation, recreation, employment, tax and government reform, and other problems of civic concern; help organize and maintain a community orchestra, theater, literary club, or art workshop; serve as consultant to the local library; organize and participate in public forums; or conduct lectures or courses in programs of adult education. Young, vigorous communities growing up on the edge of metropolitan centers, in which many college teachers make their homes, are especially in need of such services, and almost every resident teacher can make a contribution.

As a rule no monetary compensation should be expected for such service. Public-spirited members of other professions are also called upon to make contributions from their respective competencies. A teacher should not, of course, devote more energy and time than he can conveniently spare from his primary duties, including the duty to obtain relaxation and enjoyment with his family. There are teachers so dedicated to their principal scholarly activity that they have no expendable time for community service, and with good reason these may exempt themselves.

Participation in Civic Living. If a broad generalization may be forgiven, it does not seem that college teachers take advantage of their position to exert as much civic influence as do their colleagues in some comparable professions. Individual teachers may be active and influential in community affairs, but as a professional class they are not a telling force. Partly accounting for this is the nature of the teachers' calling: their contact is with youth rather than adults; their theater of operation is a campus removed from the economic and political marketplace; their principal concerns are intellectual and cultural rather than material; and they are not conscious of their group identity. It is not unnatural for other callings to be more sought out for leadership. Perhaps this is as it should be: leadership belongs to those who have earned the public's confidence, and the teaching profession has no greater claim to civic eminence than any other. Nevertheless teachers are qualified to make a more positive civic contribution than they do, and the values, insights, and knowledge they bring from their profession could be of greater social benefit. What detracts from teachers' effectiveness as citizens is a tendency to remain in the background of everyday events, emerging in periods of crisis to take their place in support of dramatic or special causes, acting in a sense as society's moral conscience. A conscience is most laudable when it operates continuously and not in sporadic or invariably admonitory fashion. Teachers' effectiveness would be enhanced were they more actively involved in the continuum of civic life.

In further pursuit of this thought some plain words need to be spoken. The place to learn to work with adults is not the classroom, library, or laboratory but in less academic settings outside the college. In dealing with persons from other walks of life it is well not to be too sensitive to intellectual differences. People respond well if, regardless of differences, they are treated as equals, naturally and honestly, without condescension or false humility. The greatest mistake the college teacher can make is to underestimate the effective intelligence of nonprofessional fellow citizens in relation to his own. Not many are likely to be as well-schooled as he, but in native ability, alertness, creative energy and specialized aptitude he will find many peers and some superiors. The point is not to look for intellectual parity but to establish a compatibility of interest based on participation in common civic service.

SELECTED BIBLIOGRAPHY

Arbuckle, Dugald S., *Student Personnel Services in Higher Education.* New York: McGraw-Hill Book Company, 1953. 352 pp.

Barzun, Jacques, *Teacher in America.* Boston: Little, Brown and Company, 1945. 321 pp.

Bragdon, Helen D. *et al., Educational Counseling of College Students.* Washington: American Council on Education, 1939. 61 pp.

Carman, Harry J., "Teachers of Tomorrow," *Association of American Colleges Bulletin,* 25:306–16, May 1949.

Cowley, William H., "A Century of College Teaching," *Improving College and University Teaching,* 1:3–10, November 1953.

Cronkhite, Bernice B. (editor), *A Handbook for College Teachers,* Chapters X–XIII. Cambridge: Harvard University Press, 1950. 272 pp.

Dennison, C. P., *Faculty Rights and Obligations in Eight Independent Liberal Arts Colleges.* New York: Teachers College Bureau of Publications, Columbia University, 1955. 186 pp.

Henderson, Algo D., *Vitalizing Liberal Education,* Chapter XIII, "The Instructor as Educator." New York: Harper & Brothers, 1944. 202 pp.

Highet, Gilbert, *The Art of Teaching,* Chapter II, "The Teacher." New York: Alfred A. Knopf, 1952. 291 pp.

Shank, Donald J. *et al., The Teacher as Counselor.* Washington: American Council on Education, 1948. 48 pp.

Spalding, William B., "The Professor as an Educator," *Journal of Higher Education,* 21:293–8, June 1950.

Taylor, Harold, *On Education and Freedom,* Chapter 2, "The College President" and Chapter 4, "Philosophy and the Teacher." New York: Abelard-Schuman, 1954. 320 pp.

Tead, Ordway, "Integrating Personnel and Teaching Functions in College," *Educational Forum,* 17:401–11, May 1953.

Wilson, Logan, "Scholar as Teacher," *Journal of General Education,* 8:86–92, January 1955.

III. *Professional Growth of the College Teacher*

The Ideal of Professional Growth. Professional excellence is not entirely a function of experience, nor is assiduous pursuit of one's duties a guarantee of distinction. The road to professional mastery lies in utilizing one's intelligence, energy, and opportunities of experience in a steady, deliberate effort to foster growth. It is self-training on the job which converts a promising but half-prepared beginner into a passable teacher and impels him toward continuously higher attainment.

Growth in a desired direction is not fortuitous. It needs to be planned and guided. Rudimentary proficiency may result from normal involvement in teaching experience, but this is only a small part of total possible growth. The possibilities and range of growth are as extensive as the teacher's own capacities within the limits of a spacious profession. The goals may lead into realms of creative scholarship, educational philosophy, theories of learning, experimental teaching practice, government of the college community, and other useful professional activity.

The agent of growth is the teacher himself. In a profession not dominated by competition from within or pressure for immediate results from without, the teacher is the keeper of his own conscience. His resolution must be strong enough to enable him at times to compensate for shortage of time, energy, or resources, or even for indifferent support by institutional superiors. Other useful activities compete for his time and attention, tempting absorption in immediate routine to the neglect of less obvious but more urgent needs. It is not easy, after a busy day of college activity, to resume in the evening one's interrupted thought on a research paper or monograph in preparation. Yet this often has to be done if the teacher would be fair with himself and the profession. The best people in an institution are frequently the most overworked, and unless careful to reserve some energy for creative activity are likely to expend themselves in work which is useful but nonproductive of growth.

All professional activity does not have equal potentiality for growth. The person who has reduced his teaching to practiced routine and fails to set for himself new goals of endeavor ceases after a time to develop. Professional enrichment results from reinvestment of intelligence and energy in new learning experience, refreshment with new knowledge, acceptance of new challenges, or new ways of approaching familiar tasks. A teacher need not change jobs frequently in order to sustain growth; he needs only to enlarge and improve his conception of his job and strive for better ways to do it.

Individual Differences in Growth. Like others, college teachers differ in capacities, interests, and inclinations for various aspects of their work. Some prefer classroom contact with students and shun administration, others find an absorbing interest in administrative assignments. In general a person's promise of growth is more through development of his relative strength than correction of weakness. While an effort should be made to remedy shortcomings in competency and maintain balance in positive accomplishment, the greater proportion of one's energy should go toward cultivating his best talents. Narrow and one-sided concentration is undesirable; on the other hand, an attempt to distribute one's resources impartially among all teaching functions is not likely to be most productive.

In the light of the requirements of his job and his known qualifications the teacher should reach for a high level of general competency, yet pursue with greatest zeal the tasks toward which he is most inclined. It is important for a scholar to be a good course instructor, to associate with students in extracurricular activity, to contribute his scholarly insights to extra-instructional institutional undertakings, but he can learn to do these things well without sacrifice of scholarly proclivities. The gifted extrovert can cultivate his specialties in human relations without neglecting the demands of scholarship. There are many kinds of excellence serviceable to education and many ways of achieving them. Only the rare person is exceptionally good in all things: let each teacher learn to do best what suits him most.

COLLEGE TEACHERS' PREPARATION

A Professional Paradox. Considering their preparation, the professional performance of college teachers is unwarrantedly good— a circumstance which may have distracted from long-needed improvement in pre-service training. A recent survey [1] supports the empirical judgment that college teaching is not as good as it might be. The wonder is that it is good at all. The explanation must lie in the caliber of person attracted to the profession, the practical efficiency of current teacher-selection practices, imperfect though they seem, and the transfer values of scholarly training carrying over into development of new competencies. Otherwise it would be difficult to explain why a young specialist in mathematics, chemistry, or Germanic literature can enter a profession whose specialty is educating youth, face responsibilities for which he is not well prepared, and acquit himself honorably and in time with distinction. Perhaps the discipline of winning a Ph. D. degree has greater selective properties than many of us suspect.

It is unnecessary to dwell in detail on shortcomings of present practice in preparation of college teachers.[2] There is general agreement that the typical graduate program pursued by prospective teachers falls short of the mark: commendable as a means of training in specialized scholarship and contributing also toward broader discipline, it does not offer direct preparation for the fundamental professional responsibility—teaching. More serious than the omission of training in the technical aspects of instruction is a failure to impart broader concepts of education, human development, the learning process, and the teacher's mission. These things the teacher must obtain for himself through experience. Yet while much can be

[1] See Paul Klapper's "Problems in College Teaching" in *The Preparation of College Teachers,* Theodore C. Blegen and Russell M. Cooper, editors (Washington: American Council on Education, 1950), pp. 40–54.

[2] An excellent discussion of the subject is afforded in *The Preparation of College Teachers, op. cit.,* and Fred J. Kelly's *Toward Better College Teaching* (Washington: Office of Education, Federal Security Agency, 1950).

learned on the job, college teaching is too advanced a profession to be mastered en route. In the first place, students learning from an apprentice teacher may not get the education to which they are entitled, though they respond to his eagerness and enthusiasm. Second, there is danger that the teacher will acquire more readily the technical skills of his craft than its basic understandings. Third, though no teacher can long maintain himself without an educational philosophy, it makes a great difference whether the philosophy is based on ascertained fact and tenable assumption or a mixture of empirical knowledge and doubtful opinion. What the self-prepared teacher may lack is not proficiency to maintain himself in the class room but vision of the possibilities of education, a deeper sense of purpose, and realization of how it is attainable.

Despite weaknesses in preparation many teachers do a fine job. Alert and sensitive, they are able to capture the spirit of the profession and become accomplished craftsmen. Teaching is not a standardized process conducted according to uniform "rules": there is freedom for individuality in approach and style, for personal discoveries and values. Existing gaps in the "science" of teaching can be filled only from personal experience. This affords added reason why many teachers succeed in training themselves. But self-training would progress further if it were based on more substantial and explicit earlier preparation, and many a teacher of moderate self-guided accomplishment would be enabled to reach a higher professional level.

An explanation of the gap between preparation and professional need is not hard to provide. The evolution of the college in educational function, organization, and practice has outdistanced developments in teacher-preparation. Scholarship is properly the principal ingredient in training college teachers; there was a time when, reinforced by capacity and willingness to learn by experience, it alone served the purpose. This is no longer true: the required preparation needs to be extended to include allied professional knowledge too important to be left to individual resources in informal learning. Even the expectation of continuing to enlist into professional service superior types of persons cannot compensate sufficiently for existing gaps in preparation.

Recruitment and Selection. Although practices in recruitment of college teachers are workable, they are not characterized by system, organization, or coordinated effort. With a membership now numbering some 200,000 and further increase in prospect, the time is approaching when the college teaching profession must consider a more deliberate and dependable long-range program of teacher supply along with clarified standards of selection. Assurance of continuity in staffing without sacrifice of quality cannot indefinitely be left to the conscience and enterprise of individual institutions, teaching departments, or administrators. Already in some fields, notably the sciences, it has become difficult to recruit first-rate persons against the competition of more remunerative opportunities in industry and government. A complicating factor is the decentralized and individualistic organization of higher education which, despite notable advantages, is a liability in recruitment. Regimentation in teacher-placement is undesirable: to legislate national or state certification requirements would certainly be unwise, and it is questionable whether even learned societies or regional accrediting agencies should undertake more than to *suggest* standards of teacher selection in any field. The answer may lie in voluntary working arrangements between undergraduate and graduate institutions.

If comprehensive provisions for teacher recruitment are still in the offing, an immediate need exists as Klapper has stated,[3] for forthright assumption of responsibility by individual institutions. Centers of graduate study engaged in supplying teachers should, in addition to furnishing an appropriate type of preparation, make a vigorous effort to attract and identify students with interest and promise in teaching and accord them special attention. This is now being attempted by an increasing number of graduate institutions, but more rapid progress is contingent upon clearer understanding of the personal and professional qualities desirable in teachers, more explicit knowledge concerning what has been called the "sociology" of the college teaching profession,[4] and agreement on the essentials of suitable training programs. Correspondingly, undergraduate colleges absorbing teachers need to cooperate more closely with gradu-

[3] Paul Klapper, *op. cit.*, p. 40.
[4] See Logan Wilson, *The Academic Man: A Study in the Sociology of a Profession* (New York: Oxford University Press, 1942).

ate centers, advising the latter of their needs, assisting in recruitment efforts, and joining in formulation of training policies. A college should not look toward a single university or a small number for continuous replenishment of its staff; its working relations should be with a wide range of graduate centers possessing distinctive interests and strengths. Each college should try to maintain access to a corps of recruits whose interest and aptitude for teaching have been demonstrated and for whom an approved program of training has been provided.

Teacher-selection practices vary among institutions, and even criteria of selection differ in the emphasis and rigor with which they are applied. Apparently most institutions have well-defined standards of preparation at least in announced policy,[5] and a generalized if broad description is possible. What is sought in a candidate is evidence of quality as a person and fitness as a scholar demonstrated by some record of achievement and personal and professional recommendation; in only 21 per cent of over six hundred institutions was preparation in professional courses for college teaching found to be considered "of great importance."[6] Graduation from a "prestige" institution or high testimonial from a distinguished scholar is a telling factor, although a candidate may improve or impair his chances by the impression he creates in a personal interview. For appointment to senior academic positions scholarship requirements are correspondingly higher, over 95 per cent of institutions insisting on the doctorate as prerequisite for a full professorship and possibly also further publication. Distinguished or "name" professors invited to join a faculty are not subjected to such close analytic scrutiny, their reputation and known achievement being surety for their worth. In general a teaching record is appraised whenever information concerning it is available, but, with beginners at least, a searching attempt to assess technical competence in instruction is not made.

Training and selection go together. More direct criteria of selection cannot be employed until the preparation of college teachers is

[5] "Instructional Staff Practices and Policies in Degree-Granting Institutions, 1953–54," National Education Association *Research Bulletin,* Vol. XXXII, No. 4(December 1954), p. 166.
[6] *Ibid.,* p. 167.

itself more directly focused on fundamental professional needs. Until such time colleges must necessarily continue to choose the best educated, scholarly, and personable applicants, hoping that in time they will also come to be good teachers. When universities undertake more direct training programs for college teaching, colleges will be enabled to add to their criteria of selection a tested indication of instructional worth.

Essentials of Preparation. Universities have begun to experiment with programs of college teacher preparation.[7] The programs vary in substance and form, and some time may elapse before any agreement is reached on essentials. Whether training takes the form of organized professional courses is at this stage less important than that there be direct, sustained preparation, including an attempt to screen candidates and to attract and encourage the more promising. In this spirit and without reference to formal organization, some elements likely to be considered essential in such preparation are here proposed in the hope of stimulating discussion of the subject.

One essential is knowledge of the function of the college. Without minimizing issues in theory or practice it is possible to convey an understanding of the educational role of the college and the manner of its fulfillment. This the prospective teacher needs, his own understanding being bounded by his experience as undergraduate and later as graduate specialist. The object of training should not be to indoctrinate with one set of principles but to expose prevailing views for examination. With this information and accumulating experience, the beginning teacher should gradually develop his own educational philosophy by discriminating selection of values and principles which he can approve. In the meantime he has some knowledge of the broader meaning of education, the relation of educational theory to social philosophy, the function of the college as a stage in the process of education, and his own expanded role as educator. These things do not come naturally to a graduate student engaged primarily in mastering and advancing a specialized field of scholarship.

[7] See Fred J. Kelly, *Toward Better College Teaching*, Chapter IV. Also, Foreword to *A Handbook for College Teachers*, Bernice B. Cronkhite, ed.; and H. B. Hill, "The Teacher Training Program for Doctoral Candidates in History at the University of Wisconsin," *Improving College and University Teaching*, Vol. II, No. 1 (February 1954), pp. 5–6.

A second requirement in preparation is introduction to study of the learning process and the nature and needs of college students as learners. Not much is known with certainty regarding the mechanics of learning on higher intellectual levels, and a good deal of accepted information is empirical or even speculative. But the increasingly assured facts, principles, and insights which the science of psychology has succeeded in gathering relative to the educational development of college students should be communicated to the teacher-in-training. Valid knowledge exists on the nature and growth of intelligence, personality development, dynamics and conditioning factors of human conduct, laws of learning, significance of individual differences, and nature and needs of adolescence. Even with existing gaps in knowledge there is more to be learned than the graduate student is usually asked to master within his period of preparation.

It should be possible to impart to the prospective teacher some basic understandings of human nature and the learning process. To learn, for example, to view the student in terms of his individual needs would be a great gain. To recognize human development as a continuous process would help the teacher start instruction from the point of actual student achievement, and avoid slippery footholds on assumed foundations. Awareness of problems in learning would foster more conscious selection and arrangement of teaching methods. Untenable notions regarding unlimited transfer of training, the inviolability of subjects of instruction, or the potency of sheer reason in dictating human conduct could be replaced with more reliable fact or theory. Once started on study of the learning process, the new teacher could more easily carry forward on his own.

A third requirement in preparation is actual practice in teaching under the friendly supervision of an able teacher. The value of this in launching the beginner on a higher plane of professional effort is inestimable. Some things the new teacher needs to know can be learned only through personal experience, and it is better that unavoidable mistakes be made where they can be sympathetically noted, discussed, and corrected. Of even greater importance is the opportunity from the beginning to induct the prospective teacher in sound values of professional workmanship which he can later cultivate under his own direction. Emphasis in practice teaching should center on this rather than on correction of elementary mistakes. Many a self-trained teacher has learned the rudiments of instruction without acquiring any aspiration to higher levels of performance which could have increased his effectiveness immeasurably.

Jointly with practice teaching opportunity there should be some systematic study of instructional method. Technical knowledge is more easily acquired during experience than apart from it, and even in the practice teaching stage only a beginning can be made. Emphasis at this stage should be on fundamentals rather than technical niceties: how the teacher conducts himself in the classroom, objectives of teacher-student relations, main points in planning and organizing instruction, patterns of teaching and their uses, employment of teaching aids, and principal methods of evaluation. Whether such study is pursued informally or in organized courses, it should be related to each trainee's personal experience in teaching, and immediately applied. It follows that the practice teaching opportunity should be utilized for real teaching and not for service as "helper" in clerical or routine chores; and that the experience should be graduated so as to enable the trainee to sample teaching problems step by step.

A fourth essential in preparation [8] is information regarding the wider scope of the college teacher's responsibilities, their rationale, and the manner of their performance. This should afford a practical orientation to the tasks in which the new college teacher, almost from the beginning, may be called upon to share—in advising students, course planning, institutional research, and the like. The prospective teacher needs to know how to maintain proper balance among these tasks. For training purposes it is unnecessary to engage in intensive study of these matters: consideration of salient principles and, whenever feasible, opportunity to apply them in practice teaching experience should suffice. The fundamentals of educational counseling can be developed in a series of discussions, supplemented

---

[8] No mention is made of proficiency in a field of scholarship as an essential element in preparation; this is assumed. Scholarship should be broadened but accent on it should not be diminished. The extent of the beginning college teacher's experience in scholarship is popularly exaggerated. According to the survey report earlier cited, in 637 reporting institutions 11 per cent of those in the rank of instructor have the doctorate, and 27 per cent have less than a master's degree. (N.E.A. *Research Bulletin*, Vol. XXXII, No. 4 [December 1954], p. 164.)

by observation of counseling procedure and personal contact with undergraduate students.

The art of curriculum making can only be learned through prolonged first-hand experience; what the trainee can acquire is some understanding of the curriculum as an instrument of educational policy, values in different fields of study, and ways in which subject matter can serve instruction. Other related functions of college teaching may be similarly approached, with greater emphasis on formation of attitudes sympathetic to their acceptance and later on-the-job mastery than on operational details.

Whether elements of training such as have been suggested are acceptable or others and better ones conceived, it is important that a more adequate program of preparing college teachers be instituted. The profession is already moving in this direction. The criticism made in 1947 in the Report of the President's Commission on Higher Education is too vital to be ignored: "College teaching is the only major learned profession for which there does not exist a well-defined program of preparation directed toward developing the skills which it is essential for the practicioner to possess." [9]

THE BEGINNING TEACHER

The Beginner vis-a-vis the Experienced Teacher. The beginner is under greater self-compulsion to develop than is his more experienced colleague. The advantages of youthful vigor and enthusiasm are heightened by an eagerness to succeed in the face of the challenge of probationary status. The fact that young teachers are sometimes found inadequate is less due to complacency than to fundamental shortcomings of capacity or training. The first years of teaching are often the best from the standpoint of growth.

If the "twenties" are the awkward age of college teaching, the "thirties" are the more dangerous: it is then that the leveling off process begins. Having gained a measure of stature and self-security from growing proficiency in his job, acceptance by colleagues and institution, and sense of ease with students, the teacher may be inclined to relax, trustful of future success without the necessity of

[9] *Higher Education for American Democracy* (New York: Harper & Brothers, 1947), Vol. Four, Chapter II, p. 16.

constant exertion. Many a teacher has enjoyed a life-time of professional activity without rising above the level of journeyman in his craft. The danger is well-known and exploited in argument by opponents of the principle of academic tenure who, in obviating one problem, would create others. The answer is to induce continued self-growth by positive means, not by threat of economic insecurity.

While the danger of stagnation is real, its incidence need not be exaggerated. If one may judge by observation, the majority of teachers are not so affected: they remain alert to their duties, conscious of their need for growth, and anxious to improve. Seasoned teachers worry as much about an occasionally "flat" lesson as any conscientious novice. The beginner may work harder and "stimulate" his students more, but the experienced teacher has incomparably more to offer in instruction. It takes professional maturity to distil wisdom from knowledge, broaden perspective, and discriminate between greater and lesser ends. It takes art to conceal art, and the practiced teacher can actually influence students more by appearing to "stimulate" them less. Yet the experienced teacher must continuously fight the temptation to slacken in growth.

Conditions Favorable to Growth. The beginner's objectives in growth differ from those of his colleagues with greater professional experience. Except in the small college the beginner is not at once plunged *in medias res* but allowed to confine his efforts to a few principal activities. It is expected that he acquit himself creditably in instruction, form good relations with students and colleagues, show sensitivity to the special character and purposes of the institution, and reveal in his own person promise of future development. If the beginner can satisfactorily demonstrate such capacities he will normally, unless institutional policy dictates otherwise, be retained. His subsequent objective should be not only to add to his institutional usefulness by increasing his range of responsibility but also to move gradually toward a higher plane of total accomplishment.

A factor conducive to growth is willingness to accept into one's professional province any responsibility pertinent to the education of students which one is qualified to perform, and to set out to learn it. It is important at the outset to establish a realistic priority of effort in terms of institutional needs and one's own capabilities. The most important thing is to become increasingly aware of opportunities, problems, and needed skills in teaching. Of next immediate importance is to accept normal auxiliary responsibilities in organized campus living, professional group activity, and administrative routine, and to resolve to do them well. Following this in priority are the specialized institutional tasks to which the young teacher may be assigned by virtue of need or special qualification. The young teacher must not be impatient with these additional obligations nor underestimate their challenge.

A further requisite for growth is readiness to learn from others. The young teacher should be quick to avail himself of opportunities to learn, informally or otherwise, from teaching colleagues, administrative staff members, and students. It is a mistake to compare the scholarship of one's new associates with those on the front lines of university research: they are not competing with university scholars but using scholarship as a tool in educating students. Nor should the beginner indulge in comparison of his new academic surroundings with those previously experienced without reflecting on differences in institutional purpose, composition of students, and financial resources: teaching impecunious but able students in a struggling small college is often more professionally rewarding than working in a materially richer setting. A young teacher has something to give his new institution, more to get from it. He brings fresh knowledge and enthusiasm beneficial to students and colleagues, but can learn much from them about the use of knowledge in teaching. Helping to freshen their interest, he may in turn absorb their "know-how."

Means of Growth. Anticipating the beginner's needs, colleges have begun to make systematic provision for his induction and early in-service training. At this stage the program is little more than rudimentary. A relatively ambitious effort may include, in addition to the amenities of social introduction, formal briefings by college officials on various aspects of institutional activity followed by opportunity for personal observation; specific colleges or large departments of instruction may hold instructional orientation conferences, or place the beginner for a time under the guidance of a more experienced colleague for informal consultation on such problems as may arise. In small institutions where new appointees are fewer and more widely spaced in time, it is easier for a department head or senior colleague to take a personal interest in a newcomer, supervising his immediate needs and fostering longer-range growth.

Whatever institutional provisions are formally made they can only be supplementary to the beginner's own efforts. The opportunities for learning are many, the place of learning is everywhere on the campus, and the agents of learning all those with whom he makes contact. Observing classes taught by colleagues and in turn inviting observation of his own, he can improve his teaching: talking with them and listening to discussion at conferences and informal gatherings, he can acquire much of value in general teaching theory and practice and specific learning problems and needs of students. By studying the educational program of the institution and familiarizing himself with its aims, scope of instruction, and special features, he can become better informed concerning the requirements of his own job. Most of all he can learn from students by observing them in classes, talking to them informally, and dipping into record files; and by sensitive assessment of their reactions to his teaching—not so much by direct expression of comment as by less direct means— he can ascertain the direction of needed improvement.

These things may be done without neglect of principal pursuits or sacrifice of long-range interests to the expediency of immediate success in adjustment. An inordinate expenditure of time and energy in order to learn "much in a hurry" is not required; what is required is alertness to such opportunities as normally present themselves or may be created without strain, and resolution to apply what has been learned. In his eagerness to succeed, the beginner should be careful not to burden his colleagues with his presence: even the most sympathetic weary of engaging in "shop-talk," answering questions, or opening their classrooms to observers. One needs to develop professional patience. In many matters there is no substitute for experience, and some valuable accomplishments can be acquired only in the course of service. There is no quick way of becoming a seasoned teacher: one must work at his craft a long while and patiently absorb the lessons of his own and others' experience. Similarly, in order to become familiar with a complex institution one must live in it.

Except in limited ways the beginner cannot expect to share in the government of his institution—sit on its policy-making bodies, influence its actions, or administer its laws—until he has secured his position by earning the confidence of colleagues and responsible officials. Similarly he cannot exercise wider leadership among the profession and the public until he has come to be known. Opportunities will develop in time, and it is well not to hurry them too much. The young teacher can err in seeking to extend himself beyond the limits of his experience and accomplishment.

THE EXPERIENCED TEACHER

While no clear demarcation exists between the close of apprenticeship and the beginning of professional maturity, increasing experience gradually liberates the maturing teacher from problems which beset the beginner. As these problems diminish, the teacher is freer to concentrate on growth of a higher sort: knowing the institution, he can better help to improve it as a center of education; having learned the conventions of teaching, he is in better position to develop original techniques; feeling at home in a field of scholarship, he can with greater assurance move in less trodden paths.

The growth process does not proceed in mechanical fashion from the conventional to the original, from the imitative to the creative. The promising young teacher, regardless of his inexperience, is from the beginning an original and creative worker in many respects. But to establish one's mastery in a craft one must learn its rules, and this is the primary task for the beginner. The experienced teacher should not be content with applying the rules more expertly or reaching for "superior levels of the commonplace" but strive for qualitatively different and higher achievement. Education is improved both by doing familiar tasks better and by envisioning and attacking new tasks.

Improving Instruction. The better the teacher, the greater the challenge for improvement that he sees. Even the accomplished teacher will find worthy targets in the endeavor to effect better course organization, planning of instruction, conduct of lecture and discussion, guidance of study, and evaluation of achievement. However familiar the subject and fluent the instruction, teaching and study aids, practice exercises, and reading lists are never so good that they cannot be improved. Better ways of adapting teaching to the individual needs of students, engaging superior students in more exacting and enriching activity, and stimulating the slow or uninterested learner to better achievement can almost always be developed.

An equally important goal is learning to deepen and liberalize one's influence as educator. Extending the educational potential of one's courses and one's activities as instructor will lead students toward broader personal development. Success in such effort is proportional to the teacher's continuous self-enrichment as person and scholar, his broadening perspective in education, and participation in the cooperative life of his institution. He cannot afford to maintain an academically provincial outlook, nor isolate himself in the classroom or laboratory away from other academic responsibility. He needs to join with colleagues in discussions of problems of teaching, learning, and administration, become involved in educational issues, and keep informed of developments outside his own discipline. Academic isolationism has operated to prevent many a well-qualified teacher from attaining the stature of educator.

The profession of college teaching has so developed in general and specialized phases that, however much he is occupied in personal scholarly pursuits, the college teacher must regularly share in common discoveries, accomplishments, and problems. Issues such as those arising from increased enrollments are not the concern of one professional group but of all. No one can afford to ignore the contributions to general educational thought of John Dewey, Bertrand Russell, or Alfred N. Whitehead but even more specialized writings in educational psychology, curriculum, and evaluation must be sampled if the teacher is to remain abreast of his profession. The publication in 1945 of Harvard's *General Education in a Free Society* deservedly attracted attention, yet studies and reports of comparable significance by colleges, teachers' associations, and government agencies within the last twenty-five years have been all too neglected. The college teacher, for example, who has not discovered for himself the series of publications sponsored by the American Youth Commission misses an opportunity for an enlightening look into the minds of students. In recent years the profession has been active in promoting conferences such as those of the Association for Higher Education [10]

---

[10] See *Current Issues in Higher Education*, Proceedings of the Ninth Annual National Conference on Higher Education (Washington: National Education Association, 1954).

and the Survey of Medical Education.[11] To the existing fund of periodical literature in higher education [12] a journal of distinction has lately been added in *Improving College Teaching and Learning.* All of these, as well as publications by the Educational Policies Commission, the American Council on Education, and other agencies, deal with matters of urgent import to the college teacher. There are practical limits to opportunity to engage in active collaboration and even to gain information through reading, but the college teacher should eagerly divide his attention between activities in his own discipline and those in the wider field of education.

One gains in professional understanding through knowledge of students, and for this purpose the classroom setting alone is insufficient. The teacher needs to associate with students in out-of-class activities. The need is admitted in principle, but as the teacher becomes more deeply involved in his primary and collateral responsibilities he finds it increasingly inconvenient to find time for "socializing" activity. The higher he advances in the profession, the farther removed from students he is apt to become. The result is that older faculty members who have more to contribute to students pass less time in such association than junior colleagues. A teacher's first business is with students, and whatever his eminence none can afford to be so busy as to be unavailable for informal association with them. Attending students' social events, participating in their activities, sharing their company at meals, inviting them to a weekly "coffee hour," accompanying them on excursions, or simply "visiting" with them during chance meetings are part of the normal routine of professional living. Students are pleased and benefited by these contacts, and teachers may learn much that is useful in teaching and conducive to mental vigor and alertness.

Productive Scholarship. Even the teacher who publishes little can by sustained pursuit of study, extracting knowledge and relating it to instruction, refresh himself and invigorate his teaching. The teacher who can periodically produce scholarly work of pub-

[11] See *Preparation for Medical Education in the Liberal Arts College,* A. E. Severinghaus, H. J. Carman, and W. E. Cadbury, Jr., editors (New York: McGraw-Hill Book Company, 1953).

[12] Notably the *AAUP Bulletin, Journal of Higher Education, Journal of General Education, Educational Record, Higher Education, School and Society,* and *Harvard Educational Review.*

lishable quality—a report of a significant experiment or investigation, a monograph on a subject of importance, a learned paper—helps not only to advance knowledge but to infuse his instruction with a sense of excitement reserved for an originator or discoverer. Standing to profit most of all is the teacher who makes continuous productive scholarship an absorbing hobby while maintaining himself in other phases of his responsibility. The discipline of exploring a problem, determining a line of investigation, following through in research, organizing findings, and giving them clear and effective expression offers an unmatched opportunity for growth.

Those interested in dedicating themselves to productive scholarship should not make the commitment lightly. The exercise of productive scholarship is exacting, requiring an abundance of energy with which to satisfy also concurrent teaching obligations. A teacher should begin by realistically appraising himself and the circumstances under which he works. If by temperament he finds intensive application to a long-term task irksome, if he finds the company of people more congenial to his interest than solitary devotion to study, if writing comes hard and the discipline of learning to write is unappealing, or if the institution makes such professional demands as to leave little time and energy for systematic research and writing, perhaps he should explore other more promising avenues of service.

There is a great difference in personal investment between preparing an occasional piece for publication and producing a more extended work of scholarship: the latter is not often turned out by working weekends and during short vacation periods. One must be willing with real austerity to "strip down" to the essentials in living, foregoing many social and professional interests. Even the pressure of family responsibilities may have a bearing on the outcome. The implication is not that the productive scholar must prepare himself for a rigorous existence without the normal amenities but that, like the artist or creative writer, he must live under professional discipline, rationing himself so as to make productive work possible.

Growth through Civic Experience. Contact with the community offers an opportunity to be of service, a constructive outlet for the teacher's talent and energy, and a means of personal and professional enrichment. The community is a social workshop and laboratory in which products of instruction are used, raw materials for later instruction produced, new educational needs revealed, and provisions for meeting them tested. Many of the college disciplines, particularly the social studies, have their roots close to the surface of community living and are shaped in their growth by the immediate social climate. The teacher must derive nourishment from contact with the public environment outside the college. It is not enough to be a "student of society" in the abstract; the teacher needs to be close to people and to an understanding of them. From such proximity and understanding he will gain in knowledge of his students and the nature and possibilities of his subject. In the Middle Ages the "Seven Liberal Arts" were taught as dry encyclopedic knowledge divorced from events of contemporary life; only the unremitting efforts of dedicated scholars kept them from extinction. Today the liberal studies in the college program are richer from contact at all points with people and their ways. To an extent the work of the college teacher is by nature confining; all the more reason why he —the physicist or the metaphysicist—should cultivate opportunity for community experience if he is to grow in capacity for liberal instruction.

RECIPROCAL OBLIGATIONS OF THE COLLEGE

Professional growth is not a one-sided undertaking. For its part the college has important obligations to fulfill if it would help the teacher realize his professional potentiality. Over and above its human complement of teachers and students the college has a corporate existence and character shaped, in some cases, over generations. It has influence and prestige carrying beyond the physical confines of the institution, and resources above those of material possession. The coporate life of the college should be so conducted as to encourage the development of students and teachers, and its strength brought to bear in their support. Of the many obligations which the college has to teachers, a few have been chosen for special mention.

1. *To employ wise policies of teacher selection, retention, and promotion.* Sound personnel policy is essential for the maintenance of a healthy institutional life. The best way for a college to achieve excellence is to find and appoint good teachers. Students would be better educated and teachers' professional development enhanced if

the latter were selected on the basis of criteria more intrinsically related to their responsibilities. The right people in the right jobs do not need much external stimulation in order to fulfill their aspirations. In the absence of more reliable indices of potentiality it is the obligation of the college to recruit people with the highest qualifications of intelligence, character, and training, trusting the probationary process to permit further evaluation of their fitness. The probationary period, usually of at least three years' duration, should be made a rigorous test of a young teacher's capability and longer-range promise. Success should earn retention. Current practices tend to be inconsistent: on the one hand, some institutions release all but the most brilliant newcomers after a few years of service, while in many others, retention after a nominal probationary period is almost assured if the young teacher "seems all right."

Academic promotion policies are also in need of reassessment. The need for considering skill in teaching as a factor in promotion is self-evident, and in principle more and more colleges have come to accord it equal ranking with scholarly attainment.[13] But good teaching is not as measurable an accomplishment as productive scholarship, and the practical result is to tip the scales in favor of the latter. This is professionally unfair and unrealistic. Without withdrawing recognition of acknowledged scholarship, promotion standards should in practice include good teaching and other professional attainments.

Although opportunities for promotion may necessarily be competitive, the principle of competition should not be carried too far. It is not a fruitful exercise to rank teachers of different accomplishment in different fields of instruction. A teacher should be appraised in terms of his professional contribution, and where a wider scale needs to be established, it should be weighted in terms of all of the teacher's functions and not a selected few.

2. *To afford adequate remuneration.* No person enters the teaching profession in order to become rich, but there is a functional relationship between adequate salary, job security and expectation of a sufficient retirement income, and maintenance of high standards

---

[13] "Instructional Staff Practices and Policies in Degree-Granting Institutions, 1953–54," N. E. A. *Research Bulletin,* Vol. XXXII, No. 4 (December 1954), p. 172.

of professional achievement. College teaching offers rewards sufficient to attract first-rate persons to the profession, but people cannot be expected to be single-minded in devotion to their job when its salary has to be supplemented by earnings from various part-time occupations College governing boards recognize the problem and do their best in the face of mounting odds, but its full resolution is beyond their control. The matter calls for vision and statesmanship on high levels of public policy so that higher education may be granted the subsidy it needs without admission of outside interference.

Arguments for improving teachers' salaries are often presented as a plea for public generosity and civic idealism, as if proper compensation were a matter of upholding the prestige of a profession. Actually more fundamental laws of economics are operative. To get and to hold persons of high professional caliber it is necessary to take account of competing opportunities in the employment market. It would be catastrophic for American society if its colleges were staffed with teachers of mediocre quality satisfied with low-paying employment. The public would not long tolerate paying physicians reduced fees for inferior medical service nor low-cost housing that fails to stand up. The costs of maintaining education should be viewed in the same way; failure to do this presents even greater risks since a decline in the educational product is less perceptible immdiately and more destructive in the long run.

3. *To foster a climate conducive to good teaching and learning.* On the whole American colleges have done an exemplary job in supporting teachers in the exercise of their rights as scholars and citizens and in resisting intrusion of occasional repressive influences from outside. A comparable job needs to be done in making every campus a stimulating and productive place in which to live and to work. Absence of restraints is not enough; to be intellectually invigorating a college should be hospitable to new ideas, new projects and endeavors, and to change. It should not only use its people skillfully for its own ends, but encourage them to conceive and seek ends of their own, expressing their distinctive talents in professionally useful ways. It should promote sound orthodoxy and promising heterodoxy, and having tried some things and failed, try again. No institution can afford to rest on its past or present accomplishment.

By continually reviewing its goals and the processes designed to serve them, imaginatively assigning creative people to creative tasks, pursuing institutional research, sharing with other institutions the product of its experience and learning, and being responsive to new developments in society, a college can retain its vitality and help its teachers to grow.

Much argument has centered on the extent to which faculty participation in institutional government is desirable. Faculty management has its limitations but also the incomparable advantage of broadening the scope of responsible college citizenship.[14] It impels concern for educational tasks outside one's immediate sphere of instruction, and fosters civic pride and sense of professional belonging. Government by committees may be awkward, but the quality of ideas is improved through friction of minds, and in the long run coordinated group activity is more productive than streamlined individual effort. The atmosphere of democratically decentralized rule is wholesome for liberal education, and the freedom it offers for responsible dissent is an influence for growth. Not every college is in position to grant the organized faculty broad powers of educational authority, but so far as possible it should invest teachers (and students) with responsibility for the conduct of institutional affairs.

4. *To assign teachers to instruction and other service in ways that take account of their special capabilities, interests, and needs for growth.* Industry has learned the importance of placing the right worker in the right job; the college is perhaps more careful in initial selection of its people than in their subsequent specific utilization, even with regard to their primary responsibility in teaching. Assignment to courses often follows the path of least resistance, the basis of course allotment being continuity in status quo, teachers' indicated preference, and seniority, combined naturally with scholarly attainment. The result is to keep teachers in the same courses for a a longer time than may be desirable, depriving them and others of an opportunity to extend their teaching competency. Young teachers are at a disadvantage in carrying a heavier burden of elementary or "leftover" courses and delayed from entering those for which they may be more suited.

[14] See also James K. Munford, "Case for Faculty Committees," *College and University*, 25: 424–31 (April 1950).

Little within the supervisor's province of responsibility is more important than fostering the proper professional utilization of man-power. A teacher's satisfaction in his work and continued impulse for self-improvement depend upon the challenge and interest in his assigned duties. One needs to feel that the courses he offers are "right" for him and that, in general, his program of professional activity has been planned with care, looking toward his long-term good. Since institutional needs occasionally conflict with personal interests, it may be necessary at times to compromise to the extent of accepting a course lying outside one's sphere of preference. But a teacher needs to feel convinced that his long term needs for growth are not being overlooked.

The paramount consideration in determining assignment to courses is that students shall have the best instruction available. Subject to this qualification, other considerations are admissible, chiefly the teacher's own preference, need for representativeness or balance in viewpoints, and training requirements of younger teach-ers. At this point the supervisor's insight into the potentialities of teachers and his leadership qualities come into evidence—in creating new and better growth opportunities and inducing colleagues to avail themselves of them. Some teachers are less venturesome than others in accepting new responsibilities, and may need to be con-vinced of their desirability. Particularly in the rapidly developing program of extra-instructional educational services it is possible for an alert supervisor to conceive new tasks promising to be useful to the institution and at the same time to engage special capacities of teachers.

From the teacher's viewpoint a good teaching schedule has—in addition to the intrinsic worth and challenge of its courses—variety, coherence, and balance. It is unwise to assign more than two "sec-tions" of the same course lest instruction become routinized; it is equally undesirable to include completely disparate offerings so that the teacher has difficulty in finding a focus for scholarly interest and application. An ideal teaching schedule consists of perhaps three different courses, on different levels to enable the teacher to work with students over a range of educational maturity, yet involving a common area of scholarship or related divisions of that area.

5. *To maintain a reasonable work schedule and satisfactory con-*

ditions of work. Within their financial capabilities colleges endeavor
to keep the individual service load down to workable size, and the
vigilance of accrediting agencies and professional organizations has
helped to enforce proper standards. College teaching should be distinguished by quality of production rather than volume of activity.
A heavy teaching schedule, oversized classes, extra-instructional assignments, and burdensome "housekeeping" duties have an adverse
effect on professional quality. Needing special protection are the
ablest and most promising teachers and those whose distinctive interests require more painstaking application. Many an able young
teacher has been checked in fulfilment of a promising career by being prematurely saddled with too many responsibilities. It is reas-
suring for an administrator to assign an important task to a person
who invariably performs well, but it is more important that such
work be apportioned fairly without excessive inconvenience to anyone. Exacting extra-instructional duties should be rotated among
those able to manage them, and few should be exempt from the
indispensable routine chores ever-present in an operation of institutional size.

Two common complaints of teachers concern the inadequacy of
work space and secretarial assistance. Such things are hard to govern
by educational principle, but in an institution's desire to expand its
academic opportunities and services, space facilities for teachers are
frequently overlooked. Spacious reception rooms and administrative
quarters are much less important than assigned space in which a
teacher can pursue work with a student, a colleague, or his own
thoughts. Similarly it is false economy to use teachers in clerical
tasks they are untrained to perform; it is cheaper to liberate them
for professional responsibilities. The physical preparation of instructional materials—course outlines, bibliographies, study exercises, examinations—as well as necessary administrative reports should be
the responsibility of a shared or centralized secretarial service.

6. *To orient the new teacher to his job.* A beginning has been
made in this direction but the organized effort is far from adequate.
Entering a new institution, even an experienced teacher requires
systematic orientation to changed responsibilities and routines. A
beginner needs more thorough in-service training not only in functions specific to his job but also in broader professional practice. The

college should provide a planned program of activities familiarizing the beginner with its educational aims, the nature and scope of its curriculum, essential information relating to students' background, current concerns and problems, and, in a more detailed way, with the teacher's individual responsibilities. This training should include planning and organizing instruction, preparing instructional materials and aids, proper use of various lesson patterns, guiding independent study, and evaluating learning. Training may be conducted in individual or group conference held in conjunction with actual supervision of the beginner in his job. If more general interest warrants the conferences may be organized on a large seminar basis with an invitation to participate extended to all faculty members.

7. *To give every teacher the benefit of constructive supervision.* Every professional person, regardless of maturity and attainment, needs at many points in his career the benefit of a colleague's advice, help, or criticism. In the college such supervision has special character and requirements. It is exercised more by the teacher himself and a voluntary group of associates than by a designated executive officer or senior colleague, its function is advisory rather than managerial, and it operates more indirectly, informally, and unobtrusively. In practice it must take account of the teacher's sometimes superior qualification in an academic field, of the rights of academic freedom and the dignity of the profession, and—not least—of the absence of standard criteria of merit. Nevertheless there is an indispensable place in college teaching for the "supervisor"—a dean, department head, or senior colleague—on whom rests special responsibility for promoting and aiding in individual and group efforts at self-improvement.

Observation of college teaching is better conducted under the auspices of teachers themselves, exchanging visits and discussing their own and one another's teaching problems. Instruction during such visits is less constrained and the subsequent conference between teachers more free of tension. Students becoming aware of the practice of faculty intervisiting will be less self-conscious. The supervisor's role is to stimulate interest in such a program, help organize and maintain it, and assist teachers in utilizing the results.

A correlative means of supervision is systematic group discussion of teaching problems on a college-wide, department, and course-committee basis, organized and led by teachers. Criticism of teaching practice and proposals for improvement, emanating from group deliberation and impersonally directed, have greater effect than those passing from supervisor to teacher—and hurt much less. The supervisor's role is to sponsor and support these conferences, promote participation, play an active though not dominant part in the proceedings, and assist in carrying out the proposals. The supervisor himself, meeting in informal sessions with individual teachers, can make direct contributions of inestimable value, whether in dealing with instructional problems of the moment or matters of longer range. On the college level such meetings should be free of official formality and didactic tone: they are explorations of ideas between equals.

Good supervision stimulates the initiative, imagination, and intelligent effort of others. College teachers need less to be corrected and guided than released for creative work. The college supervisor makes his best contribution not by trying to recast colleagues in his own image but by giving them leeway to develop in theirs. It does not much matter whether the supervisor is privately in agreement with what a teacher attempts: if the latter is convinced of the worth of an idea, provided no prohibitive consequences impend, the supervisor should accord assistance and support, although he is free to express his reservations. Some undertakings may not succeed, but it is important that the teacher keep trying, and from the effort may come growth.

8. *To protect the teacher in the exercise of his professional duties.* This obligation may not need to be invoked often, but when a critical situation arises the institution should take an unequivocal stand. A college teacher is professionally dedicated to the task of stimulating thought and guiding it in the direction of truth, in pursuing scholarship and according it free expression. There are times when, in the practice of his calling, he may arouse opposition from public groups on grounds of offense to patriotism, religion, morality, race, or economic belief. Insistent protest by even a small vocal group can make a large institution uncomfortable. It is easy then for the institution to make its public peace by assuring that the teacher will be restrained from further giving offense; but the proper course is for the institution to ascertain whether the teacher's action has been professionally correct and, in the event that it has been, to give him

unqualified support whether or not it agrees substantively with what has been said or done. Only in this way can the teacher's (and the profession's) freedom to grow be assured. All too often a teacher's manner rather than substance of expression may be the cause of the difficulty; such offense is unnecessary, and steps should be taken to obviate its recurrence. Teachers are bound by the same obligations to good taste and civility as other persons and, when they become careless or insensitive it is the institution's supervisory responsibility to correct them and restore harmony.

An institution should be slow to intervene in matters of teacher-student relations, yet avoid a policy of complete noncommitment. For a college to dignify every complaint against a teacher with a formal hearing would have the effect of fostering educationally undesirable habits: haggling about examination or course grades, for example, would be certain to increase. Solicitous parents may write to a college executive expressing grievance against this teacher or that; in trivial cases reply should be made without even notifying the teacher; in cases warranting more complete explanation the complaining letter should be forwarded to the teacher with a request for reply. Only when charges are unmistakably serious is thorough investigation justified. If a teacher is qualified to hold his teaching position, he is qualified to work his way out of the occasional difficulties that arise in teacher-student relations. The "official" judgment of the institution should not supplant the teacher's own judgment except for cause.

Teachers have been known at times to behave capriciously and to be guilty of unjustifiable actions in dealing with students. In such cases the institution has an obligation to rectify the mistake. Incidents in which students seem to have been treated unfairly should be investigated and, if the teacher proves to have been at fault, amends made to the student without degrading the teacher or compromising his future effectiveness. A good teacher grows from the mistakes he has made, provided they have been brought to his attention without incurring his lasting resentment.

SELECTED BIBLIOGRAPHY

Anderson, Paul R., "The Preparation of the Teacher in General Education," *Journal of General Education*, 3:98–106, January 1949.

Association for Higher Education, *Current Issues in Higher Education, 1954,* Proceedings of the Ninth Annual National Conference on Higher Education. Washington: National Education Association, 1954. 321 pp.

Blegen, Theodore C. and Cooper, Russell M., editors, *The Preparation of College Teachers,* Report of a Conference Held in Chicago, Illinois, December 8–10, 1949, Sponsored by the American Council on Education and the U.S. Office of Education. Washington: American Council on Education, 1950. 186 pp.

Carman, Harry J., "Teachers of Tomorrow," *Association of American Colleges Bulletin,* 35:306–16, May 1949.

Eckert, Ruth E., "Some Neglected Aspects in the Preparation of College Teachers," *Journal of General Education,* 3:137–44, January 1949.

Edmondson, James B., "Improving the Effectiveness of College Teaching," *School and Society,* 76:209–13, October 4, 1952.

Gilbert, Amy M., "In-Service Education of the College Faculty," *Journal of Higher Education,* 20:192–97, April 1949.

Gray, William S., ed., *The Preparation and In-Service Training of College Teachers,* Volume 10 of the Proceedings of the Institute for Administrative Officers of Higher Institutions. Chicago: University of Chicago Press, 1938. 230 pp.

Kelly, Fred J., ed., *Improving College Instruction,* Report of a Conference Held at Chicago, Illinois, December 7–9, 1950, Sponsored by the American Council on Education and the U.S. Office of Education. Washington: American Council on Education, 1951. 195 pp.

————, *Toward Better College Teaching,* Bulletin 1950, No. 13, Office of Education, Federal Security Agency. Washington: U.S. Government Printing Office, 1950. 71 pp.

Klapper, Paul, "Problems in College Teaching," *American Association of University Professors Bulletin,* 36:53–63, March 1950.

————, "Professional Preparation of the College Teacher," *Journal of General Education,* 3:228–44, July 1949.

National Education Association, Research Division, "Instructional Staff Practices and Policies in Degree-Granting Instsitutions, 1953–54," *Research Bulletin,* 32:159–214, December 1954.

President's Report on Higher Education, *Higher Education for American Democracy,* Vol. IV, "Staffing Higher Education," 63 pp. New York: Harper & Brothers, 1947.

Reed, Anna Y. *et al., The Effective and the Ineffective College Teacher.* New York: American Book Company, 1935. 344 pp.

Russell, John Dale, ed., *Problems of Faculty Personnel*, Volume 18 of the Proceedings of the Institute for Administrative Officers of Higher Institutions. Chicago: University of Chicago Press, 1946. 146 pp.

Tead, Ordway, *College Teaching and College Learning: A Plea for Improvement*, Frank Ellsworth Spaulding Lecture for 1947–1948. New Haven: Yale University Press, 1949. 56 pp.

Wilson, Logan, *The Academic Man: A Study in the Sociology of a Profession*. New York: Oxford University Press, 1942. 248 pp.

Woodburne, Lloyd S., *Faculty Personnel Policies in Higher Education*. New York: Harper & Brothers, 1950. 201 pp.

IV. *The Teacher and His Students*

The profession of college teaching has placed less than due emphasis on learning the nature of the student. Current knowledge of students is largely empirical, with a relatively small core of scientifically ascertained and verified fact. We do not have enough precise information about the kinds of persons who populate the colleges and our classrooms, their educational backgrounds, motives for study, and how they learn. Lacking such information we are compelled to rely upon past and continuing experience, inspired insight, and rationalized hypothesis. This is not the safest way for a profession to operate, even with teachers who are sensitive and discerning in judgment. The psychological foundations of learning and teaching need to be extended and deepened, empirical "home truths" replaced by secure knowledge, and the sociological and educational backgrounds of college students more systematically explored. Progress is being made in these directions but the goal of *knowing the student* is still distant.

This chapter deals in a necessarily general way with information about students pertinent to classroom instruction. The reader is cautioned against applying generalizations concerning a multitude of students to specific cases. No psychological doctrine is better established than the fact of individual differences, even in populations more homogeneous than that of the college. The experimentally derived principles of development, learning, and behavior have wider applicability than descriptive sociological and educational data, but even the former must be interpreted in light of the modifying influences which enter into a particular situation. The best purpose served by general findings of group attributes and behavior is to provide

78

easier access to study and understanding of the individual and a standard of comparative reference. The need for recognizing individual differences holds also as between institutions: survey findings of institutional populations are not transferable unless they are seen as modified by significant similarities and differences. In the final analysis experimental psychology has to be supplemented by institutional research probing into special problems and needs of respective college populations.

WHO GOES TO COLLEGE?

Recent Changes in College Population. Anyone whose teaching career spans the period since the first World War has witnessed profound changes in higher education. He may recall the relatively small, select academic college of his early years; the great buildup of the 1920's with its expansion in numbers of students,[1] size of institutions, course offerings, and divisions of instruction; the hard years of the Depression when enrollments slackened, students shifted from academic to technical and applied studies, and specialized institutions gained at the expense of liberal; and the recent resurgence in the World War II period when colleges became centers of specialized war-service training, mathematics and science came to the fore, and returning veterans and other entrants strained the facilities of colleges both physically and with demand for new educational services.

The central phenomenon throughout this period has been the rise in enrollment. Though one may weary of statistics, their story is impressive: there are in resident attendance in American colleges and universities over $2\frac{1}{4}$ million students, of whom $1\frac{3}{4}$ million are undergraduates, about one-third women; while the national population in the first half of the twentieth century has approximately doubled and the number of institutions increased about 85 per cent, the enrollment in these institutions has grown 1000 per cent; from 4 per cent of college-age youth in attendance in 1900, the percentage in 1950 had risen to 28.4 inclusive of veterans, and 18.4 without them.[2]

[1] In the decade between 1920 and 1930 the undergraduate enrollment more than doubled, increasing from approximately 370,000 to 790,000. *Higher Education in the Forty-Eight States* (Chicago: The Council of State Governments, 1952), p. 39.

[2] *Ibid.*, p. 30.

Indications are clear that growth in enrollment will continue. Experts differ in the measure of their predictions, but none deny the trend.

Assuming that there will be no further increase in the *percentage* of college-age youth attending our colleges and universities and that the only increases will be caused by an increasing number of college-age young people, we may look forward to an enrollment of more than four million . . . by 1970. In the face of past experience and present trends, this would appear to be entirely too conservative. . . . If the trend of increasing proportional attendance continues at the rate of approximately one percent a year until 1962, following the pattern established over the last twenty years, and remains at that level, we shall have enrolled in our colleges and universities by 1970 approximately five and one-half million students.[3]

In addition to magnifying the enterprise of higher education in its total and separate institutional aspects, the growth in enrollment has been a paramount influence in extending and complicating the program of studies. A college Bulletin listing some seven or eight hundred courses together with information concerning prerequisites, course patterns, and credit allowances makes formidable reading. One may remember the time when the college teacher was fairly familiar with the titles of offerings by his own institution; it now takes considerable application to college-wide curriculum activity to achieve the same familiarity. The program has been opened to many subjects not previously included, concentration of student interest among studies has shifted, and new combinations of course patterns have emerged. A teacher of an old established discipline may suddenly find himself intellectually not "at home" with an institution he has long served, and not a few become disaffected by the educational changes.

The most patent evidence of change is apt to be in the teacher's own classroom—in the composition of the class, the quality of students, their educational preparation, and readiness to learn the subject. At one time it could more easily be taken for granted that college students, whatever their scholastic shortcomings, were equipped with aptitude and preparation for language study. "Fresh-

[3] American Association of Collegiate Registrars and Admissions Officers, *The Impending Tidal Wave of Students* (1954), pp. 22–24.

man Composition" was offered as a review of fundamentals of language and expression prior to an incursion into more creative activity, not—as it is now for some students—as a first course in formal grammar. Foreign-language instruction presumed familiarity with the linguistic structure of one's native tongue as well as some earlier foreign-language preparation. Although most colleges still have foreign-language requirements for admission, the presumption cannot now be made to the same extent. Language facility remains relatively important in the entering students' intellectual equipment for college study, yet institutions find it increasingly necessary to lower the level of beginning foreign-language instruction and to institute such remedial facilities as "clinics" and "workshops." More students enter with only the most rudimentary secondary-school foreign-language preparation.

In general the teacher is bound to note that the students' range of abilities is greater and their interests are more variegated. Perhaps most conspicuous is the larger number of "average" learners and those of marginal quality whose capacities would not have earned them admission or retention a generation ago. The latter element evokes the not uncommon complaint that secondary education has deteriorated and that colleges too are going downhill. It is true, to a greater extent than formerly, that student motivation for learning some specific subject cannot be taken for granted, that extrinsic attention-holding devices may need to be employed in instruction, that simple exposition of a topic may not suffice to assure understanding, and that provision for remedial instruction may occasionally be necessary. Deficiencies in preparation are in evidence not only in language study but also in mathematics, science, history, and other disciplines. This does not hold for all students, as any fair-minded teacher will admit: superior students are numerous, and there are others to whom these real or attributed shortcomings do not apply.

The conclusion toward which this seems superficially to tend is deceptive. All things considered, there is no justification for complaint about the current college population. In the first place, the new college population now represents a fair cross-section of the American public. Such representation is not yet complete or even adequate, but there are in the colleges not only prospective recruits for the traditionally higher professions but young people with farther-ranging interests in agriculture, the arts, business, public service, technology, and other occupational categories. There is diversity in cultural origin, socio-economic background, aptitude, and interest. Higher education gains in vitality from the impact of varied minds, interests, aptitudes, and personalities; institutions grow in vigor as they open their doors to capable young people from all walks of life who stand to profit from educational opportunity.

Second, though students today may be lacking in some essentials of preparation, they have other attributes and accomplishments in greater abundance. Contemporary living tends to instil a more mature and responsible outlook and a more realistic sense of values. Also, pre-college education, however it may be criticized for lack of academic rigor, accentuates certain aspects of personal and social development which cannot be shrugged off as unimportant to higher education. Students are healthier, better balanced, more experienced, more at home with the world of practical things, better acquainted with music and the arts, and their range of knowledge, particularly of contemporary matters, is greater.[4] Their values are apt to be more worldly, respecting fundamental qualities of kindness, generosity, integrity, and good sense more than intellectual subtlety. They have a better sense of their own needs and are more appreciative of what education can do for them.

Finally, it would be wrong to generalize that as a population they are academically inferior to their predecessors although, owing to the higher enrollment, some inferior material is necessarily included. The program of secondary education has been broadened so as to distribute students' preparation over many subjects rather than concentrate it in a few. To a teacher analyzing his students' background of accomplishment it may seem as if training in *his* subject has been neglected, and in the case of some students it has been. But available evidence does not support the conclusion that either the intelligence or the scholastic achievement of entering college students is declining.[5] There are more bright students in the colleges today than

[4] See also Arthur Mizener's "The Undergraduate of the 20's Was Less Mature," *New York Herald-Tribune Sunday Supplement,* September 19, 1954.

[5] Comparative evidence of past and present accomplishment is not easy to produce. One such study by Philip A. Boyer and Hans C. Gordon ("Have High Schools Neglected Academic Achievement?," *School and Society,* 49:810–12 [June 24, 1939]) fails to find, on the basis of the same tests administered to graduating students in the academic curriculum of Philadelphia high schools in

previously, and more of those whose mental caliber approaches genius. With the possible exception of linguistic studies, the preparatory accomplishment of most students is as good as it ever was. The larger number of marginal students with conspicuous shortcomings tends to distract from others whose attainment is substantial.

Generalizations regarding the relative merits of past and present secondary education are also hard and profitless to make. The modern secondary school is so different from the older as to render comparison inept. Even the college-preparatory curriculum today addresses itself not specifically to college-entrance requirements but to broader objectives including the developmental needs of a large adolescent population. Much of what the student learns in the high school relates primarily to the making of a man and a citizen, and only indirectly to later college experience. This is as it should be: an educative institution cannot afford to be exclusively preparatory. The value of the college would diminish were it to serve as no more than a preparatory establishment for the university. It should be enough for the secondary school to send to the college good young people capable of rising to higher levels of study.

Social Composition of College Population. The total number of students involved and the differences in institutional constituency make necessary a cautious approach in the treatment of available data. "In general, the population of a specific college tends to be rather homogeneous. Socio-economic and cultural differences within a group appear to be of less magnitude than the differences between total populations of different types of institutions." [6] Institutional

---

1928 and again in 1938, any significant differentials in achievement; Ralph W. Tyler's study ("High School Pupils of Today," *Ohio State Educational Research Bulletin*, 9: 409–11) showed that high-school graduates in Ohio in 1930 did better in physics and mathematics and as well in English composition as graduates of the same schools had done in 1922 or 1924; E. C. Seyler's comparative study of the scholastic achievement of freshmen at the University of Illinois in 1949 and the combined achievement of three classes entering in 1935, 1936, and 1937 (*College and University: The Journal of the American Association of Collegiate Registrars and Admissions Officers*, 27:90–106) showed the 1949 freshmen better qualified for college work. A summary of evidence favoring present-day education is offered by Archibald W. Anderson "The Charges Against American Education: What Is the Evidence?," *Progressive Education*, 29:91–105 (January 1952).

[6] Daniel Feder *et al.* in the *Encyclopedia of Educational Research* (Revised ed.; New York: The Macmillan Company, 1950), p. 1294.

homogeneity is, of course, relative; it may be explained by the fact that students' attraction to an institution is largely influenced by location and accessibility, suitability of fees, family interest and tradition, appropriateness of its offerings to given purpose, and academic eligibility for admission. A study by the Office of Education for 1949–50 showed that four out of five undergraduate students attend institutions in their home states, and most of the remaining fifth in adjacent states.[7]

So far as "class structure" can be identified in American society, repeated studies have shown that college students are drawn largely from the "middle" and "upper" classes of the population.[8] A much larger proportion of college youth comes from the upper socio-economic reaches than from the lower: of 910 youth with an IQ of 110 or above surveyed in a Pennsylvania study in 1936, 57 per cent of those in higher socio-economic groups attended college, and only 13 per cent in the lower;[9] Helen B. Goetsch's study of 1023 students with an IQ of 117 or better who were graduated from Milwaukee High School in 1937 and 1938 produced similar findings;[10] W. S. Hoffman's analysis (1932) of occupations of parents of students in 55 junior college, liberal colleges, and universities revealed that in three-fourths of the cases the fathers were engaged in four major types of occupations—proprietary, agricultural, professional, and managerial;[11] and more recent studies have corroborated this evidence. In the last generation the social base of the college enrollment has been extended: children of workers, skilled and even unskilled, enter college in greater numbers than formerly. But, as late as 1950,

[7] Cited in *Higher Education in the Forty-Eight States* (Chicago: Council of State Governments, 1952), pp. 42–43.

[8] The Time Magazine study, *They Went to College,* by Ernest Havemann and Patricia Salter West (New York: Harcourt, Brace and Co., 1952) states the case somewhat optimistically. "The picture of the college campus as the exclusive preserve of rich youngsters is an illusion. The campus is inhabited by a broad cross section of American life . . ." (p. 166). No exception can be taken to the first part of the statement; the second is probably intended to be interpreted figuratively, qualified as it is by the authors' own findings.

[9] Cited by Warner, Havighurst, and Loeb, *Who Shall Be Educated?,* (New York: Harper & Brothers, 1944), pp. 51–52.

[10] *Op. cit.,* p. 52.

[11] See "Student Personnel Work—I. Student Population" in *Encyclopedia of Educational Research* (Revised ed.; New York: The Macmillan Company, 1950), p. 1294.

the estimate still was that "students whose fathers are engaged in manual labor rarely exceed five per cent of the total enrollment." [12]

As indicated, discrepancies among institutions are considerable. Exclusive and costly "finishing" schools continue to maintain a financially select clientele; some of the older Eastern institutions with "Ivy League" standing attract a more than representative share of young people of wealth. On the other hand, the majority of American colleges, large and small, public, independent, or church-connected, while drawing students from average or above-average income groups, also contain youth of less than moderate means. Assistance in the form of scholarships, grants-in-aid, and opportunities for part-time employment has enabled impecunious young people from city, town, or country to pursue a higher education. Even select private colleges have been generous, within the limits of their resources, in furnishing subventions to talented students who otherwise would have been denied an opportunity for college study.

The influx of veterans following World War II not only raised the maturity level of the college population but broadened its base. The "G I benefits" affording tuition expenses and moderate personal and family subsistence influenced veterans who might otherwise not have done so to seek a college education.[13] In the fall of 1947 veterans constituted 48 per cent of a total college enrollment of some 2.34 million.[14] During the five-year period from 1946 to 1951, the college came closer to representing a real cross-section of American society than ever before. The social gains of this experiment in subsidized higher education have been enormous, despite some publicized wastage and the discreditable tactics of a few individuals and "schools." In modified form the experiment continues, and not only veterans themselves are its beneficiaries but also colleges and the society they serve.

[12] *Ibid.*

[13] Many of these veterans had not completed their secondary schooling prior to entrance into military service. Some were admitted into colleges on the basis of studies pursued in the Armed Forces education program which enabled them to earn a high school diploma or Equivalency Certificate. Colleges cooperated by liberalizing their entrance requirements and accepting veterans with generous "conditions."

[14] *Statistics of Higher Education,* 1947–48, Office of Education (Washington: Federal Security Agency, 1950), p. 20.

The college population still remains more representative of the economically favored portion of society. Parental occupation continues to be an important index of the child's prospects of going to college. But socio-economic status is not the only selective factor: another is geography. There are disparities among regions, states, and localities in financial ability to support higher education and in consequent availability of colleges. The state of California with its numerous junior colleges is more apt to draw into these schools youth from lower income groups than are states with less extensive educational facilities. The Southern states with the highest ratio of children to adults do not have a corresponding representation in the colleges, and in all states the incidence of college enrollment among rural youth is smaller than for those residing in cities, as the Time Study confirms.[15]

No special virtue attaches to educating the poor as against the rich, the rural as against the urban dweller. The virtue is in affording opportunity for higher education to whoever with superior intellectual capacity can profit from it. As yet no such equal opportunity exists.[16] Standards of admission to college operate to insure a student body intellectually above the average regardless of whether its individuals are rich or poor. It cannot be said therefore that colleges suffer by the existing preponderance of students from well-to-do families; but colleges are being deprived of the presence of equally capable young people who cannot afford to attend. The President's Commission on Higher Education in 1947 stated the case bluntly.

The old comfortable idea that any boy can get a college education who has it in him, simply is not true. Low family income, together with the rising costs of education, constitutes an almost impassable barrier to

[15] *They Went to College,* p. 14.

[16] As this is being written, the National Merit Scholarship Corporation has been set up with funds donated by the Ford Foundation, the Carnegie Corporation, and private industry "to conduct the hunt for talent in the nation's 25,000 high schools. A series of screenings and tests will winnow out the most promising students. The amount of each winner's scholarship will vary according to his or her needs. An honorarium of $100 will go to those able to pay their own way through college. Those unable to pay will get four years of higher education . . . the National Merit Scholarship Corporation will also make grants to the colleges which its winners attend . . . to make up the difference between the cost of educating a student and the tuition charged." *New York Herald Tribune,* September 11, 1955.

college education for many young people. For some, in fact, the barrier is raised so early in life that it prevents them from attending high school even when free public high schools exist near their homes.[17]

In the Commission's estimate the number attending college prior to the second World War represented "less than one-third of those who demonstrably can profit from higher education." This bespeaks a lamentable loss to the nation. No society can afford to deprive itself of the potentialities of its best people, whatever their economic origin.

The bar to equality of opportunity in higher education is chiefly insufficiency of funds. Money is needed to improve the resources of public and private agencies providing education and to aid bright individuals otherwise unable to maintain themselves in school. No better social investment can be made. To a fine mind college education is a necessity. To a society desirous of promoting its democratic way of life investment in higher education is buying insurance for a better future.

Why should the individual teacher be concerned? As teacher and scholar he is interested in imparting learning to those best fitted to receive it and whose development can be furthered thereby. An artist likes to work for an appreciative audience, a teacher to teach those who can profit most from instruction; currently many with such promise do not come within his reach. As educator the teacher looks beyond his immediate classroom toward the broader ends of education, and the sight of qualified young people handicapped in the opportunity to serve themselves and society should be disquieting.

Intelligence and Academic Preparation of College Entrants. Somewhat more than three-fourths of the nation's youth reach the secondary school, more than half of those entering remain to be graduated, and about a third of the latter proceed to college. Despite the size of the college enrollment and taking into account discrepancies in institutional standards, college entrants as a group are well above the intellectual average of the high-school population. A generation ago, before the secondary school had advanced to the status

[17] *Higher Education for American Democracy,* Report of the President's Commission on Higher Education (New York: Harper & Brothers, 1947), Vol. I, p. 28.

of a near universal institution, its students ranked above the average of the general population in intelligence; currently there is little if any difference, the mean IQ of high-school students being slightly above 100. Informed estimates place the mean intelligence of students entering liberal-arts colleges in the neighborhood of 115 (signifying an intelligence level exceeded by fewer than 20 per cent of the general population), of those entering technical colleges somewhat higher, and teachers' colleges lower. Within the liberal-arts program an intelligence differential exists as between students in the physical sciences, English and foreign language, and those in education, home economics, and physical education. The range, however, "between the highest field, physics, and the lowest, physical education, is less than the difference between physical education and the population average." [18]

With the recent increase in college enrollments it might be reasonable to assume a decline in the mean intelligence of the college population. This is not borne out by the findings. In a ten-year analysis of results on American Council of Education Psychological Examinations Traxler [19] noted a slight but steady upward trend in scores made by entering students from 1935 to 1944. Assuming constancy in the level of testing, this suggests that the reservoir of able youth being drawn into the colleges has not been depleted. It further suggests that the larger number of patently mediocre students admitted is offset by a corresponding increase in those of superior quality. One may guess that colleges can continue for some time to admit *selectively* increasing numbers of students without incurring a drop in intellectual level. Discernible weaknesses in the college population are probably less a function of the number of students than of their manner of selection.

College entrants have usually completed a course of "preparatory" study in public or private high schools or more specifically preparatory institutions. The trend toward liberalized and flexible college admission requirements has removed much of the ground of the old

---

[18] Dael Wolfle and Toby Oxtoby, "Distribution of Ability of Students Specializing in Different Fields," *Science,* 116: 311–14 (September 26, 1952).

[19] Cited in "Student Personnel Work—I. Student Population," *Encyclopedia of Educational Research* (Revised ed.; New York: The Macmillan Company, 1950), p. 1295.

argument that the academic high-school curriculum is college controlled. Nevertheless, despite expansion of total offerings, change and modification in specific subjects of study, and differences in individual institutions, the academic high-school program remains fairly standardized. A summary description of the typical preparation of candidates for college admission will be attempted.

High-school study of Greek has largely disappeared, the enrollment in Latin has greatly declined, and new studies have been added in modern foreign languages. Heavier accent has been placed on the fine arts, music, health and physical education, and practical shop activity, and the extracurricular program has been extended. Elective courses have been made available in many fields of study, and it is now possible for a high-school student to "major" or "specialize" in mathematics, science, or even art or music. In all studies there have been changes of emphasis in objectives.[20] But the chief elements of the curriculum remain English, history and the social studies, mathematics, science, and foreign language. Changes in objectives have in varying degree affected the substance of instruction, with the result that students learn more that is not specifically preparatory for college study along with subject matter directly pertinent. In some subjects departures from earlier convention have not been radical: instruction in algebra, geometry, trigonometry, chemistry, and physics, except for greater emphasis on "lay" or "consumer" values, remains essentially unchanged. However reorganized, each of the principal subjects of study contains a core of knowledge upon which the college can build.

English instruction has shifted from its former emphasis on rhetoric and declamation, theme writing, compositional exercises in narration, description, exposition, and argumentation, grammar and linguistic study, substituting more experience in the functional use of language as a means of communication and self-expression, oral and to a lesser extent written. Something is lost in mastery of language as a precise tool of thought and expression, something gained in its potentiality as a medium of personal and social development.

[20] A general objective summed up as "education for life adjustment" has especially drawn the fire of critics in college circles who feel that it detracts from intellectual discipline and thorough scholastic preparation. Comment on the criticism of the objective as such was made earlier in the chapter.

Literature is taught primarily to cultivate the habit of reading and the power to learn from the printed page, secondarily for appreciation of literary content and form. The course of study has been popularized by the addition of contemporary writings, and by material conforming more closely to the interests of adolescents in biography, adventure, travel, science, nature, sports, and other favorite themes. Attention to established classics has been curtailed, in some cases without detriment to students' educational development at this stage, in others (if curtailment is at the expense of Shakespeare's *Hamlet* or *Midsummer Night's Dream*, Elizabethan poetry, or Milton's or Wordsworth's sonnets) with genuine loss. Foreign-language instruction has been slower to change, although there too emphasis on "reading" or "speaking" objectives has replaced the earlier concentration on language structure, and more time is spent on cultural *realia*. During the third year of foreign-language study the student has a better opportunity to become acquainted with some of its literary masterpieces.

Great variation exists in the content and organization of history and other social-studies offerings. Aimed at fostering better understanding of the modern world and particularly of American society, and at cultivating better democratic citizenship, the course of study has been in almost continuous process of reorganization. Study of American history as well as "world backgrounds" and recent European history remains a constant element in the social-studies offerings, but whether the treatment of subjects is "separated" or "integrated" or whether the development of topics is chronological or topical depends on particular school policy. The trend is toward integration or synthesis of subject matter under large categories of experience or learning—problems of community living, democratic society, industrial order, national expansion, international relations and the like. The framework of study may differ from school to school and in the same school may change several times in the course of a few years. In general, emphasis is on the contemporary scene rather than the past, and disciplined continuity of study has been subordinated toward providing a larger and more integrated perspective. The subject is in many ways richer and more significant, but its educative effect is weakened by constant shifting and the difficulty of finding and retaining a central focus of attention.

The more adventurous secondary-school programs have not been the general college preparatory but those designed for specialized purposes. High schools offer a variety of such programs for students not planning to continue in higher study as well as for those headed toward liberal or specialized higher institutions. Included are courses of study in agriculture, business, fine arts, mechanics and technology, and a host of skilled trade fields. Some of the best high schools, from the viewpoint of student quality and achievement, are technical or academic "special purpose" institutions such as, for example, the High School of Science in New York City. Vocational high schools, while dealing with students of lesser academic adptitude, have proved themselves enterprising in developing courses and modes of instruction appropriate to the needs of their population. Thirty-one vocational high schools in New York City, for example, combine general educational training with specialized preparation in fields ranging from aviation to seamanship and the theatre arts. In many cases close links are maintained with industry, study in school is coupled with concurrent paid work-experience, and instruction is realistic, stimulating, and effective. A small proportion of graduates go on to college study, and a few to liberal institutions.

The foregoing is not intended to glorify the high school or exculpate its shortcomings. A college teacher should know as much as possible concerning the educational background of his students, and in college circles this background is too often dismissed slightingly, without sufficient sympathetic understanding of what the high school seeks to achieve. Such general information as has been given is not a substitute for learning the specific background and needs of each student, but it may help to make the college teacher more realistically aware of aims and positive accomplishments as well as shortcomings. The chances are that the college is not fully utilizing students' educational equipment particularly in aspects not directly involved in the academic program of instruction. The scholastic shortcomings of the college entrant, though regrettable, are rarely catastrophic: most of them can be overcome through sufficient exertion by students and teachers without much loss of time or significant impairment of college standards. Deficiencies in knowledge of grammar, for example, may be corrected in the course of language instruction, perhaps more effectively than was possible earlier. The added expense in effort and time can be charged against economies effected elsewhere in dealing with more mature, responsible, and well-rounded students.

WHY STUDENTS GO TO COLLEGE

The fact that a student applies for admission to an institution does not assure that he is willing to be guided by its aims. Students seek college education for various motives and occasionally without any clearly understood motive at all. Objectives in college study are clarified, refined, and sometimes substantially altered in the course of college experience: purposes which seemed important at the time of entrance may have been discarded before the student gets to the senior year. In retrospect dominant purposes may be defined still differently. The questions "Why do students go to college?" and "What in consequence should the college do?" are not as easily answerable as may appear at first sight. The first cannot be entirely satisfied by survey of student opinion; the second involves choices among educational values more than application of simple logic.

In order to help students utilize their educational opportunities, it is important to know as much as possible concerning their initial purposes in college study and at subsequent turns in their college career. These purposes are not always good but, if they are to be assessed, they must be identified. They cannot be ignored: if judged worthy and important, they should be fulfilled; if unworthy, they should by common consent be altered. Furthermore, if students' objectives in study are found substantially at variance with ours in instruction, it might be wise also to reexamine the latter. Teachers' objectives may be in error, not so much for lack of theoretical merit as of realistic prospects of fulfillment.

Motivation for college study is an individual matter not ascertainable on a mass basis, although general trends may be explored. The literature of higher education has in recent years contributed helpful "leads" to the question of why students go to college. It remains for each institution to canvass its own students and base its policies upon its findings. Equipped with general data concerning students' purposes, the teacher or counselor will be in a better position to explore the specific needs of students under his instruction or guidance and govern his practices thereby.

Practical Motive in College Education. Specialized colleges have a more assured and definite understanding of students' reasons for attendance than do institutions of general education. A student enters a college of engineering primarily to learn this profession, although along with professional training he expects and receives general education. The same logic does not hold for entrance into a liberal college: it is naive to assume that all such entrants are impelled by purely intellectual interest in fields of learning. This motive does exist, combined in most cases with other extrinsic objectives. Relatively less often is it the only or even predominant reason.

Whether or not we make the admission, practical motives play an important role in college attendance. Students from higher-income families regard college education as a normal stage of their upbringing and a means of reaching their expected status in society. Others look toward college education as an avenue for improving opportunities for a career, a desirable marriage, or other ambitions. Students driven by urge of scholarship alone constitute a small minority. The inference is not that all others are utility-minded, but that utilitarian considerations are also present.

The potency of the economic motive should not be underestimated. Most students do not enter college primarily to seek vocational training, but the incidental attainment of this objective is implicit in their intentions. Vaguely at first and more distinctly later, they expect the college to provide a foundation on which a successful career may be built and some definite preparation for gaining entry to a chosen pursuit. They expect college education to enhance their occupational qualifications and prospects, and should be disappointed if it failed to do so.

Support for these conclusions was furnished some years ago in a comprehensive study at Syracuse University by Katz and Allport,[21] and more recent studies at other institutions have tended to corroborate the evidence. In their survey of "attitudes, opinions, and practices" of students at Syracuse, Katz and Allport sought to discover, among other things, "reasons for coming to college, for selecting a certain college, and for remaining in college." Over 3500 students

[21] Daniel Katz and Floyd Henry Allport, *Students' Attitudes* (Syracuse, New York: The Craftsman Press, 1931). The report is based on data collected in 1926.

(1080 in the College of Liberal Arts) responded to an inquiry directing them to check, from a list of ten, the *three* most important reasons for coming to college; 72 per cent of the students included as
one reason "In order to prepare for a certain vocation." Because
other reasons offered have bearing upon this discussion, a summary
of the findings is here reproduced.[22]

Reasons for Coming to College (*Listed in order of frequency of response*)	Students in Liberal Arts %	General University Population %
In order to prepare for a certain vocation.	72.1	71.8
For general improvement in culture and ideals.	69.7	64.5
Because a person with a college degree can obtain a better position and can earn more money.	42.6	47.6
Because of my interest in specific studies and my de- sire to pursue them further.	33.2	31.9
Because a person with a college education has more prestige and a higher social standing.	31.4	31.8
Because my parents wished it.	20.0	20.8
For some other reason not mentioned.	10.0	9.9
Because of the social attractions or athletic oppor- tunities of college life.	7.2	8.2
Because so many of my friends and relatives had gone to college that it seemed the thing to do.	6.0	5.4
In order to show people I have as good a mind as anyone.	2.0	2.3

The authors noted that the principal reasons for coming to college seemed to be (1) utilitarian, (2) scholarly or cultural; that of
thirty-six possible combinations of reasons, only one combination
appeared persistently—that of the first three reasons listed above;
and that students in liberal arts did not differ significantly from the
pattern of the general college population including students in business administration, fine arts, applied science, forestry, home economics, and the graduate school.

Almost the same reasons seemed to apply for staying in college,[23]
except for a reversal in rank order between the third and fourth: the

[22] *Ibid.*, abstracted from Table I, p. 11.
[23] *Ibid.*, p. 18.

first two reasons were checked by 70 and 69 per cent of the students respectively; "interest in studies" was reported by 45 per cent, and "market value of degree" by 42 per cent. Of one or more reasons indicated for *specifically choosing to attend* Syracuse University, the most common was "proximity" (41 per cent), followed in order by "opportunities for self-support" (28 per cent), "educational advantages" (19 per cent), "reasons unknown" (18 per cent), and "influence of persons other than parents" (17 per cent).[24]

It is unlikely, as the authors make clear, that these findings would fit specifically any other population of students. Change the institution (and the period) under study, and the relative "percentages" would almost certainly be changed; the rank order of indicated reasons might also be affected. Conceivably these findings are not applicable to small colleges with select constituencies or distinctive educational purposes. Moreover, the study is handicapped by normal limitations of the checklist technique which *suggests* rather than *elicits* reasons: as indicated earlier, students may not be clearly aware of the motives which brought them to college. Still, it is noteworthy that so large a proportion of students in one institution expressed themselves as strongly influenced by the vocational or practical value of a college education.

Vocational Choices of Students. Particularly in liberal colleges most students at entrance do not have a fixed vocational objective. There are broad preferences as to fields of study and possible occupational pursuits, and expectation that in time the area of preference will be narrowed and the occupational objectives more clearly defined. This is as it should be: the liberal college does not owe students a rigid course of study conforming to specialized interests, whether professional or scholarly: it is however obligated to provide opportunity to explore various fields of study, determine special capabilities within them, and develop interests and accomplishments useful professionally and in other aspects of living. The practical motives for college education are healthy and should not be suppressed; they need to be balanced by other less utilitarian motives, and directed along lines broadly beneficial to society and the individual.

[24] *Ibid.,* pp. 20–21.

Some students do enter with a definite vocation in mind. It is perhaps harder for a liberal college to educate such students even if their choices are well-founded: they are apt to be impatient with studies unrelated to their fixed interest and to resist efforts to promote their broader development. The task of the college is to help the student expand his decided interest and join it with others newly formed. More troublesome is the student whose practical ambitions are definite but unrealistic, who overestimates his suitability for a field of endeavor or invests real talent in an area barren of promise. Such a student needs help from the college in the way of honest disillusionment and sympathetic positive guidance.

College students are drawn from a cross-section of business and professional society at middle and higher income levels and as graduates may normally be expected to arrange themselves at the same levels. Specialized colleges yearly feed into society graduates trained in many occupations for which special training as well as general education are a necessity. In the arts and sciences alone, the nation's institutions of higher education in 1951 granted baccalaureate degrees to students majoring in more than seventy subject fields.[25] Students' expectations of economic and vocational advantage from their college education are justifiable, and from the teachers' point of view there is no reason to feel that such expectations are inconsistent with the purposes of higher education.

Cultural and Scholarly Interests. The findings indicate that such interests are not lacking. In the Katz and Allport study almost 70 per cent of liberal-arts students and 65 per cent of the total university population checked "general improvement in culture and ideals" as one of three reasons for coming to college, and almost a third of the students indicated "interest in specific studies and desire to pursue them further." The fact that the last-stated reason improved its position in the course of students' college experience is encouraging. The college needs and has students attracted principally by scholarly interest and a desire for knowledge: the future teachers, scholars, writers, and men in dedicated professions. It is also important that all students, whatever their further motivations, possess an intrinsic interest in academic studies, and this appears to be true of a substantial portion.

[25] *Higher Education in the Forty-Eight States, op. cit.,* pp. 40–42.

Academic interests, if not prominently present at entrance, can be developed in the course of college education. Students are not immune from such interests even if apparently preoccupied with preparing for a career, extending social contacts, developing athletic capabilities, or merely enjoying life on the college campus. Stimulating instruction can foster interests just as dispirited teaching can debilitate those once flourishing. Many mathematicians, scientists, linguists, and historians were initially inspired by their subject in college, not in the high school. The college should not be diverted from its task of disclosing to the student the possibilities of fields of learning and of trying to secure his commitment to them even in the face of initial disinterest. The task becomes easier if instruction realistically takes the student's measure, and keeps account of elements in its favor and those against which it must contend.

On the other hand, the college cannot relax with students who have decided academic interests. These too need a balanced education looking not only toward their intellectual but also personal, social, and economic life. Strong interests in special studies are often a fine means of general educational development, but occasionally may lead the student down narrow, closed-end paths. A student excelling in a favored field of study may find too late that he has neglected other requirements for educated living. Not every scholarly pursuit need have, for example, a vocational or economic outlet, but a student's scholastic pursuits should *in the aggregate* serve to fit him for major life contingencies. In a college population containing so many "in obvious need of assistance" it is easy to overlook the student who fulfills his academic obligations and apparently knows where he is going. Such a student also needs help in evaluating his interests and objectives, and broadening or redirecting them when necessary.

Other Purposes in College Attendance. Where college education has become a conventional requisite for membership in a social or economic group, often the path of lesser resistance is to conform. Especially where parents are college-trained it is difficult for them to become reconciled to a child's failure to follow suit. A family's ambition for its children, considerations of social prestige, the mores of a community or social circle may be factors in influencing youth to attend college. Sometimes the young person may not himself be conscious of these motives, feeling only a vague and disquieting lack of positive purpose.

Not all these young people are poor or indifferent college material; some may be promising by any standards. But each year the colleges admit an indeterminate number of half-willing or moderately equipped students whose expectations for college success are not good. That some youth are driven more by convention than real purpose to seek a college education should not militate against their eventual success. Where intellectual capacity exists it should be developed: interests may be aroused, intellectual ambition awakened, and positive educational goals implanted. Where intellectual capacity is insufficient colleges should be firm in denying admission, previously having assured themselves that in all their varied course offerings there is no real opportunity for the student to succeed.

Other motives for college attendance are well known: following in the footsteps of friends or admired persons, desire to be identified with institutions which attract sports headlines, willingness to take financial advantage of an athletic "scholarship," and the like. These extrinsic motives need not impinge upon the student's real suitability for college. The general guiding principle should be that where a student exhibits intellectual ability and willingness to learn the college has some basis for undertaking to educate him.

EXPECTATION OF SUCCESS IN COLLEGE STUDY

On this subject much more is certain to be learned in the coming years than is now known. Specialists in testing and evaluation centers have been active in collating and analyzing information obtained from entrance examination testing and reports of high-school achievement, and comparing them with records of accomplishment in college study. It would be most helpful if at the time of application for admission there were available a reliable means of estimating students' probable chances for success in college. Not that such success could ever be predicted with certainty: even with a trustworthy predictive index at hand we should have to guard against too deterministic an attitude in initially judging applicants. There are too many variables in educational experience to enable us to produce a mathematically certain formula. But given a better predictive index, colleges would be able to develop more discriminating admission practices, reducing the probabilities of student failure, providing greater educational advantages to those admitted, and redirecting those denied admission to other more promising forms of education or training. The conscientious and fairly effective job which colleges currently do in this respect would be improved were more refined instruments of selection available.

Intelligence and College Success. In the final analysis a student's intellectual capacity establishes his fitness for higher education. Yet study after study has disclosed that intelligence is not in itself a reliable index of probable college success. An IQ of 110 is estimated as the minimum requisite for passable college work, and this may be accepted readily enough. But the correlation between students' intelligence and achievement after admission to college is no higher than 0.5,[26] which is insufficient to warrant the use of intelligence as a predictive index. "Accumulated evidence indicates that the degree of intelligence needed for success in college cannot be stated categorically. Hartson and Sprow found that while 80 per cent of the freshmen who had an IQ above 126 became seniors, 64 per cent of those with an IQ below 116 became seniors also." [27] Many students who fail in college studies have psychological examination scores above the institutional mean, and some of those dismissed for poor scholarship are by no means among the intellectually least promising.[28] Factors such as health, physical energy, motivation to study, outside interests, suitability of the college program, quality of teaching, and degree of industrious application account for existing discrepancies between intellectual potential and actual college achievement.

The implication is not that the intelligence factor may be dis-

[26] "Educational Prognosis in College," *Encyclopedia of Educational Research* (Revised ed.; New York: The Macmillan Company), 1950, pp. 882 ff.

[27] *Ibid.*, p. 883.

[28] A study of intelligence and entrance examination scores of 955 students dismissed for poor scholarship from Brooklyn College over a five year period from 1944 through 1948 concludes: "The pattern of high, mean, and low scores, while slightly lower for this group, indicates that it is not scholastic aptitude, as measured by these criteria, that is lacking. The cause of failure probably lies in the areas of economic adjustment, social adjustment, personality adjustment, home adjustment, and related problems." La Verne Buckton, *The Prediction of Student Success at Brooklyn College,* 1949 Report of the Testing Bureau, Department of Personnel Service, Brooklyn College, p. 14.

counted but that, along with intelligence data, a good deal of other information is relevant. The way to ascertain whether a student is suitable college material is to learn as much as possible about him, relating intelligence to factors of known achievement, health, personal history, educational purpose and interests, appropriateness of proposed program of study, and opportunities and methods of work. Selection for admission is the first step in a process of continuous appraisal seeking to estimate and improve the student's chances for success. The task requires close observation and follow-up of the student at work, particularly in the freshman year, systematic gathering and recording of personnel data, and a sustained program of wise and sympathetic counseling.

Reliable Indices of College Performance. At the time of admission the most reliable *single* factor in predicting college success, with a correlation coefficient of approximately 0.6, is the student's achievement in high-school studies, based not on a specific set of subjects but on the total course. The special pattern of high-school studies pursued does not seem to affect the reliability of this index. The next best single factor are scores made on a battery of entrance achievement tests. Combining the two and obtaining a cumulative index based on average high-school grade and mean entrance examination score, weighted equally or with heavier accent on the former, colleges have found an improved criterion for determining the admissibility of students. Supplementing this mathematical yardstick by information gathered from the candidate's personal history, the testimony of guidance officials in the high school, and impressions gained during a personal interview, college admission officers can make more intelligent discrimination between promising and unpromising college material.

On the assumption that past accomplishment is a fair index of probable future performance, colleges are showing greater interest in obtaining from high schools qualitative evaluations of the applicant's character, personality, scholarship, and general fitness for college study. Some colleges have gone further in according recommendations by responsible officials of reputable schools an almost decisive role in determining acceptance of candidates. As high schools improve their personnel programs and systems of record-keeping, and colleges gain familiarity with the work of the individual schools, this practice should become more common. In the meantime an increasing number of colleges have been admitting a specified top portion of a school's graduating class without entrance examination or irrespective of completion of a prescribed pattern of preparatory studies. The University of Denver, for example, admits without examination applicants in the upper quarter of their graduating class in high school without reference to pattern of study; the University of California and the University of Minnesota admit applicants from the top 10 per cent of their classes.

The final test of a student's capacity for college study is not in any predictive index but in the quality of his continuous college performance. A student's work in the freshman year offers a better indication of what may be expected throughout the college course than any of the indices mentioned earlier,[29] and each succeeding term provides mounting evidence. This argues strongly that admission to college is not the final step in the selection process; selection based on demonstrated achievement and guided by good personnel practice should be continued well into the college period, not so much to safeguard correctness of institutional policy as to afford the student every advantage for success and to redeem those who are redeemable. It also argues for liberalizing traditional formal entrance requirements so that a student intellectually and socially at home in a college may be permitted to do college work, regardless of how many Carnegie "units" he has accumulated.

(For Bibliography See the End of Chapter V)

[29] LaVerne Buckton, "The Interpretation and Use of Test Results at Brooklyn College," paper read before the National Council on Measurements Used in Education, February 17, 1954, at Atlantic City, N.J. On the basis of ten consecutive years' study Buckton found the correlation coefficient between the Freshman index and success in the last three years of college to range between 0.675 and 0.722.

V. The Teacher and His Students: Continued

This chapter carries the discussion into aspects of student development and learning behavior and their implications for teaching. The chapter is organized under three headings—college students as individuals, as learners, and as adolescents—which while not strictly logical afford a convenient basis for a reasonably orderly presentation. The discussion aims not at summarizing available information pertinent to these subjects,[1] but at pointing up some matters of special practical interest to the teacher.

COLLEGE STUDENTS AS INDIVIDUALS

The Nature of Individual Difference. A group of people is never truly homogeneous except in a restricted sense, and at no time in its history has the college possessed a homogeneous student body. Individual students differ from one another in various ways—as whole persons and in special attributes, in natural and in acquired traits. As the aggregate enrollment in the colleges has grown in size and social representativeness, the range of differences has been increased and the *kinds* of differences have been compounded. A wider gap

[1] It is hard to select from the extensive literature a few works for special reference. An authoritative source on psychology of learning is Ernest R. Hilgard's *Theories of Learning* (New York: Appleton-Century-Crofts, Inc., 1948). Charles H. Judd's *Education As Cultivation of the Higher Mental Processes* (New York: The Macmillan Company, 1936) contributes important insights into the nature of higher-level learning. Raymond G. Kuhlen's *The Psychology of Adolescent Development* (New York: Harper & Brothers, 1952) is a standard work on that subject.

now exists between the best and the poorest students, the oldest and the youngest, the most scholarly and the least academic, but more important is the greater variety in the kinds of specific attributes represented. Advances in psychology have made us more keenly aware of the educational significance of differences. If the latter complicate our task of instruction, they also offer positive opportunities for strengthening and enriching the education of students.

Human traits can sometimes be measured or estimated quantitatively, represented on a graph, or rated on a point scale. Intelligence is commonly represented in IQ units, and differences in intelligence stated in numerical terms. But intelligence is a quality of mind rather than a quantitative value. A person with 150 IQ differs from one with 125 IQ not so much in size of mental capacity as in the *way* he thinks and the *kind* of thinking he does. Two persons of equal IQ need not resemble each other at all in kinds of intellectual aptitude, manner of thinking, and even rates of learning. Psychologists favor the use of intelligence tests as a general indication of a person's promise rather than as basis for comparison. Somewhat the same holds for other differences we attempt to measure quantitatively. Educational achievement may be symbolized by term grades or achievement test scores, and differences in achievement inferred therefrom. But these differences signify qualitative variations in ideational content achieved through study. They are not quantitative differences except to the statistician.

The qualitative nature of human difference is more readily evident in such attributes as values and ideals, attitudes, interests, and purposes. Although quantitative measures have been developed even for some of these, the aim has been to facilitate more precise characterization of the individual rather than comparison with others. To understand qualitative differences it is necessary to understand *people* in the context of their personality and experience. All this points to the conclusion that awareness of differences is of greatest importance because it enables us better to learn and understand each person.

Educationally the most significant traits do not readily lend themselves to comparative assessment. Having determined that a student is more intelligent than another, how much do we know about the intelligence of either? We know even less when attempting to compare people with respect to moral and esthetic values, intellectual interests, and educational objectives. Tabulating differences is not as important as understanding them, and the business of rating individuals on a single trait or accomplishment is frequently overdone. It is understandable that a football coach, in selecting his varsity team, must rate his players on ability to run, tackle, block, pass, receive, and kick a football; to estimate his own accomplishment in teaching as well as to meet the administrative needs of an institutional program for orderly progress of students, a teacher of geometry or physics needs to grade students on their course achievement. But these necessary incidentals should not be identified with the main task of education, which is to educate each student according to his needs, without regard to the diverse needs of others.

Individual differences among persons are too numerous to be catalogued, and many of them are not commensurable. To equate students on the basis of one characteristic is to incur the risk of making partial and unjust characterizations. In the interest of fairness a Dean's List citing students of academic distinction should be matched by others identifying those who have demonstrated civic worth, creative accomplishment in artistic activity, or unusual perseverance enabling them to surmount handicaps of opportunity in order to achieve even modest academic standing. These qualities may figure as much in education as those which more commonly attract academic notice.

Individuality and Difference. A more constructive approach than focusing on specific differences is to view each person as distinct from every other. People differ more in their total complexion than in particulars; though alike in height, weight, manual dexterity, or mechanical skill, no two are perfectly alike as people. Persons with similar esthetic or religious values may respond differently to a given esthetic or religious experience. The configuration of traits in human personality makes for individuality in thought and behavior.

Preaching to teachers the doctrine of students' individuality is much like "carrying coals to Newcastle"; it is a fact they are rarely allowed to forget. The way a student enters a classroom and from that point proceeds to involve himself in the work of the course is distinctly his own, matched precisely by no other; what he derives from the course is also his own. Educational counselors never fail to be impressed by differences in the students they face in daily procession, each with his own way of viewing and interpreting experience, of assessing problems and pursuing their solution.

If one may not try to compare "unlikes," we should be spared the unprofitable task of comparing people. A great deal has been written on the subject of human equality, not all of it instructive. People are neither equal nor unequal; they are different. In an ethical, social, or political sense they are equal before God, before the law, and in the exercise of their civic franchise. They are unequal in strength, intelligence, beauty, earning power, and political influence. But in their essential quality as human beings they are simply different from one another. Each is entitled to receive respect, to be accepted into society without handicaps or privileges, to live on his own terms and be protected in the enjoyment of his human rights so long as he does not violate the rights of another. The doctrine of brotherhood reconciles the ideal of equality with the undeniable truth of individual differences. We need to use our knowledge of disparities for understanding better the nature and needs of each person.

If the task of education is not thereby reduced, it is possibly clarified. Let us agree that it is unprofitable to weigh people against one another, to keep a close account of observed differences, and to attempt to provide splinters of educational experience conforming to this or that individual trait. It is of greater moment that the integrity of the individual be recognized and sustained in whatever educational experience he may be engaged. Provided each student can obtain what he needs, it does not matter whether a course of study is shared by few or by many. Occasionally a program offering may be unsuitable, and another will have to be found; but more often, by knowing the student we can conduct instruction and guidance in such a way that even a common educational experience is profitable. Students enter a course of instruction as different people seeking different things, and to the extent that his quest is worthy, each student is entitled to help in pursuing it.

The foregoing is not an endorsement for a uniform curriculum for all students. With the present college population this is impractical, even were we more certain of what such a curriculum should contain. But it does argue against extremes of educational division and subdivision in the form of specialized schools, departments of instruction, course offerings and study programs. Extreme specialization does not necessarily serve the interests of the individual, and in affording it we more often indulge ourselves than our students. A broad common foundation of educational experience permitting some variation, complemented and balanced by concentration in a more limited elective field of learning, offers adequate opportunity for individualizing education. How we receive and teach the student in any course of instruction has a greater bearing on meeting his needs than surrounding him with specialized subject matter.

Strengths and Weaknesses. In his own person each of us represents a mixture of capacities, aptitudes, and interests extending in non-uniform degree in various directions. Even some qualities apt to be regarded as constants—intelligence, creativeness, poise, and others—vary in effectiveness in specific situations. Intelligence, for example, is conceived as a general quality, yet a person's capacity to think in verbal terms may exceed his ability to reason mathematically, distinguish spatial relationships, or understand mechanical operations; one's academic aptitude may be at variance with his aptitude for understanding people. The tendency is for the specific aspects of intelligence to correlate positively with one another: a bright person tends to be bright in most respects, and his "brightness" may be reflected also in manifestations of behavior—gentleness, courtesy, kindness—not ordinarily termed intellectual. But in the same person discrepancies may be noted in the operation of specific aspects of intelligence, and even intellectually superior people may suffer from some special intellectual disability. Similar disparity may exist with respect to aptitudes not identifiable with intelligence such as physical agility, stamina, motor coordination, facility in games and sports, and with respect to interests and tastes.

It is fortunate for society that people differ in their potentialities and in the outlets afforded for their talents. Efficient and stimulating social living demands such variety. A complicated world needs as much diversity of aptitude and talent as it can get, and a healthy democracy thrives on individuality of character, thought, and action. And if variety is necessary and desirable, what better basis is there for its development than to encourage each person to concentrate on the things he can do best, provided they are educationally serviceable and socially worthy?

Human excellence cannot be reduced to a single, definable quality.

In a democratic society which intends to broaden the base of its young people's educational interests and competence as whole persons, quality is *not* correctly definable in terms exclusively of ability to handle abstract ideas with verbal facility, valuable and greatly needed though such ability is. Mental quality is assured by insistence on high standards of excellence, thoroughness, persistence, cheerfulness and originality of attack in whatever areas of subject matter the colleges decide there is challenging intellectual content. . . . All types of mind are important; they are necessary; they can be qualitatively significant; their fullest development is essential. A pharmacist, a veterinarian, a nurse, a secretary, a housewife—all can manifest quality in their mental effort and performance. . . . Excellence, in short, is not an abstract attribute; it is the total adroitness and elegance with which the necessary activities of life are carried on by giving thought to them.[2]

The different and unique qualities that each student presents can be an asset in his education, and his special potentialities the most promising avenue of development. We should remove disabilities and settle differences obstructive of personal development and social integration; but it is even more important that we identify potential strengths, and guide and foster their growth in promising directions. To do this, we must be prepared to recognize talent in whatever form it may be revealed: in musical, artistic, or literary power, linguistic, mathematical, or scientific achievement, human relations, even in athletic performance. Our aim should be to produce not the accomplished professional—athlete, musician, artist, or for that matter mathematician or scientist—but the accomplished person using his special abilities as a means of enhancing his general competence. This is the only defensible reason for the current practice in liberal-arts colleges of having students concentrate in the latter part of the course on "a field of major interest," not thereby to produce specialists but to educate students better through studies in which they are interested and more apt to succeed.

The alternative to this conception of strengths and weaknesses

[2] Ordway Tead, "Looking Ahead at the Role of the College," Speech at San Francisco State College, October 16, 1954, 15 pp. mimeo.

does not seem promising. It is to accord equal importance to abilities and disabilities, giving each the educational attention needed to raise the student to a respectable level of general attainment. The non-language minded student with a positive inclination toward science or engineering would divide his effort between acquiring language facility and making headway in science or engineering; the scholarly but socially inhibited youth would be encouraged to apportion his time between study and fraternization. This would be truly an education for "uniformity and mediocrity." Even as a practical plan of educational strategy this alternative is unsound. People cannot be held to the same educational standards nor led to education by the same paths. They cannot be expected to ration their interests and energy among a multiplicity of educational tasks. There must be some unifying principle or central purpose which gives relevance to their educational experience and sustains them in their educational effort. Such purpose can be derived from students' growing recognition of their emerging talents and interests. The latter need not be given full rein, but harnessed in the interest of a balanced education which yet recognizes distinctions among people.

Not all students display a single, positive talent overriding all others. The term needs to be applied in a relative sense. Certain of a person's capacities, aptitudes, and interests are greater than others: the problem is to identify them, and put them to work for education. As a profession we are adept at discovering students' shortcomings and conscientious in seeking to correct them. We need to sensitize ourselves as much to their positive potentialities. That some potentiality exists in every case is not to be doubted. The tendency is to confine our view within the natural boundaries of our own subject; few teachers have not been surprised, at one time or another in their career, by the later rise to distinction in the world of practical or cultural affairs of a student who had been just ordinary in *their* classes. It is easier still to overlook a minor talent which promises no such distinction particularly if unrelated to the instruction at hand. But if talent can be identified wherever and in whatever degree it exists, it may become the key to better knowledge of the student, and the means of stimulating his greater involvement even in a course of study to which it appears unrelated. The approach to learning is many-sided, and prospects for success are better if entry is made through strength rather than weakness.

COLLEGE STUDENTS AS LEARNERS

Professional experience has accumulated a fund of practical knowledge concerning the process of higher learning. Our methods of teaching are founded on empirical judgment and reasonable hypothesis as to how students learn. Occasional works of gifted colleagues have added to the clarity of our understanding,[3] and experimental psychology is steadily increasing its contribution. But our total knowledge is incomplete, insufficiently verified, and not well organized for use. Understandably the young science of psychology has devoted the greater portion of its effort to study of the earlier stage of a person's development and to lower levels of the learning process. We know more about the psychological development of children and young adolescents than of older adolescents and adults, more about how children learn in the elementary school than how students learn in college. Relatively few studies have concerned themselves with phases of older adolescence and with adult learning on higher operating levels.[4]

The assumption that college students learn as others do is tenable only to a degree. General principles or "laws" of learning apply to college students, subject—as in the case of others—to individual variation. The need for motivation for study, "readiness" to learn, organizing elements of learning in meaningful patterns of ideas, finding satisfaction in learning experience, and opportunity for functional application of learning obtains for them as it does for others. But college students are an intellectually select population, and the college program of study a select body of learning experience. It cannot be assumed that higher learning is a simple extension of the

[3] We refer to such writings as John Dewey's *How We Think* (New York: D. C. Heath and Co., 1910), and Alfred North Whitehead's *The Aims of Education* (New York: The Macmillan Company, 1929).

[4] The outstanding work on the subject is E. L. Thorndike's *Adult Learning* (New York: The Macmillan Company, 1928). Investigation of adult learning has since been continued by Professor Irving Lorge of Columbia and others. For citations of studies of later adolescence, see *Adolescence,* 43rd Yearbook, Part I, National Society for the Study of Education (Chicago: University of Chicago Press, 1944).

lower, that learning calculus is a continuation of learning arithmetic, or theoretical physics of junior-high-school science. Nor may it be assumed that superior minds follow the same paths in learning as do ordinary, the difference being mainly in distance and rate. There are qualitative changes in the learning process concerning which we know little.

The contribution of psychology to knowledge of higher learning has been twofold. Employing as rigorous experimental procedure as possible, it has tried to test the validity of certain empirical doctrines, and even in the negative role of disproving unfounded claims has rendered important service. Secondly, working from different perspectives and with different postulates,[5] it has tried to formulate principles of learning derived from scientific evidence. It has thus far made creditable headway, though not to the point where it is capable of furnishing the teacher with organized knowledge sufficient to his need. "The studies of educational psychologists," writes W. H. Cowley, "have produced significant facts and generalizations, but no adequate arrangements have yet developed for bringing them to the attention of college teachers or of prospective teachers. The defects badly need remedying."[6]

Mental Discipline: Tenable and Untenable Assumptions. A once widespread doctrine which experimental psychology has largely discredited is that of formal discipline, with its corollary of automatic transfer of learning. For a long time higher education was guided by the idea that there was an assured way of training the mind through the offices of "mind-forming" disciplines such as the classical languages, mathematics, and science. It was assumed that the mind trained in this way could be depended upon to give a good account of itself in whatever situations demanded good thinking, whether in personal or social living, the pursuit of a vocation, economic management, politics, constructive use of leisure, or anything else. This theory, though no longer widely credited, is by no means extinct.

[5] As the reader well knows, there is no "psychology" of learning but there are "psychologies." Hilgard distinguishes nine systems of learning theory plus additional variations. (*Theories of Learning* [New York: Appleton-Century-Crofts, Inc., 1948].)

[6] "A Century of College Teaching," *Improving College and University Teaching,* Vol. I, No. 3 (November 1953), p. 7.

At the beginning of this century Thorndike and Woodworth (and subsequently others) sought to test this hypothesis experimentally,[7] and although their experiments were not sufficiently definitive to dispel all argument, their findings confirmed what common sense alone should have perceived: that intellectual effectiveness in all types of life experience is not achieved easily. Since then psychology, whatever its special approach, has agreed in repudiating the notion that the mind is constituted of "faculties"—such as attention, memory, reasoning, imagination—which can by general training be made effective for all purposes. So extreme has been the reaction against *formal* discipline, particularly on the lower school levels, that the possibility of *mental* discipline in its larger sense has also been discounted. This is unfortunate.

It must be possible to help form good intellectual habits, sharpen mental perception, and increase mental power, else higher education would be substantially wasted. If it were not already in existence, the concept of mental discipline would have to be invented. Less tenable, however, is the supposition that disciplining follows naturally from activity in certain courses or fields of study. There should be no question that physics, properly taught and learned, can impart to the student scientific attitudes and modes of thought, and greater skill, clarity, and precision in ordering facts, distinguishing relationships, and separating truth from error. But these must be systematically sought as objectives of instruction, learned and demonstrated in the course of study, generalized and applied in life experience as well as in further pursuit of physics: they do not result simply from enrolling in the course, listening to lectures, solving problems mechanically, and reproducing "experiments" in accordance with the laboratory manual. Similarly with language study and mathematics: the disciplinary values are there; they need to be identified, sought out by instruction, achieved, and used.

Nor is it plausible that only certain subjects possess disciplinary potency. *Any* study can contribute to the disciplining of the mind provided instruction focuses on attainment of quality in thinking and power in relating knowledge to experience, not on the verbal re-

[7] E. L. Thorndike and R. S. Woodworth, "The Influence of Improvement in One Mental Function Upon the Efficiency of Other Functions," *Psychological Review*, 8:247–61, 384–95, 553–64 (1901).

production of facts. Humanities, sciences, social sciences, and applied studies can, each in its own way, not only increase the student's knowledge but enhance his competence to operate effectively in any context of experience by developing his intellectual abilities. This is mental discipline in its broader sense; and by whatever special theories modern psychologists choose to explain "conceptualization" or "generalization" of learning and "transfer of training," they agree that these things not only are possible but happen.

The college student is at the point of his normal development where he can consciously cultivate intellectual habits and skills, generalize his learnings, and apply them to life situations. He needs to be made aware of the importance of doing these things, and helped in doing them properly. Faced with a multitude of specific instructional tasks, the teacher may sometimes be distracted from the main purpose of instruction which is the cultivation of the students' intellectual growth. It helps, therefore, if the teacher can keep in the foreground two questions: What disciplinary values greater than acquisition of subject matter are inherent in my course of instruction? How can I teach my course so as to make these latent values more realizable?

Satisfaction in Learning. Faith in formal discipline was accompanied by an equally simple and attractive belief in the potency of effort. It mattered not so much what one learned provided that in the learning he expended hard and persistent effort, preferably enforced by "power of will." This theory contains a commonsense truth which few would question: there can be no great accomplishment without exertion; the greater the investment of effort, the better one is likely to learn. But this is not identical with maintaining that special virtue accrues from expenditure of effort per se, particularly in doing what is uninteresting or disagreeable. Character can be built through adversity, but it can be built more effectually through satisfying experience; learning may result from determined self-application to uncongenial tasks, but more can be accomplished through pleasurable tasks willingly pursued. It is not the importance of effort which is here challenged, but the assumption that "willed" effort is somehow more potent educationally than doing "what comes naturally."

Modern psychology has maintained that, however indispensable to learning effort may be, it is also important to understand why one is learning, have a sense of personal motive in learning, and find satisfaction in the task. The scientific antecedents of this principle are found in Thorndike's famous "Law of Effect": learning is more effective when accompanied by a feeling of satisfaction, less effective when accompanied by a sense of annoyance. This "law of learning" is now recognized as an oversimplification of a more complex principle. Pain as well as pleasure can stimulate learning; much less effective than either is learning experience accompanied by little emotion or feeling of any kind. The "annoyers" which are deterrents to learning can be other than physical sensations of distress, fear of disapproval, or threat to self: indifference, lack of incentive or interest, failure to look with pride toward accomplishment are even more inhibitive. Satisfaction in learning is more often psychic satisfaction which comes from believing in what one is doing, from having a personal stake in learning, from making progress especially when the going is rough. Not effort alone but *purposeful* effort is the key to successful learning.

Interest and effort are paired in education. The one stimulates the other, gives it direction, and propels it forward even in the face of difficulty. The teacher works with both; he seeks to energize the student, and can best do so by stimulating interest and helping to make the study of his subject a rewarding experience. There comes a time when a student must continue learning for himself; the safest assurance that he will do this is if he finds the experience intellectually satisfying.

The fact that we teach on the college level does not reduce the need for motivation. Some students approach a subject of study with sturdy and well-formed sense of purpose; our task in such cases is to speed the student toward his objective, strengthening and extending his interest. Other students do not have the same degree of positive incentive. A college program of study includes a greater range of intellectual purposes than one person can naturally accept. A purpose, after all, is personal: to a mathematician nothing may be more obvious than the need for understanding rational and irrational numbers; to a student this need may be enveloped in mystery. Our task with such students is to attempt to convey the need for learning our subject, and to promote a satisfaction in learning which comes from accepting a challenge and making headway with it. This is motivation: not discussing the virtues of a subject, but teaching it in such a way that its meaning and the intrinsic need for learning it become clear and are accepted by the student.

However industriously we try, we find it hard to reach some students. In such cases little can be done except to keep trying. Fortunately interest and effort serve each other: not until some investment in effort has been made may interest appear. The development of interest can also be gradual and imperceptible, taking place in unexpected ways. It is not uncommon to hear from a student heretofore slow to respond to instruction, "I think I see now what this course is driving at."

Learning and Experience. As college teachers we tend to view learning mainly in intellectual terms. We take pride in the fact that college studies deal with ideas rather than techniques, with "pure" knowledge rather than its application. Each college discipline represents the intellectual distillation of the products of much human experience. Our instruction is normally designed to appeal to those senses which translate *things* into concepts and ideas. We lecture, explain, demonstrate, question, and otherwise lead the student toward understanding; the latter listens, sees, talks, reads, and thinks —and if he thinks well, we are satisfied. Learning tends to be identified with comprehension, and often is pursued no further.

In general, this emphasis on the intellectual aspects of learning experience is unavoidable, else in the short time available we should never succeed in educating the student in needed respects. Furthermore, the college student is capable of working with ideas—of receiving, assimilating, and responding to them. What is overlooked, however, is that this approach to learning is a short cut, and short cuts are sometimes so arduous as to be impassable. However clearly presented by the teacher a subject may not be understood by students, and even repeated explanations may not help. As every teacher knows, momentary understanding does not always produce learning: what is understood today may be forgotten tomorrow, and never successfully applied.

Teachers are interested in inducing not the symptoms of learning but learning itself. "At its best and most complete, learning combines thinking, feeling, acting, and expressing appropriately in relation to the demands of a confronted situation of need, desire, drive, or aspiration." [8] The consummation of learning is found in the change of the student's thinking, feeling, and behavior, and the test of learning is in his ability to use what he has learned in thought and in action. True learning begins and ends in experience; the intellective process is an intermediate step. It is not true that we proceed first to form concepts, then to apply them. The two work together: practice clarifies and refines theory, theory intelligently directs practice. A student learns better if he has a chance to apply what he is learning at the time he is learning it.

The implications for college teaching of these general statements are numerous. Experiential learning certainly deserves a greater place in higher education than it has received. As science teaching discovered, not all of its subject matter can be conveyed verbally; field and laboratory experience is needed to supplement lecture and recitation. Instruction in the fine arts and music customarily also combines theory with practice. In teaching the social sciences and the humanities more can be done to involve the student in direct learning experience. A course in abnormal psychology gains in effect when verbal instruction is coupled with periodic clinical observation of patients in medical centers. A sociology student enriches his understanding of the subject by participating in the work of social-service agencies. The realities of political science are better grasped when textbook study is combined with on-the-spot experience with governmental and other public operations. There is hardly a subject of instruction which cannot be improved through more extended contact with primary sources of experience.

This is not anti-intellectual doctrine. We are not disparaging the efficacy of verbal instruction and book learning, only noting that these can be more effective when combined with direct personal experience. As a self-sufficient method of learning on the college level, the latter has decided limitations, and even as a partial method is not equally applicable to all subjects. What we are suggesting is a more balanced use of diversified learning methods. The goals of instruction need not be affected: emphasis should still be on cultiva-

[8] Ordway Tead, *College Teaching and College Learning* (New Haven: Yale University Press, 1949), p. 24.

tion of intellectual powers and broader understandings rather than on minor facts and skills pertinent to specific situations.

The interrelation of learning and experience suggests also the need for a clearer recognition of the supporting and permeative role of feeling and emotion. A person thoroughly involved in an experience learns not only with his mind but also with his "heart," and as a result whatever is learned is learned better. Our appeal in instruction is and should be to the intellect, but the rational learning process is strengthened when accompanied by proper feeling tone. Instruction should aim to develop not only ideas but emotional acceptance of them and pleasure in them—as much in teaching the "cold-blooded" sciences as in the more value-laden social sciences and the appreciational arts. A student is likely to learn better the elements of scientific thinking if he feels a strong personal attachment to them, and is then more likely to use them in non-science situations.

Democracy means more when accepted as a personal creed than when merely understood and impersonally judged as a form of social procedure. Much as we like to avoid indoctrination, retain our own objectivity, and help students to think and act dispassionately, our concern fundamentally is to teach values and ideas along with principles and facts. Man is not so utterly rational a creature that he invariably follows the logic of his thinking even when that logic leads in one direction. When principles and emotions are in conflict, the former sometimes lose out. We need to recognize that fact, and when convinced of the truth of an idea lead the student to accept it not only intellectually but sympathetically. At the same time we should be clear in distinguishing between such "truths" and other categories of knowledge in which definitive judgment is not attainable. Even in such cases objectivity or open-mindedness can be fostered more readily when the student is inclined to accord it emotional approval.

Independence in Learning. One of the great educational needs of the college student is for growth in intellectual independence. In this undertaking the student's native intelligence is a marked asset, and the knowledge and skill gained from previous schooling a reasonably promising starting point. Students admitted to college can read, make some independent use of sources of knowledge, identify and formulate problems in academic and real life experience, and think through some of them to conclusions. Naturally there are limitations to their intellectual power, deriving partly from inadequacies of previous learning, partly from their relative immaturity. However bright and proficient the student, he cannot in the secondary-school stage be expected to develop the quality of independence which should characterize a mature educated person.

Intellectual independence rarely is a fortuitous achievement; it requires systematic cultivation. The teacher must accept it as a major objective and direct his teaching so as to place upon students the responsibility for learning. This means providing opportunities for students to work independently, encouraging and evaluating their efforts. Progress toward independence is gradual, assuming different forms at different educational levels. A senior course should be distinguished from a freshman course, among other ways, by the extent and quality of independent learning. But in a freshman course also, as in every college learning experience, there should be opportunity for graduated exercise of independence. No one subject occupies a privileged position as a potential contributor to such growth; all the disciplines working coordinately toward this end can make its realization possible.

The term "intellectual independence" should have definition. It suggests more than mastery of tools of learning and competence in their use. One must think for himself, and the substance of thought is even more important than the method of achieving it. "How to read a book," trace a fact to its source, solve a practical or academic problem, and pursue independently a subject of special interest are important accomplishments but in themselves do not add up to the highest kind of intellectual independence needed. More is involved than operation of the intellect alone: not only knowing how to think, but having the courage to state one's ideas even in the face of possible social disapproval, to stand by one's principles, and to express one's personality in ways that may not conform to conventional patterns. Intellectual independence involves having a sense of values, and not only the clear-sightedness but also the moral strength to respond to the facts of experience in the light of one's values and beliefs, not merely as others respond. At its best intellectual independence embraces also a sense of social responsibility, personal humility, and commonsense regard for reality.

It follows that training for intellectual independence presumes more than teaching the student how to study and pursue independent learning in a specific field. The teacher needs also to help the student emerge as a person—develop a sense of his own integrity, think and act for himself, "be himself." This will occur more readily as the teacher creates opportunities to stimulate original and independent thinking and to encourage responsible and controlled self-expression. In most subjects of study "truths" are not so rigidly cast as to allow for only a single answer. Recognition of the student's freedom to assume a responsible position of difference does more to foster intellectual independence than any number of satisfactory or "pass" grades. Teaching him respect for truth wherever it exists, for knowledge and fact, for methods of thinking which limit personal bias and reduce the chances of error is equally indispensable in promoting positive independence. And for providing the student with intellectual substance—the "wherewithal" of independent thinking —perhaps nothing is more effective than arousing interests and encouraging their intensive cultivation as a means of personal development, so that in time the student may come to feel, "These things I know, and for these things I stand."

Levels of Thinking, Learning, and Teaching. The nature of the thought process is still in large part unknown; our teaching would be surer were we more definite in our knowledge of it. We use freely such terms as idea, concept, judgment, evaluation, and problem solving without awareness that they are more indicative of the overt result of thinking than of the thinking process. We can tell when a person reasons well, but what he does in the act of reasoning is a matter of hypothesis. Nevertheless, teaching cannot be suspended until all the facts are in; we necessarily proceed on the little we know and on what we can plausibly assume.

Compared with the person of average intellect the college student is more adept in analyzing experience, elaborating meanings into ideas, relating ideas in coherent patterns of thought, and bringing these to bear in evaluating, reorganizing, and directing his behavior. He can comprehend faster, penetrate more deeply into abstract thinking, distinguish subtle differences in meaning, and more effectively work his way toward and from generalization. Depending upon his individual quality of mind, he may or may not follow "normal" or customary steps in reasoning, telescoping thought processes, combining or omitting steps, or inventing pathways of his own. All this is, of course, relative: only the rare student possesses all these qualities to a great extent. But the characterization may roughly fit the large percentage of students whose aptitude conforms to the requirements of college study.

The college long ago accommodated itself to the thinking, supposed or real, of the superior individual; this is reflected in the content of study and the mode of instruction. A college course of instruction deals not so much with *things* as with meanings, relationships, principles, and generalizations. College teaching begins not on the ground floor of experience but on a higher level, and continues to work upward. To appreciate the difference one should spend some days observing elementary or secondary classes or instruction of adults in evening schools. There teaching is denotative, descriptive, and explicit; much of the time is utilized in building the concrete basis for thought; the avenue toward comprehension is through multi-sensory appeal; sojourn with pure thought is necessarily limited.

By contrast college teaching is connotative, suggestive, dealing with implication. Not only basic experience but fundamental meaning derived from such experience is assumed a priori. The subject matter is derivative, abstract. Exposition is for the most part economical, terse, concept-laden, and to a high degree verbal, aided only by such multi-sensory devices as are judged essential for comprehension. The appeal is to higher and subtler forms of thinking— forming concepts, discerning relationships, deriving principles, testing, evaluating, and refining ideas. The ultimate objective of instruction is to have the student learn better to perform these operations for himself.

So far as we know this is as it should be, except for two things. Even superior students need at times to fall back upon simpler thinking processes and forms of learning; and not all students are generally superior. To assume that instruction should always be on a uniformly high level of abstraction is a mistake. "Nothing indeed," writes Jean Piaget, "could be more superficial than to suppose that the construction of intelligence is already accomplished on the practical level, and then simply to appeal to language and imaginal representation to explain how this ready-made intelligence comes to be internalized as logical thought." [9] An intelligent art teacher knows that his capacity for high-level thought might be reduced were he to become involved in discussion of nuclear fission, synthesis of organic compounds, or the solution of integral equations. By the same token a student in an art course cannot develop a meaningful appreciation of works of Greek sculpture or Italian Renaissance painting until he has had a chance to live with these works on lower levels of experience, perception, and thought. To be technically competent, instruction must range over various levels of thought and learning, adjusting to the level of the student's need and working upwards from there.

The object is not to simplify teaching so as to make it conform to the thinking of the less able students; rather to raise their thinking to higher levels.

There are many levels of intelligence and of intellectual achievement. There is no reason for distinguishing merely two levels, a very low and a very high. There is an uninterrupted series of steps leading up from the experiences which are externally conditioned, simple, and immature to the experiences which are higher because they emphasize systematically relations, abstractions, and broad generalizations. It is to the advantage of society that all individuals be stimulated to climb these steps as rapidly and as far as possible.[10]

COLLEGE STUDENTS AS ADOLESCENTS

Influencing the teacher's attitude is the knowledge that the young people with whom he deals are in the later stages of adolescence. Adolescence suggests an unsettling stage of growth and development: the "storm and stress" associated with biological coming of age, uncertainty in realization of self and quest for self-understanding, unpredictiveness in behavior, alternating self-assertiveness and self-effacement, idealism carried to logical but unnerving extremes, teen-age romances and an occasional crush on the teacher, and all

[9] *The Psychology of Intelligence* (New York: Harcourt, Brace and Company, 1950), p. 120. The whole of this brilliant book should be read.

[10] Charles H. Judd, *Education As Cultivation of the Higher Mental Processes* (New York: The Macmillan Company, 1936), p. 193.

sorts of interesting behavior at times attractive, at other times exasperating.

Recent studies of adolescence have tended to de-emphasize the *sturm und drang* aspects of adolescent behavior and to offer a more plausible accounting of adolescent concerns and problems. Behavioral phenomena associated with biological change and maturation have not been discounted, but anthropological studies by Margaret Mead and others have shown that they need not be so intense and disturbing but for causative factors within the culture itself. With the change in emphasis, the sociological problems of adolescence (as distinct from those induced by mainly physiological causes) have come into prominence. These days adolescents are often judged as more "sinned against" than "sinning."

Possibly both the biological and the sociological dogmas exaggerate. Adolescence is not quite the peculiarly difficult period that popular belief supposes; childhood too has its difficulties, and middle age, and senescence perhaps most of all. Modern psychologies tend to seek the key to graceful or difficult adjustment in the make-up of the person interacting with the forces of his life experience, rather than in inherent crises of any one stage of growth. Individuals do differ in the manner of their passage through adolescence: those who were difficult as children continue difficult as adolescents, and probably will remain difficult as adults. Nor are adolescents the only ones to suffer from society's inadequacies and imbalances: in periods of severe unemployment youth find it hard to be placed in jobs, but so do people of forty-five years of age or over; abstinence from the normal marriage sex relationship may be hard for unmarried young folk of twenty but it is hard also for older spinsters and widowed men and women. Insecurity is common among adolescents but it also faces many of us during much of our lifetime. Society has problems which it imposes generously upon all of us, and to say that it singles out adolescents for especially severe treatment is an overstatement.

Some Problems of Older Adolescents. Without therefore magnifying or belittling adolescent problems it is necessary to understand them. Adolescents require neither excessive sympathy nor tolerance but they do need understanding and help in solving their problems. Inasmuch as these problems occur during the growing-up process when youth are in school and college, they are inseparable from education, and concern with them is a necessary function of the teacher.

1. *Anxiety concerning self.* The term is used in its normal rather than clinical or pathological sense. College students are approaching the threshold of maturity; they are confronted with the task of establishing themselves as individuals in society, of proving their worth to themselves and to others. There is naturally a degree of concern as to whether they will be successful as people, make their economic way, attract a suitable partner in marriage, make and hold friends, and become generally accepted and respected as adults. Their current state of health, physical attractiveness, popularity, financial well-being, adjustment to school and college, and satisfaction with study is the index by which they estimate probabilities of future success. Not all young people show equal concern: some face the future with confidence, others at one time or another experience deep misgivings. Less serious limitations such as lack of conspicuous "good looks" in girls or athletic physique in young men are apt to be viewed with exaggerated concern; temporary setbacks may be counted more heavily than they should be. Even when no negative portents exist, youth may be doubtful of future adequacy.

Seen in retrospect, much of this concern is unjustified. Nevertheless young people need reassurance as to their competence to cope with the demands of adult life experience. Such reassurance may occasionally take the form of verbal encouragement, but it is more important that they be provided with opportunity to demonstrate their capability to meet such challenges as arise. Confidence in the future is built not by anticipating life demands, seeking to forestall possible contingencies, taking experiences out of context and dealing with them prematurely, but by living successfully in the present.

The college should do everything possible to make the student's educational experience a success; failure may have penalties more severe than those immediately obvious. Studies may be designed in part as a test of intellectual strength, but youth should be helped to meet the test successfully. Outside the formal program of study there should be other opportunities for youth to achieve recognition as persons, establish themselves in relation to their fellows, and make a contribution to community living. The lonely student, the unwanted, the socially maladjusted is as much a problem to the teacher and counselor as the one academically in arrears. It helps also to provide students scope for activity outside the college community proper— in gainful part-time employment, civic improvement, child care, social work, and the like.

2. *Need for proper sex adjustment.* The mores of society may play a role in aggravating problems of adjustment; safeguards that society sets up for itself are sometimes a hazard for the individual. The problem of sex adjustment is a case in point. Surrounded by a conspiracy of silence and subject to social taboos, important problems in sex relationships must be handled by indirection. Whereas other cases of infringement upon social custom may be regarded merely as a transgression of youth, ignorance or violation of the social code in sex matters is punishable more drastically by the sense of shame or disgrace it evokes.

In the United States [writes Kuhlen] the opportunity to become an adult economically is delayed far beyond the age when an individual is physically and mentally capable of doing productive work, and marriage is delayed far beyond the age when biologically the young person is capable of reproduction.[11]

For both sexes the average age of advent of pubescence is roughly 14; the average age at marriage is approximately 24.[12] The interval affords the adolescent ample time to wonder, speculate, learn well or badly, form wholesome attitudes or ways of thinking and acting which may be hard to correct later. At an age when youth in former times prepared to marry and support a home and family, the college student is in school, living at family expense supplemented perhaps by earnings from part-time employment, with prospects of a career and marriage in many cases not yet visible. Sexually mature, youth must postpone for some time entrance into normal adult sex relationship. "Dates," dances, socials, companionship with members of the other sex are wholesome compensatory activities, but not an adequate substitute.

This prolongation of childhood was not accomplished by fiat, nor

11 *The Psychology of Adolescent Development* (New York: Harper & Brothers, 1952), p. 180.
12 *Ibid.,* p. 182.

can it be retracted in that way. In our society with its requirement of extended schooling this prolongation is unavoidable, and even as such has compensations: if we have extended childhood, we have also succeeded in extending the span of life, and both are traceable to the same causes. Naturally there is nothing the college can do to influence the period of waiting for marriage except to educate the individual to adjust to it: help him build healthy attitudes and social relationships, dispel fears and superstitions, reduce tensions that arise from worry about self, and provide constructive, pleasurable activities through which the normal urge for companionship with members of the opposite sex may be satisfied. For this purpose activities of many sorts are serviceable, on campus and off, and the more natural and unobtrusive the mingling of sexes, the better: joint club activities, community and civic drives, musicals, amateur theatricals, discussion of good books, as well as individual and small group sports such as hiking, skiing, tennis, and golf. Especially should noncoeducational institutions make efforts to organize such activities and dignify them by institutional sponsorship. For the individual student in need of help with his own problems of adjustment, there should always be available understanding, non-inhibitive counseling.

3. *Conflicts with adult society.* The view that many youth have of the world and the prospects it holds for them is, understandably, not enchanting. Born into an economic depression, sharing in childhood the anxieties of war, experiencing the tensions of the war's aftermath, some of them have never known real security of mind. Now of college age, boys face the prospect of temporary disruption of the start of a career by the obligation of military service; girls have to endure separation from their young men and share in the uncertainty of their future. Except for a few technical fields demanding qualifications of superior intelligence and training, entry into a professional career is not easy. The world is in seeming constant discord: "small" wars are being fought almost continuously, and even within one nation segments of the population regard each other with unfriendliness and suspicion. There is talk of a better world to come, of a brotherhood of nations to be united in peace, and some fundamental arrangements have been made to bring this world into being. But its concrete materialization is terribly slow, and deep ideological chasms still separate nations and individuals.

Under the circumstances, how are intelligent young people supposed to feel about the future they will inherit?

Young people tend to be idealistic and, being limited in experience, to follow the logic of their idealism; this brings them into disagreement, and sometimes difficulty, with older people. Adults are tolerant of the trespasses of youth provided their own prerogatives are not involved. They can view with amusement incidents of "goldfish swallowing" and midnight raids on girls' dormitories, but react with greater exasperation to youth's occasional incursions into serious social problems such as civil rights, employer-labor relations, and the like. Let college students, motivated by what they consider a sense of fair play, join a picket line and they become objects of suspicion and vocal rebuke. It is not so much youthful pranks which bring premature gray hairs to college officials, but occasions of real or potential conflict with the adult community in matters of serious social concern.

Fortunately this nation is relatively free of "professional" students who in academic guise serve as instigators of civil discord. College students are usually motivated by a sincere idealism rather than a desire to stir up excitement and make trouble for their elders. They are impelled by principles taught to them by adults and they insist that the principles be accepted in fact as well as theory. Lacking the broader vision of adults, they sometimes fail to see all aspects of a problem, or to understand that by pressing the enforcement of some rights they may deny or imperil others. A college campus can be a restless place, and the urgency of youth occasionally translates itself into idealistically motivated but imprudent action.

Youth tend to see things in black or white, not so well in shades of gray. They are impatient with imperfection and contemptuous of compromise. This is what so often creates friction with adults who are more likely to take a longer and more balanced view, estimate the risks, and proceed with greater caution. What makes youth good soldiers in battle tends often to make them too impetuous citizens. Driven by what they regard as unjustified provocation, elements in the adult community and sometimes even teachers, who should know better, may be impelled to rear and strike back—to exact penalties and impose curbs.

Educators should be careful to avoid this sort of reaction. Youth should be protected in their idealism; we *want* them to be spirited. The objective is to educate them, not to break them. What a poor world this would be if young people were bereft of spirit and ardor and became safe, shrewd, conservative operators! Rarely should institutional authority be pitted against the forceful self-expression of students. Even in the face of immoderation, college officials and teachers should persist in retaining their educational perspective, and apply the tactics of patience and moderation. The problem is to educate students toward broader, more balanced and responsible understanding, to give them responsible experience along with intelligent principle, so that with growing maturity there may be added to idealism the virtue of wisdom.

These are a few of the problems which concern college youth. There are others, some more personal and specific to the individual. The adolescent seeks to make adjustments which strike him as reasonable and satisfying, and which give him a sense of standing and self-respect as a person; possibilities of difficulty or mistakes are many. Human relations with parents, family, or outsiders are frequently a source of irritation; so is the need for conformity to many of society's conventions. Whatever the problem—common or individual, academic or personal—it should be scrutinized by the college for possible effect upon the student's educational development. If the student seems to need help in its resolution, the college through its resources of personnel should try to provide it.

SELECTED BIBLIOGRAPHY

Cole, Luella, *The Background for College Teaching,* Chapters VI-XIII, "The College Student." New York: Farrar and Rinehart, Inc., 1940. 616 pp.

Council of State Governments, *Higher Education in the Forty-Eight States.* Chicago: The Council, 1952. 316 pp.

Crawford, A. B. and Burnham, P. S., *Forecasting College Achievement.* New Haven: Yale University Press, 1946. 274 pp.

Fine, Benjamin, *Admission to American Colleges.* New York: Harper & Brothers, 1946. 225 pp.

Havemann, Ernest and West, Patricia S., *They Went to College*. New York: Harcourt, Brace and Company, 1952. 277 pp.

Heaton, Kenneth L. and Weedon, Vivian, *The Failing Student*, A Study of Academic Failure and the Implication for Education. Chicago: University of Chicago Press, 1939. 286 pp.

Hilgard, Ernest, *Theories of Learning*. New York: Appleton-Century-Crofts, Inc., 1948. 409 pp.

Hollinshead, Byron S., *Who Should Go to College*. New York: Columbia University Press, 1952. 190 pp.

Horrocks, John E., *The Psychology of Adolescence*. New York: Houghton Mifflin Company, 1951. 614 pp.

Judd, Charles H., *Education As Cultivation of the Higher Mental Processes*. New York: The Macmillan Company, 1936. 206 pp.

Katz, Daniel and Allport, Floyd N., *Students' Attitudes*, A Report of the Syracuse University Reaction Study. Syracuse, N.Y.: The Craftsman Press, 1931. 408 pp.

Kingsley, Howard L., *The Nature and Conditions of Learning*. New York: Prentice-Hall, Inc., 1946. 579 pp.

Kuhlen, Raymond G., *The Psychology of Adolescent Development*. New York: Harper & Brothers, 1952. 675 pp.

Landis, Paul H., *Adolescence and Youth*. New York: McGraw-Hill Book Company, 1945. 470 pp.

Meland, Bernard E., *Higher Education and the Human Spirit*, Chapter III, "The Nature of Thinking in Education." Chicago: University of Chicago Press, 1953. 200 pp.

National Society for the Study of Education, *Adolescence*, Forty-Third Yearbook, Part I. Chicago: University of Chicago Press, 1944. 358 pp.

Pace, C. Robert, *They Went to College*, A Study of 951 Former University Students. Minneapolis: University of Minnesota Press, 1941. 148 pp.

Piaget, Jean, *The Psychology of Intelligence*. New York: Harcourt, Brace and Company, 1950. 182 pp.

Prescott, Daniel A., *Emotion and the Educative Process*. Washington: American Council on Education, 1938. 323 pp.

President's Commission on Higher Education, *Higher Education in American Democracy*. New York: Harper & Brothers, 1947. Combined edition, 6 vols., 103 pp., 69 pp., 74 pp., 63 pp., 68 pp. and 51 pp. respectively.

Taylor, Harold, ed., *Essays in Teaching*, Chapter II, "The Teacher and the Student" and Chapter VIII, "The Individual Student." New York: Harper & Brothers, 1950. 239 pp.

Tead, Ordway, *College Teaching and College Learning: A Plea for Improvement,* Chapter IV, "The Nature of Learning." New Haven: Yale University Press, 1949. 56 pp.

Thorpe, Louis and Schmuller, Allen M., *Contemporary Theories of Learning.* New York: The Ronald Press, 1954. 480 pp.

Warner, W. Lloyd, Havighurst, Robert J., and Loeb, Martin B., *Who Shall Be Educated?* New York: Harper & Brothers, 1944. 190 pp.

VI. *The College Curriculum*

The curriculum is an instrument of education, the chief means available to the teacher for the accomplishment of his educational purpose. Over the years it has received much professional attention, yet not always with proper reference to the ends it is meant to serve. The subject matter of the curriculum tends to become absorbing in its own right and its essentially instrumental role to be forgotten. Disciplines of instruction appear to assume an independent purpose for existence, and the servant leads the master. Just as other instruments have at times outlived the needs which created them, so have portions of the curriculum sometimes remained after their usefulness diminished. Protected by tradition the curriculum has not always been subjected to the test of logic or practical sense.

It is difficult to determine when a curriculum is an efficient instrument of education and even harder to gauge its efficiency with precision: results in education are slow to become evident. They are not readily provable, and the final issue may remain in doubt. In recent years much effort has gone into redesigning the curriculum to adapt it to the needs of the times. The chances are that from this activity has resulted an instrument capable enough of serving its purpose; the probability is also that it can be further improved. Important for both current use and future improvement of the curriculum is an attitude receptive to recognition of shortcomings as well as merits, and not so restrained by tradition or by loyalty to a field of scholarship as to fail to perceive or take needed action.

To laymen a profession is supposed to hold no secrets for its practicioners; those in the profession know better. It should be admitted that there is much relating to curriculum concerning which knowledge is lacking, in which professional procedure is based on trial and error, hypothesis, or simply faith. We behave sometimes as if there were no curriculum problems that greater resources of money or manpower could not solve. Such self-assurance is not justified; it would be healthier to acknowledge that in many respects our approach toward assembling, organizing, and conducting a program of study is experimental and tentative.

The Teacher's Concern with the Entire Curriculum. The college teacher is often so engrossed in immediate tasks that he is unable, except in an incidental way, to spare the time for cultivating familiarity with the college program as a whole. Except where problems impinge upon his own or his department's courses of instruction, he is unlikely to be concerned with what are sometimes called "curriculum matters." Beyond the scope of his courses his knowledge of the organized course of study may be limited. First his professional training was not planned to focus attention on problems in curriculum; then, following his entry into teaching, his chief preoccupation was naturally with immediate preparation for instructional and other responsibilities. Thus the pattern was set. It is not unusual to find teachers of several years' service with an institution who have only casual acquaintance with its patterns of offerings, and, summoned to college-wide curriculum service, even experienced teachers are astonished to discover how much hard work as well as disputation can take place behind the closed door of a conference room.

Yet, next to teaching, there are not many matters more deserving of the teacher's attention and concern. In order that he may teach his students properly, he needs to be aware of the larger educational experience in which they are involved, of the relations among its component parts, of its values and shortcomings.

Furthermore, acquaintance with the curriculum in general terms is in itself insufficient. One should know the curriculum intimately enough to understand its shared use as an instrument of education: its rationale, the principles underlying its operation, its purported goals, major component elements, manner of operation, and determinable achievements. The teacher should, moreover, be interested in learning how the program came to be, recent developments or changes, and curriculum undertakings under way. Whether or not directly engaged in curriculum activity, he is not without influence in formulating policy and determining its future success. Often it is the collective judgment of the faculty which decides whether a curriculum proposal is acceptable, and the support furnished by the faculty which makes the difference between the success or failure of an innovation. The teacher has an obligation to use his influence responsibly to good effect.

Some Attributes of the Prevailing Curriculum. While there is no "typical" college program, it is possible to describe attributes common to programs in most institutions. In important respects the contemporary American college is distinguishable from the institution of several generations ago or even from comparable European institutions today. To check the pertinence of these attributes one has only to relate them to the institution he serves or to others with which he may be familiar. In recognizing the existence of common characteristics, prevailing differences in curriculum features of institutions need not be minimized. So much has been written on the subject that listing and brief explanation may suffice.

1. *Comprehensiveness.* The range and variety of knowledge encompassed within the college curriculum is "encyclopedic." Practically every major field of learning is represented by a course or courses, in some instances at several levels of study. The compact body of liberal disciplines which almost to the time of the Civil War "consisted chiefly of studies in Latin, Greek, mathematics, logic, and moral philosophy, with occasional smatterings of Hebrew and elementary physics and astronomy,"[1] has given way to a program of extended dimensions. To the traditional subjects—classical languages and literatures, mathematics, philosophy, and physical science —modern languages and literatures, the biological sciences, the social sciences, the fine arts, music, health, and physical education have been added, and the increase of knowledge within each subject has led to multiplication of courses of instruction. Most recently even liberal institutions have been introducing studies in such occupational fields as business, home economics, journalism, social work, and teaching. So extensive is the college curriculum that a student can hope to master only a fraction of it.

[1] Richard Hofstadter and C. DeWitt Hardy, *The Development and Scope of Higher Education in the United States* (New York: Columbia University Press, 1952), p. 11.

The vast expansion in the scope of knowledge that has taken place in modern times is not the only reason for the comprehensiveness of the curriculum. In every age the sum of organized learning has been much larger than that which the college could or cared to include in its program. Much of the time, however, the theory under which higher education operated placed a premium not on inclusiveness but on selectivity of learning; under formal discipline, for example, a few well-chosen formative subjects could accomplish the purposes of college education. When this theory lost ground, a formidable barrier against less discriminating admission of studies was removed. Under the advancing pressure of science, social science, and new professions, and with the mounting enrollment of students with differentiated interests, the gates were further opened and in a short time the college curriculum became virtually a panoramic representation of man's knowledge.

2. *Number of separate offerings.* The amount of knowledge enclosed by the curriculum inevitably presents problems in organizing instruction. Paralleling scholarly and research practice in the different fields of learning, curriculum disciplines have tended to be organized and conducted in limited allotments, within the larger boundaries of departments, divisions, and "schools" of instruction. The number of separate course offerings in liberal colleges alone, if a cumulative nonduplicating list could be assembled, would run well into the thousands. A single large college may have twenty-five or more departments of instruction and may list upward of five hundred or six hundred courses; a large one with several branches may have twice the number. In one semester a student may pursue six or seven courses, and in four years of study "complete" between fifty and fifty-five. A mathematical credit system keeps track of the student's progress through the forest of studies and indicates when he has accomplished enough to merit graduation.

College teachers are aware of the difficulties inherent in this proliferation of studies. The condition is not an outcome of design but of evolutionary development to which a number of influences contributed: the increasingly specialized nature of scholarship, pressure for admission of new fields of learning, desire to satisfy the differing interests of students, introduction of the elective principle, and others. Teachers themselves are not without responsibility, as all should admit who have at various times pressed for inclusion of a particular course representative of their specialized interest.

3. *Disparity among courses*. Equally evident is the discrepancy among courses in range and depth of subject matter and in structure. In effect there is no common yardstick by which a course is definable. In the same semester and for an equal number of credits a student may be enrolled in a "general" course of broad content, a specialized course of delimited area but considerable depth, and a "tool" course in speech, writing, foreign language, or mathematics. In his junior year he may take courses less rigorous than those pursued as a freshman. Some courses are logically self-contained units, others a framework of convenience enclosing selected beginning and terminal points for instruction, as, for example, "History of Europe from 1815 to 1865." Most courses are specifically within one field of learning or department of instruction, others are interdisciplinary. The duration of courses varies among and within institutions, and may range from a "quarter" of six or eight weeks to a period of a year or two.

There is no virtue in uniformity as such, and some disparity among courses is necessary and desirable. Differences in levels of study, conduct of instruction, and outcomes of learning should be cultivated if we are to provide students with variety of learning experience. Weakness occurs when diversity is fortuitous rather than planned, when no definite standards obtain as to what constitutes a good course of study.

4. *The elective principle*. Most liberal colleges adhere to the elective principle. They differ in the degree of elective freedom granted, the nature of elective offerings, and the manner in which student selection of courses is regulated. Elective study is commonly associated with "concentration" in a major field of study, and represents a recognition of the worth of different varieties of learning experience as well as a practical concession to the divergent interests of the students. The realistic alternative to limited election is not a uniform course of study for all students but either multiplication of specialized colleges or greatly curtailed enrollment in higher education. It is no coincidence that pressure for elective study developed when the colleges began to attract more students and that the recent

growth in enrollment has been accompanied by an expansion of elective opportunity.

Further justifying the elective principle is the theory that higher education must fulfill also an exploratory function, that is, enable the student to explore himself in relation to various fields of learning. Elective opportunities are not limited to the field of the student's "major" concentration but are present to some extent in other phases of the program of study. No single feature is more characteristic of the contemporary American college and its concept of higher education than the elective system.

5. *The prescribed core.* Paired with the elective principle is the complementary practice of designating a portion of the curriculum as "prescribed." Prescriptive offerings vary widely among institutions in substance, form, and extent. In some cases prescribed courses may be few, consisting of several "tool" subjects and content courses such as "History of Western Culture" which are judged indispensable. More often the prescribed program is of greater extent, containing representative courses from major divisions of study embracing the humanities, science, and social science without a definite organic interconnection. The prescription may be stated in terms of listed courses or as a required "distribution" of credits among given course groupings or "areas" of study. The sum of prescribed course credits may range from a small fraction of the total needed for graduation to more than half.

The prescriptive principle is founded in the belief that a common body of educational experience is basic to the development of all students regardless of individual differences, and that the best interest of each requires that a balance be maintained between common and differentiated study. The prescriptive principle as such has not incurred as much criticism as its elective complement. The problem is to determine what constitutes proper balance and, even more serious, to identify and assemble the elements of a good prescribed core.

6. *Internal regulation.* The multiform nature of the curriculum imposes a need for greater institutional regulation of study than may in principle be desirable. American institutions of higher education have been criticized as being over-regulated: there are rules governing admission to courses, attendance, fulfillment of prescriptions, choice of electives, preparation of programs of study, retention or

dismissal, and eligibility for graduation. To institutional regulations departments of instruction may add requirements for their own "majors." Having satisfied the college foreign-language prescription a student may be faced with an additional language requirement set by his elective department; or, having selected a field of concentration, he may find himself pursuing patterns of elective courses not primarily of his own design. Extensive use is made of the device of labeling courses prerequisite to others, though the strict necessity of such linkage may not always be apparent.

Some regulation is necessary to safeguard coherence and continuous progression in study and balanced education. Amid the variety of curricular offerings it would be unsafe simply to turn the student loose to shift for himself. Unrestricted election of studies could readily degenerate into the practice of sampling courses at random or, contrarily, into overspecialization. But the prevailing abundance of regulation does lend a "lock-step" quality to college education. In an attempt to break the lock-step some colleges have taken measures to insure greater individual freedom in programming and progression in study, using for this purpose placement and exemption examinations, comprehensive tests of achievement, and independent reading courses.

Curriculum Strengths and Weaknesses

The foregoing discussion of general curriculum attributes suggests both strengths and weaknesses. It is well to make an explicit distinction between the two, since current proposals for reform threaten at times to sweep away much that is good along with the elements that should be eliminated.

Strengths. 1. *Adaptability to individual needs.* The college curriculum has evolved in a manner responsive to the needs of a mixed student population. Its value lies not only in the richness of its offerings but also in their adaptability to students. Though the reality falls short of the ideal there is inherent an effort to make available to each person an appropriate education. A science-minded student can, with adequate guidance, develop his potentiality in science and at the same time secure a broad training in the humanities and social sciences. The musically gifted student, the artist, future mathematician, psychologist, or teacher can similarly select studies consistent with his special aptitudes while pursuing others addressed to the demands of more general education. The student without pronounced aptitude or interest has a chance to explore his capacities in several fields of study. No single common course of study could serve all these students, even were it possible to prescribe one which would meet with general approval. In the absence of indisputable authority indicating otherwise, a diversified, multipurpose curriculum seems best.

2. *Dynamic quality of the program.* Whatever its failings the curriculum of the American college is alive, responsive to change in society and to the growth and development of knowledge. Advances in scholarship and its application to the service of mankind are reflected in adaptations of the course of study. It is not true now, as it may have been in past periods, that institutions of higher education are out of touch with intellectual and creative progress in the world outside. Without surrendering its function of conserving the best in tradition, the college is involved in the discovery and acquisition of new subject matter. To be sure, not everything admitted into the curriculum has proved worthy of retention. But the prevailing experimental approach to curriculum making is wholesome, and the willingness to change, appraise, and change again is evidence of professional alertness and determination to improve.

3. *Intellectual freedom.* The elective principle has introduced a radical change in the concept of curriculum and in basic educational philosophy. Liberal education can hardly stress freedom as an objective without admitting freedom into the learning process, and without opening up a wider intellectual universe for investigation and study. A closed system of thought, whether it relates to science, political philosophy, or educational theory, is intellectually confining; minds do not operate at their best within strictly delimited boundaries. Whatever advantages the older fixed curriculum may have had in greater order and clarity, it also approximated a closed system of thought which in time became involuted, narrow, and illiberalizing. For long periods the liberal college curriculum was liberal mostly in name; the most creative intellectual work in the eighteenth century was done by individuals who broke away from the barren fields of institutional learning. The current curriculum is open-ended, fostering a variety of approaches to education and

encouraging experimentation. The goal is education for every student, but associated with it is a healthy assumption that what is good education for one may not be good for another, and that our chances of determining a *uniform* good education for all are negligible. A philosophy of education which is realistically cognizant of the limitations of its own claims to truth and which is willing to try to educate different individuals in different ways is compatible with the goals and interests of democracy.

4. *Elective influence on instruction.* Where the student has a measure of freedom in choice of studies, the effect upon instruction is bound to be good. This does not mean that teachers consciously engage in competition for trade or need a competitive incentive in order to teach their courses well. A degree of competition for the interest of students is healthy. Choosing teachers and courses was an ancient prerogative of university students and, although historical records attest to abuses, it is regrettable that at least in American colleges this privilege was for a long time withdrawn. Both teachers and students acknowledge that a different spirit exists in elective as against prescribed courses, the difference being not wholly attributable to the greater selectivity and maturity of classes, or the teachers' fondness for their courses. Voluntary student enrollment and participation in course activity is itself a factor for good morale which facilitates the teacher's task and improves its effectiveness. Too many prescribed courses have the unpleasant habit of "going dead." The small element of competition introduced by the elective system, while insufficient to threaten teachers, serves to put them on their mettle. We take pride in keeping up the level of enrollment in our elective courses, and perhaps subconsciously work harder to make the experience rewarding to students.

Weaknesses. Some weaknesses in the educational program result from the functions it seeks to fulfill, and are an extension of properties which have been identified as "strengths." The difference between "strength" and "weakness" may be only a matter of the degree to which a condition exists; carried to extremes, a commendable practice may engender its own problems. Thus, a profusion of curricular offerings allowing an opportunity for enriched educational experience may also be confusing to students; a pluralistic approach to education may be necessary and justified but it may foster undesirable conflicts in aims and purposes. Good educational principles do not in themselves insure against difficulties and abuses in practice.

1. *Difficulty in organizing for the student a balanced, unified, and coherent program of study.* The wealth of course offerings is in a sense embarrassing. From this diversified domain it is not easy to carve out individual programs of study which meet the specifications for good education. A program of study is not merely a succession of courses; it implies relevance to purpose, internal coherence, balance, and continuous progression of educational experience. While curriculum regulations may be helpful in insuring at least minimal adherence to principles of program organization consistent with individual variations, the problem of planning and shaping a pattern of study for each student remains. The student may be unable to plan such a program for himself, or may be influenced by preformed interests to concentrate on some fields of learning to the neglect of others. For the lazy or indifferent student there may be too much opportunity to "shop" for easy courses, and to assemble a program of study that is hardly true education. A mediocre student can find courses suited to his mediocre abilities, and be graduated without ever having been challenged to rise above mediocrity. These are not hypothetical limitations; they are apparent in the records of many students.

2. *Lack of clarity in aims of studies.* The curriculum may at times resemble a patchwork of courses unrelated by any unity of purpose or common sense of mission. Instruction in different courses may be guided by mutually irreconcilable aims or, in some cases, by no clearly definable aim at all. In the final analysis the choice of instructional aim is made by each teacher. One teacher of literature may guide his instruction so as to center on developing appreciation and independent reading interests; another may concentrate on literary and biographical facts of authorship, content, and style. A science teacher may conduct his course with a view toward acquainting nonspecialists with some fundamental discoveries and concepts of science and methods of scientific procedure; another may labor to produce prospective scientists, and a third may not go beyond stressing memorization of the contents of the textbook and laboratory manual. Furthermore it is not exceptional to find teachers indulging in classroom criticism of studies whose purposes do not suit them:

the historian may express dissatisfaction with a less "disciplined" social science, and the teacher of philosophy find fault with "bread-and-butter" subjects which have invaded the academic field. To the student on the receiving end of these doctrines, the aims of college study must seem confusing, if and when he stops to think.

Though return to a monolithic curriculum structure is hardly desirable, some clearer definition and greater consistency of educational purpose in specific course offerings would be helpful. A diversified curriculum need not be a disorganized one. Different approaches to instruction can be maintained provided they are known, identified, and coordinated as far as possible toward common ends. However much we differ in educational philosophy, our professional goals are not situated in diametrically opposite directions and we more often agree than disagree on desired final outcomes.

3. *Too much "splintering."* The tendency has been to divide and subdivide areas of instruction, creating narrower, more intensive, and more specialized units. Pressure from professional schools and a desire for academic prestige have operated in the colleges to promote the admission of technical and advanced courses more appropriate to graduate levels of study. The weakness is evident in purely humanistic as well as quasi-professional offerings. Some of the "splinter" courses are of questionable value as instruments of general or liberal education. Even the teacher who pursues broader objectives of instruction than those directly implicit in a course title is handicapped by having to work within the confines of overspecialized subject matter or technique.

It is true that the world's knowledge has come to be embodied within specialized fields of learning, but the curriculum need not faithfully mirror this design. The shape of the curriculum should be influenced by its function, which is primarily to utilize disciplines in educating people. To a certain extent the curriculum must conform to the existing organization of learning, but it is free also to create new syntheses more suitable as educational tools. Colleges have begun to combine and reorganize their offerings so as to present fewer course units, of greater scope and substance. The effort thus far has centered more on basic or "general education" courses than on elective studies. A cursory review of electives in some large colleges will disclose many which are still narrow and overspecialized in content.

4. *Dissatisfaction with prescribed studies.* For reasons which have been noted and for others, the conventionally prescribed courses have not provided a satisfactory core of general education. Growing by accumulation rather than design, they have increasingly encroached upon the total college program; as new fields of study developed, departments of instruction tended to strengthen their position in the curriculum through the medium of a required course or two. Unrelated to each other, prescribed courses reflected some of the common weaknesses in college studies and displayed further shortcomings of their own. Often organized as an "introduction" to a field of study or as a "general" offering upon which later specialization could be based, they were apt to be pursued without much interest and taught without enthusiasm. Perhaps with this in mind, some colleges deliberately cut back their prescribed studies to a minimum composed chiefly of essential tool subjects.[2]

Yet a substantial element of common education is necessary, along with the complementary need for some differentiated training. General education does not necessarily postulate that courses must be commonly prescribed, but since advanced studies tend to be so divergent, a foundation of common learning offers greater assurance of a balanced liberal education. Acting on this belief, colleges have been experimenting with new "programs of general education."

The precise meaning of "general education" is difficult to determine since the term has been used in various ways. Essentially the "general education" movement represents a renewed effort to design a core of studies which would meet the common requirements for educating people and at the same time provide each student with an effective foundation for further differentiated training. Departing from the conventional subject-bounded course organization, the programs seek to arrange new syntheses of learning in fewer and larger blocks of study. Instead of offering limited samplings of knowledge from many different subjects, an attempt is made to bring the student into contact with representative problems in a few major fields. The interrelationship of disciplines is recognized and brought into

[2] See also Oliver C. Carmichael's "Contemporary Trends in the Arts Colleges," *Association of American Colleges Bulletin,* 36:488–93 (December 1950).

the content of courses, and greater care is used in maintaining lateral coherence among studies. The task of formulating such programs, involving as it does a break from tradition, has not been easy; hardly any are without defects discernible to those responsible for their operation. But the experimental effort is promising, and the motives for it sound.

5. *The credit system.* The danger in attempting to record educational progress through a quantitative system of credits is patent: it lies perhaps not so much in the device itself as in the inferences it may foster. As a method of assessing the orderly progress of large numbers of students through courses of study essentially dissimilar and incomparable, the credit arrangement is feasible enough; but as a way of gauging the actual accomplishment of a specific student it is without much value. The number of course credits a student has earned reveals little concerning the extent and quality of his educational development. Learned and Wood's study [3] indicated that assumptions regarding students' real knowledge made on the basis of their credit standing are hazardous. Yet the student's progress through the course of study must be charted, and no better alternative to the credit system has yet presented itself.

The weakness of the credit system may be offset in a variety of ways. One is simply by flexible organization of study schedules and close guidance of students, enabling the college to know and evaluate students as individuals. Another is by computing for each student a special credit rating indicative of his qualitative worth along with the usual numerical total of credits completed. A third is by use of comprehensive achievement examinations as measures of progression; a number of institutions are currently utilizing such examinations with reference to prescribed studies, elective field of concentration, or the total college program. Prepared with skill and care as valid instruments for determining educational growth, comprehensive examinations are an effective offset to the limitations of the credit system. The practical deterrent to their habitual use is that such instruments are hard to devise, and their preparation is laborious and costly.

A Balanced View. In the face of interlocking strength and weak-

[3] *The Student and His Knowledge* (New York: Carnegie Foundation for the Advancement of Teaching, 1938).

ness it is difficult to maintain a balanced view of the curriculum. Some educators, unfavorably impressed by its shortcomings, have advocated complete revamping, looking toward a simplified, more logical and coherent sequence of studies, one which would minimize specialization, and exclude offerings not in the liberal tradition. Before supporting such proposals it would be well to consider the difficulty of finding an alternative serviceable to as many students in as many ways. For all its shortcomings the present curriculum does a remarkable job; and though imperfect in practice, its underlying principles are more in harmony with the needs of the student population than an attractively simplified, uniform course of study conceivably could be. (The reference is to the comprehensive liberal college serving a heterogeneous group of students; existing *specialized* colleges are not faced with the same problem and do not show these shortcomings in the same degree.)

Much can be done to improve the college curriculum. As one reviews the immediate past it is heartening to note how much has already been done to revise it and strengthen its effectiveness. Despite its size and awkwardness the curriculum has proved adaptive to change. If progress is slow at times, the slowness is more attributable to opposition by vested interests than to scarcity of promising ideas and proposals. Curriculum improvement will come only as it is actively fostered by teachers careful to distinguish the good from the bad and willing to venture experimentally into untried ways. There is no certain remedy by which to secure a good curriculum; easy formulas are apt to conceal deep pitfalls. Only in patient, continuous, cooperative trial is there assured hope of success.

How the Curriculum Came to Be

Even a brief account of the development of the American college curriculum shows the interplay of modernism and tradition, resistance and gradual accommodation, controversy and compromise.[4] The early American college was in most instances church-related and guided by religious purpose, though not exclusively a school for the ministry. In addition to training an educated clergy, its avowed aim was to perpetuate the higher learning in the persons of an edu-

[4] A good general reference is R. Freeman Butts' *The College Charts Its Course* (New York: McGraw-Hill Book Co.), 1939.

cated class of English gentlemen. The curriculum emphasized religion, the languages of religious learning, logic, natural philosophy, and elements of mathematics. Necessarily the program of study was prescribed. By the end of the Colonial Period a trend toward greater secular interest made itself noticeable, reflected by the establishment of nondenominational colleges and the reorganization of studies in older institutions. In 1779, under urging by Thomas Jefferson, the College of William and Mary revised its program, substituting new professorships in political science, medicine, and modern languages for professorships in Divinity and Oriental languages, and adding new studies in law, fine arts, and natural history. With the development of state universities in the early nineteenth century the secular influence became dominant, expressing itself, among other ways, in greater willingness to open the curriculum to admission of new studies.

A hundred years ago the college curriculum was a simple affair with a clearly organized structure of studies. Though earlier the University of Virginia [5] and a number of other institutions had experimented for a time with the principle of limited election, by the middle of the nineteenth century a single fixed pattern of study, distributed over a four-year period, prevailed almost everywhere.[6] Several institutions—notably Harvard, Yale, Dartmouth, Rochester, and Michigan—had organized separate schools or sequences of study leading to the B.S. degree. The Bachelor of Arts course, however, was the recognized liberal program, consisting in the main of Greek and Latin, mathematics, philosophy, religion, physical science, and history. A number of professorships in modern language and literature had been established but these subjects were still on the fringe of the curriculum. Biology, social science, music, and fine arts had not yet been introduced. Disciplines were not organized and conducted in course units but offered as broad fields of learning in graded sequence. The heart of the curriculum was the classical sub-

[5] The University of Virginia provided eight separate "schools" or courses of study different from one another, "but to receive a diploma from a school a student had to take all the prescribed subjects in that school and write a final examination when he was ready." Butts, *op. cit.*, p. 93.

[6] In 1856 at Harvard all studies were required except that juniors and seniors were allowed one elective (*Ibid.*, p. 114). A few other colleges also had tentatively introduced very limited election.

jects studied for the full four-year period; subjects of secondary importance such as physical science and history were fitted into the program whenever convenient, sometimes with intervals between periods of study.

As indicated earlier, the limited range of studies was not a reflection of the paucity of knowledge in the world outside; it was the effect of deliberate principle consistent with what had evolved as the prime objective of the college—training through mental discipline. As mental discipline was then understood, it was not necessary to have many subjects as instruments of education: a few "formative" studies could serve the purpose. Those with the strongest claim to disciplinary values were the classical languages and mathematics, regarded as ideally complementary in the kinds of training they afforded the mental faculties. Scientific studies were judged respectable and practically useful, but not of sufficiently high disciplinary quality to warrant the award of the A.B. degree to students pursuing a science-centered program.

As the nineteenth century proceeded it became more difficult to resist the pressure of new studies, chiefly in the expanding fields of science; and once the barrier of the traditional curriculum had been breached, new subjects entered one by one. Gradually and of necessity the elective principle was developed. In the years between 1870 and 1910, under the leadership of Eliot of Harvard, Barnard of Columbia, Andrew White of Cornell, Jordan of Stanford, Harper of Chicago, and others, the issue was fought out and a decision finally reached. By 1910 the elective system in one form or another had become accepted by the great majority of American colleges.

The principal argument used by proponents of the elective system was that an enlarged curriculum, more nearly representative of the many fields of learning, would better serve the educational interests of students; the elective system itself was the device for holding students' programs of study to manageable size. Support of the elective principle was offered even on disciplinary grounds: it was argued, for example, that by limiting the range of studies for each student, more thorough scholarship and better mental discipline could be secured. The new studies were themselves affirmed to have disciplinary value.

The victory of the elective principle was ultimately assured by the

evident social and cultural importance of the new studies, the changing educational needs in a democratic society under rapid industrial-
ization, and the upward pressure upon the college of a large new
high-school population for many of whom the traditional studies
held no special interest. In the twentieth century it became difficult
to defend a limited and exclusive curriculum on any grounds. Thus
were admitted many of the "newer" subjects now in the college program. After 1890 organization by departments was effected in order
to facilitate course instruction by competent specialists. Colleges developed different arrangements for combining prescribed and elective studies, but in one manner or another their curricula assumed
some of the general characteristics previously discussed.

(For bibliography see the end of Chapter VII.)

VII. *The College Curriculum: Continued*

RECENT PRACTICES IN CURRICULUM RECONSTRUCTION

In comparison with its predecessor the modern college curriculum has enjoyed little stability. In a sense its evolution has never ceased: under constant scrutiny by college authorities it has changed almost from year to year through the addition, withdrawal, substitution, and reorganization of courses. Aware of inherent difficulties and problems almost from the time of the inception of the elective system, colleges have been experimenting with ways and means of strengthening the curriculum. In recent years the effort has been intensified and its reach extended. No longer content with piecemeal change, institutions have undertaken basic alteration in curriculum design. Indicative of this effort is the general-education "movement" [1] aiming at an organic reconstruction of the basis of liberal education. Although current curriculum revision is not limited to general education, the latter is representative of the spirit and principles guiding the effort.

The general-education movement is widespread; in 1939, a yearbook of the National Society for the Study of Education spoke of it as "the current ground-swell in American colleges and universities." Certainly numerous colleges have been experimenting with general-education programs and several such programs will be summarized

[1] See, for example, P. F. Valentine, "General Education Programs," Chapter 6 in *The American College,* P. F. Valentine, ed. (New York: Philosophical Library, 1949) and H. T. Morse, "The Design and Operation of Programs of General Education," Chapter XVI in *General Education,* Fifty-first Yearbook of the National Society for the Study of Education (Chicago: University of Chicago Press, 1952).

in the pages immediately following. These are not represented as typical or necessarily superior, but as indicative of the kind of curriculum thinking and practice taking place.

Relative to these accounts some general observations suggest themselves. No two programs are identical in content or organizational pattern. But in various ways all center attention on the study of contemporary society and its major institutions, and on the responsibilities and problems of intelligent social living. Paralleling this emphasis on social understanding is almost equal stress on science in the modern world and on self-cultivation in the humane and esthetic arts. The subject matter is selected and taught in such a way as to enhance its liberalizing values vis-à-vis its specialized training potentialities. No effort is made to "cover" all disciplines either through multiple samplings or comprehensive survey courses. Prescribed introductory departmental offerings have given way to three or four large courses each identified with a major division of learning. An attempt is made to find new syntheses of subject matter and elements of integration within studies and among them. As might be expected, different methods of fostering integration are being tried, some (e.g., at Boston University) more pronounced than others. The tendency is to keep the programs under almost constant surveillance, resulting in steady modification of course contents. Omitting much relevant information pertaining to honors work, comprehensive examinations, remedial instruction, and the like, the following synopses will dwell principally on component courses.

COLUMBIA COLLEGE [2]

The Columbia College curriculum as now constituted did not originate as a unit but developed gradually during the period from 1919 to the present; a large portion of the course of study in the first two years is devoted to orientation courses in the three areas of the humanities, the sciences, and the social sciences. There are requirements also in the fields of English composition, foreign languages, physical education, and hygiene. The description which follows is restricted to the three orientation courses.

[2] *A College Program in Action* (New York: Columbia University Press, 1946).

Contemporary Civilization A and B, a two-year sequence in the social sciences, represents a pooling of effort in subject matter and instruction by the Departments of Economics, Government, History, and Philosophy. The objective of the course is to reveal the nature of the past and to expose the insistent contemporary problems of the present which our tradition—the living past—can help us understand. In the freshman year the course starts with the breakup of the Middle Ages and undertakes an analysis along three lines of inquiry. How have people made a living? How have they lived together? How have they understood the world and their relation to it? In the second year some insistent problems of the present are raised for consideration. It is evident from the nature of the problems studied that none of them can be fully understood and solved in isolation from the others or if only one aspect is singled out for special investigation.

Humanities A and B is a two-year sequence in literature, music, and fine arts taught by the Departments of English, Philosophy, History, Classics, and the Modern Languages. The object of this course is to introduce the students to the several "languages" of the arts, in the belief that those arts are effective in increasing the range and power of the mind. In the freshman year the students pursue a prescribed course featuring reading and discussion of portions of more than forty selected "great books"; in the sophomore year they have the option of continuing the sequence course or taking in its place other courses in more specific subject fields.

Science A and B was originally organized around the concepts of matter, energy, and radiation; the study of the earth as part of the universe; and the development of plant and animal life. This course was offered as an alternative to specific courses in particular sciences. Laboratory work was an integral part of the course and was designed to permit the students to acquire a body of facts by direct observation. In 1946 it was recommended that an integrated two-year course in the natural sciences be required of *all* students, that the teachers be prepared to conduct instruction throughout the entire course, and that the subject matter of the course should range from the principles underlying the behavior of gross and microscopic bodies to the nature and activities of living organisms.

The requirement in effect at the present time may be summarized as follows:

One two-term course from each of any two of the following groups: (a) mathematics; (b) astronomy, chemistry, physics; (c) botany, geology, psychology, zoology.

COLLEGE OF THE UNIVERSITY OF CHICAGO [3]

The College of the University of Chicago has been engaged in constructing an effective curriculum in general education for about twenty-five years. The curriculum is still undergoing revision,[4] but the general aspects differing most markedly from the traditional liberal college program may be described.

Students are normally admitted to the College upon completing two years of high-school study; following a four-year course of study in general education they qualify for a bachelor's degree. Achievement is not measured in terms of courses completed or credits earned but by passing comprehensive examinations in a number of subject fields. Attendance in these courses is optional and students may take the comprehensive examinations whenever they feel themselves sufficiently prepared. The core of the program is a group of three courses, each of which is prescribed for three years: Humanities, Social Sciences, and Natural Sciences. There is no requirement of advanced or specialized work in a given field. A schematic summary of the course of study follows:

First Year	*Second Year*
Social Sciences 1	Social Sciences 2
Humanities 1	Humanities 2
Natural Sciences 1	Natural Sciences 2
English	Mathematics

Third Year	*Fourth Year*
Social Sciences 3	History
Humanities 3	Observation, Interpretation, and
Natural Sciences 3	Integration
Foreign Language	

[3] *The Idea and Practice of General Education* (Chicago: University of Chicago Press, 1950).

[4] See "The University of Chicago Adopts New Degree Program," *School and Society*, 78:44–45 (August 8, 1953).

The Humanities sequence is organized with a view to training students in the exercise of the disciplines which contribute to an intelligent appreciation of the arts. While maintaining distinctions between the proper role of the humanities and that of other areas of knowledge, instruction seeks to avoid too narrow a conception of humanistic subject matter and method. The sequence of three courses is aimed at the following objectives:

1. Increasing the experience of students with the great products of the arts by the examination of a considerable body of the best works in the fields of literature, the visual arts, and music.

2. Training students in the exercise of analytical methods appropriate to humanistic ends.

3. Training students in the use of the arts of criticism which will enable them to recognize some of the differences in values ascribed to works . . . and, in the light of this recognition, to make responsible and sensitive criticisms.

The three-year Social Science sequence includes study of American political institutions, personality and culture, and freedom and order. *Social Sciences 1* selects for study a number of situations in which the American people have had to face critical problems of government. Students are expected to develop skill in reading and interpreting original documents and some historical sense of the American democratic tradition. *Social Sciences 2* explores the possibilities and limitations of studying human nature and society in a scientific way. Study is centered upon the relation of an individual's personality to his culture though its concern is not alone with the students' society and culture but with societies in general and with widely contrasting types of culture. *Social Sciences 3* attempts to foster the habit of deliberating rationally on problems of public policy with the help of the analytical disciplines of political science, political economy, political sociology, ethics, and social philosophy. With respect to each major problem the students are encouraged to assemble what they know of the historical background, the philosophic arguments concerning the ultimate values, and the scientific theory and facts for the purpose of drawing or appraising conclusions on practical policy.

The three years of the Science sequence are divided about equally between the physical and the biological sciences. The topics chosen for treatment are representative of these two major fields but not exhaustive. An attempt is made to relate the work of the science course to problems and matters which are the main responsibilities of the other courses in the program. The unit elements of the course are not, strictly speaking, topics but problems, and are treated with considerable emphasis on detail and questions of evidence and interpretation. The laboratory work is distinguished by a paucity of written instructions. Student teams are expected to formulate the problem to be solved, develop the details of experimentation, and proceed, on the basis of their own plans, to obtain and interpret data.

All students are required to take a course in the *History of Western Civilization* and one in *Observation, Interpretation, and Integration,* both of which are offered in the fourth year. These two courses strive to effect integration of the curriculum: the one historically by focusing attention on genesis and development, the other philosophically by concentrating attention on intellectual analysis and methodology.

There are also prescribed courses in mathematics, English composition, and foreign language but they are more limited in scope than the three principal sequences.

HARVARD COLLEGE [5]

There was widespread feeling in the faculty at Harvard that although the curriculum made adequate provision for "concentration" in a given field, it did not assure adequate distribution of the students' educational experience over all the major fields. The Harvard Report discusses in detail the theory of general education and the desired outcomes of education, and recommends methods of achieving these aims.

It is assumed that general education is distinguished from specialized education not so much in subject matter as in method and outlook. The curriculum is viewed not as a collection of courses but as an organic whole whose parts join in expounding a ruling idea and in serving a common aim. It was felt necessary first to decide what traits of mind and character contribute to responsible social living;

[5] *General Education in a Free Society* (Cambridge: Harvard University Press, 1945).

and then to choose the elements of knowledge which may be expected to nourish them. The traits singled out for emphasis were: to think effectively, to communicate thought, to make relevant judgments, and to discriminate among values.

The Report of the Harvard Committee recommended the introduction of a substantial intellectual experience common to all students and also that the principle of specialization be retained so that students might be enabled to gain a more thorough mastery of a segment of learning. The curriculum as finally adopted prescribes during the first two years of study:

1. Three elementary courses in general education, one from each of the areas of Humanities, Social Sciences, and Natural Sciences.

2. Additional courses outside the field of concentration to achieve a total of six. The courses satisfying this requirement may be selected from the group of elementary courses in general education, from the second-level general education courses offered by the Committee on General Education, or from department course offerings judged suitable for general education. The students are given considerable latitude in selecting courses in each area from a list of equivalent alternatives.

The outline of the elementary courses in general education is as follows:

THE HUMANITIES

1. Humanism in the West
2. Epic and Novel
3. Individual and Social Values
    I. In History and Drama
    II. In Fiction and Philosophy
4. Ideas of Good and Evil in Western Literature

THE SOCIAL SCIENCES

1. Introduction to the Development of Western Civilization
2. Western Thought and Institutions
3. The Growth of Modern Western Society
4. Institutions and Culture in the West

THE NATURAL SCIENCES

1. The Physical Sciences in a Technical Civilization
2. Principles of Physical Science

3. The Nature and Growth of the Physical Sciences
4. Research Patterns in Physical Science
5. Principles of Biological Science

None of these courses is of "survey" nature and no attempt is made to treat exhaustively the subjects under discussion. The humanities courses are organized around problems revealed in ancient and modern literature. The science courses center on different portions of the fields of science. The social science courses range from a straight course in the *History of Western Civilization* (*Social Science 1*) to one of sociological content and organization (*Social Science 4*). There is no formal attempt to integrate the subject matter of the various courses. It is felt that the nature of the three fields themselves provides a measure of integration which will be reinforced whenever two courses make contact with the same subject matter.

The second-level general education offerings are designed to fill in some of the gaps in elementary courses and also to provide courses which do not readily fit into an established department. The second-level offerings are as follows:

THE HUMANITIES

111. Classics of the Christian Tradition
113. Types of Art: The Representation of Nature in European and Asiatic Art
114. Art in Man's Environment
116. The Spirit of the Renaissance

THE SOCIAL SCIENCES

111. History of Far Eastern Civilization
112. Human Relations
113. The Impact of Science on Modern Life
114. Interpretations of American Institutions
115. Economics for the Citizen
116. Introduction to the Civilization of India
118. Democratic Theory and Its Critics
119. The Structure and the Growth of Law
120. Fundamental Human Rights
127. Introduction to the Civilization of the Middle East

THE NATURAL SCIENCES

111. Organic Evolution
112. Introduction to the Philosophy of Science
114. Human Behavior

In addition to the prescription in general education, the students must complete a year's work in English composition, engage in supervised physical training in the freshman year, demonstrate a reading knowledge of a foreign language, and satisfy an elective concentration requirement.

COLGATE [6]

The Colgate curriculum contains a core of courses devoted to problems drawn from the following fields: natural sciences, public affairs, philosophy and religion, area studies, music and the visual arts, literature, English communication, and the American Idea in the Modern World. Students are also required to demonstrate competence in a foreign language and satisfy a concentration requirement. In the "core" courses instruction is based so far as possible on actual "cases" or concrete problems. In seeking the solutions to these problems it is intended that the students exercise their powers of initiative in exploration and analysis, as well as their capacity to teach and to learn from others. The following are brief descriptions of some of the core courses.

Problems in Natural Science investigates problems significant in the development of the physical and biological sciences, the ways in which the problems have been attacked, the development of scientific theories, and the verification or rejection of such theories.

Problems in Public Affairs treats some important problems in the area of social organization and discusses concrete cases in industry, labor and economics, and social, governmental and international relations.

Problems in Philosophy and Religion defines problems of meaning and value and explores possible answers by examining the chief ideologies, philosophies, and faiths that lay claim to the belief and loyalty of Western man.

[6] John S. Allen, "General Education at Colgate University," *School and Society*, 53:579–82 (May 3, 1941).

Area Studies. The objective of this course is to help the students to understand and appreciate problems which lead to conflict in the modern world, and to relate these problems to the position of the United States in the world.

The American Idea in the Modern World offers an analysis of contemporary American aims and values through an examination of our fundamental cultural documents and practices to determine the validity and effectiveness of the "American Way" in the current conflict of ideologies at home and abroad.

BOSTON UNIVERSITY [7]

The College of General Education of Boston University has developed a two-year course of integrated general education, the purposes of which are summarized thus:

1. To attain through a study of our cultural heritage and that of other cultures a frame of reference which will enable the students to apply a broader perspective when they meet contemporary social problems.

2. To develop the habit of reaching decisions on social problems through the give and take of the democratic discussion method.

3. To give the students experience, not only in the habits of "scientific thinking" but training in evaluating the social implications and the consequences of rival theories.

The special distinction of the program is in its attempt to develop a comprehensive integration of subject matter in contrast to the more common tendency towards limited integration. The aim is to unify the courses of instruction so that material drawn from all fields is synchronized and correlated at every possible point. An effort is made to bring before the students actual cases and problems and to discuss them in all their relevant aspects. The major elements of the program are as follows:

Human Relations. This course seeks to give the students knowledge of themselves and the society in which they live. Beginning with a study of the nature of man, the course proceeds to analyze

---

[7] Judson R. Butler, "The Program of the College of General Education at Boston University," Chapter XII in *Organization and Administration of General Education,* W. Hugh Stickler, ed. (Dubuque, Iowa: Wm C. Brown Co., 1951).

some factors which have been involved in the evolution and institutional development of contemporary Western civilization.

Political Economy. Political and economic phenomena are treated as they are found in society, together. The principles of economics and politics are applied in both historical and contemporary situations.

English and Humanities stresses straight thinking, clear writing, and effective speaking. It aims to help the students arrive at an understanding of the worth and dignity of man as revealed in literature and the humanities.

Science. The purpose of the course is to give a clear understanding of the achievements of the principal sciences, to demonstrate the relationship between the laws of science and the world of nature, and to promote understanding of the scientific methods in order to show how scientific development has made for cultural progress and growth.

Guidance is a required course with three major objectives. It aims to help the students: (1) meet various problems of a personal, social, vocational, and educational nature; (2) determine, analyze, and understand their interests, aptitudes, abilities, limitations, opportunities, and needs; and (3) acquire sound occupational information in order that they may make wise vocational choices and decisions.

Techniques of Curriculum Revision

Curriculum revision is not an exact science or fine art; there are no strict rules of procedure to be followed. Rather, it is a careful process of applying balanced judgment supported by educational principles and looking squarely at the results. There are so many variables in education that its course cannot be predicted with certainty; results become evident in experience only after experience has been made possible. An important function of the curriculum planner is "to make educational experience possible" and to do what he can to assure a reasonable degree of success; that is, to invite and accept ideas whatever their origin, develop and improve them, and put them to work in the curriculum. It helps if the curriculum planner is hospitable to proposals for change, is venturesome rather than overcautious, recognizes the merits of a proposal as well as its defects, and uses his professional talents to minimize foreseeable difficulties. Most of us have strong convictions about the value of some college disciplines as compared with others; in working on curriculum matters it behooves us to keep our prejudices under control and prevent them as far as possible from coloring our judgment.

There are positive principles of operating procedure which are important, though the manner of their application must be influenced by the particular curriculum problem at hand. If the problem, for example, is to reassess an institution's prescriptive offerings and reorganize them "from the ground up," practically every known principle of curriculum-making will be brought into use, and even new principles may have to be devised. If the problem is limited to deciding whether a single course offering has merit, fewer considerations will be operative. Each curriculum task presents a fresh challenge to creative endeavor. It is not possible to list a routine "series of steps" by which curriculum revision can be accomplished, but attention can be directed to a few considerations which are practically necessary. In listing these considerations in the following discussion, the numerical order has no significance.

1. *Relevance to educational aims.* Neither the whole nor any portion of the curriculum can be appraised without reference to the educational purposes it is meant to serve. Though educational aims can be evaluated without reference to a stated body of subject matter, the latter cannot be weighed independently. It is not enough to say, "Here is a proposed course in Political Theory; it traces the development of concepts of the state and the relation of the individual to the state held by representative philosophers and political thinkers from Plato to John Stuart Mill; the subject matter seems attractive and there is no other course offering like it; let us, therefore, adopt it." Explicitly or otherwise, the question should be raised, "How does the proposed offering relate to the aims of our college as we understand them?"

Investigation of this question may reveal that the proposed course serves well the college's purposes and might be satisfactory if effective instruction were assured. On the other hand, study of a proposal for a course in "Field experience in psychiatric social case work" may produce a less favorable finding although the substance of the proposed course is substantial enough and its appeal to some students strong. Courses with sectarian leaning, excessively professionalized or specialized offerings, and those too advanced for undergraduate study can be spotted quickly by checking their relevance to the aims of the college. This is not the only criterion by which the validity of an offering can be established, but some of the disorder in the current curriculum might have been avoided through stricter adherence to this principle.

Institutional aims are themselves subject to examination. If the aims are stated so generally that they cannot serve as an effective criterion of relevance, it may be presumed that the curriculum and instruction also suffer because of this vagueness. Such a statement of aims needs to be reformulated in more explicit terms if it is to serve as other than academic window-dressing. It is disheartening to be confronted with a set of aims stated grandly but unrealistically in view of the actual needs and realizable possibilities of the institution's student population, or lordly references to "higher spiritual values" affording little direction to educational process. Where clearly-defined purposes prove chronically inhospitable to new learning, they should also be opened up for examination by the faculty, since a static curriculum is almost certain to depreciate in vitality.

The curriculum maker deals as much with educational aims as with program content and organization. Often he must concern himself with principles and issues of educational philosophy for which no assured basis of judgment exists. In these circumstances he does the best he can, relying upon his own convictions and beliefs and such evidence as he can secure; admitting into consideration also the points of view of others. But he cannot proceed to the practical details of curriculum development without facing the question, "What educational purpose is this meant to serve?"

2. *Ascertaining or verifying the need for change.* Curriculum revision is regarded with annoyance by some college teachers as symbolizing incessant tinkering and love of change for its own sake. Not until the teacher is himself invested with responsibility for curriculum study does he come to appreciate its importance and to develop zeal in its pursuit. Yet to the extent that curriculum makers fail to establish the need for change and to convince their colleagues of this need, they overlook an essential aspect of their obligation.

Curriculum revision should not be undertaken until convincing evidence points to the need for change. Frequently the first awareness of need is not by the constituted curriculum-making "authority" —a teachers' committee in a department or college or a specialist curriculum director—but by those involved directly in teaching and learning. Pressure for change from teachers or students may take the form of criticism of the existing offerings or constructive formulation of alternatives; in either case it is up to the responsible curriculum personnel to verify the need for change before taking further action.

The most fundamental kind of curriculum change does not, however, usually originate in this way. Concerned with immediate teaching and learning problems in their courses, teachers and students seldom have the broadest view of curriculum objectives and attainments. For this the curriculum maker is in better position: maintaining contact with proceedings in specific courses, he can also see the curriculum as a whole, from different angles and without the proximity which sometimes distorts perspective. Curriculum shortcomings and possible methods of improvement may be more apparent to him than to colleagues on the scene of action. Some of the most promising ventures in general education have grown out of recommendations by small, centrally-selected faculty committees which utilized the advantage of a "stand-off" view. The most creative contribution the curriculum maker can make is to take the initiative in fostering curriculum improvement, explain and justify his proposals to his colleagues, and convert an indifferent faculty to open-minded cooperation. This is even more important than sitting in judgment on proposals submitted by others and perhaps sponsoring their development.

One method of detecting shortcomings and determining need for change lies in study of the related ends and means in education. Not all of the college's offerings were specifically designed to suit the purposes they now serve: traditional disciplines have been re-adapted, studies originally patterned by specialists for specialized ends have been refitted, and others have for a long time been substantially unaltered. There are bound to be defects of omission and commission. By relating the accomplishment to the goals it should be possible to discover where some of the defects lie. The reasonableness of this procedure must be admitted unless one chooses to argue that education is a mystical experience with no visible connection between activity and outcome. At the risk of incurring hostility by being too specific, it might be mentioned that the conventional freshman composition course with its theme writing and handy manual in language mechanics is less than an ideal way of developing the art of written expression. Perhaps also other typical offerings in introductory science, mathematics, and foreign language, in content or course organization, fall short of their purported objectives. One way to tell is to look them over.

In this sensitive job it is better for the curriculum planner to forego a priori judgment in favor of a more scientific approach. There are signs by which curriculum weakness may be spotted: poor morale of students or teachers with reference to certain courses, repeated expression of dissatisfaction, persistent decline in enrollment, irregular attendance or excessive drop-outs, high incidence of failure or of easy success, failure to continue elective study in the same field, or evidence of background deficiency in later studies. Weakness may reside in instruction rather than curriculum, and it is necessary to distinguish between the two.

Once a trouble spot is located, the portion of the curriculum affected should be scrutinized and an attempt made to assemble all pertinent information. Talks with students, teachers, and counselors, analysis of students' programs and academic records, review of course syllabi, outlines, and study materials, and reliable standardized tests may serve to establish more precisely the nature of the difficulty and sometimes suggest the needed remedy. If curriculum change is contemplated, the evidence of weakness should be publicized to the extent that the faculty is convinced that a problem exists, but *not* in such a way as to place any particular teacher or group of teachers in a defensive position.

Verification of assumed need for change is no less essential when the curriculum maker deals with fully formulated proposals previously sent up "through channels." The fact that proposals may originate in faculty departments and carry departmental endorsement is not a certain indication of their necessity. Some departments are more eager for change than others, and without curbing the constructive efforts of their teachers it is nevertheless important to keep department offerings within workable bounds and assure reasonable stability. It is unwise to add, exchange, or withdraw courses except for good reason, and in advancing a proposal for change the reason should be indicated. If evidence cannot be furnished by those originating the proposal it should be sought by those responsible for promulgating further action. Indication of needed change is not always based on a weakness calling for correction; it may represent an extension or reinforcement of existing strength.

3. *Preparing or developing a curriculum proposal.* Curriculum change is not the only method of improving a college program. More can sometimes be accomplished by redirecting the aims and methods of instruction, improving guidance services, enriching extracurricular activities, extending opportunities for individual study, or strengthening evaluation procedures. The various contingencies should be explored for their possible contribution to the solution of a problem. For this reason it is well for a "curriculum committee" to work in concert with other college agencies performing representative institutional functions. Frequently curriculum change is and should be correlated with changes in other phases of the educational process.

Assuming that curriculum change is necessary, how does the curriculum planner proceed to formulate and develop his ideas? Analyzing the process is somewhat like analyzing thought itself, and the result is apt to be equally indefinite. Good curriculum planning is the product of creative use of intelligence, utilizing such informational resources as may be available, moderating itself by careful judgment, but necessitating eventually a "leap into the unknown." Effective curriculum change seldom consists in reproducing courses offered elsewhere, and where little precedent exists, not even imitation is easy. It is no accident that current experimental programs of general education, while resembling each other in underlying ideas and some general features, differ in details of content, structure, and emphasis. Each reflects the separate creative efforts of its authors— their ideas, hypotheses, and tentative solutions. There are and will continue to be "standard" offerings, but recent curriculum revision has sought in the main to get away from standardization.

The curriculum maker does not approach the constructive phase of his task in an attitude of naivete. His knowledge of the underlying factors creating an unsatisfactory curriculum situation may suggest alternative courses of action and point the way to a corrective plan. Beyond this is the "beacon light" of educational purpose which helps in determining a sense of direction, and general principles of teaching and learning which help to maintain even experimental effort on a safer course. The known needs and capabilities of students also guide the curriculum maker in the exercise of initiative and original thought.

While the curriculum planner is not absolved of final responsibility to think for himself, he can to some extent be guided by pertinent information. It is useful to know how other institutions are dealing with comparable problems in order to check or verify certain assumptions, gain insight into possible procedures, or discover and avoid unanticipated difficulties. A canvass of research studies will disclose findings on disputed matters such as the efficacy of large versus small group instruction, the merits of laboratory versus non-laboratory science training, or the values of integration. Standardized tests in fundamental subjects may reveal deficiencies in students' learning which must be considered in any eventual curriculum proposal. Talks with students and teachers or systematic canvassing of their ideas may produce good suggestions. By gathering and analyzing such information, reflecting upon it, and "living with it," the curriculum maker will be aided in crystallizing his own ideas and strengthening his convictions.

Consideration of proposals espoused by a department and submitted for higher approval to the college-wide curriculum agency presents fewer difficulties. Such proposals should not be merely "rubber stamped." Even after the desirability of curriculum change has been established, the proposals should be analyzed, studied, and improved in every way possible. Proposed course offerings should be scrutinized for suitability of content, range of learning covered, coherence and clarity of organization, appropriateness to instructional level, and articulation with other offerings—down to such relatively minor technical matters as course title, catalogue description, allotment of credits, and qualification for admission. Further revision, however, should not be attempted except in consultation with the colleagues originating the proposal, and with their concurrence; where objections to revision are offered, they should be carefully weighed, and if necessary a compromise effected that is agreeable to all concerned. Nothing is so annoying to teachers engaged in curriculum planning as to have a central curriculum committee highhandedly reject or alter their proposals. Yet the function of this committee is too important to permit the passive endorsement of all proposals received.

4. *Design and structure of courses.* Inevitably the curriculum maker is faced with the problem of determining what constitutes the essential attributes of a course. Course offerings in the various disciplines may differ widely in form as well as substance. To the teacher of mathematics accustomed to teaching a closely-knit body of subject matter, an art, music, or home economics workshop, a physical education course, or even one in social science may seem a loose array of planned activities without internal system and logic. No teacher can afford to think in this way, least of all one who is involved in curriculum activity. Merit in the design of a course cannot be judged by the measure of its conformity to a standard pattern.

What, in essence, is a course? It is a body of learning experience for students, selected from established fields of scholarship (and other forms of endeavor), organized and presented in such a way as to serve the maximum educational needs and interests of the students. Each course is in effect a synthetic creation, an artifact conceived and executed by teachers. No course is any less artificial than any other, although some have become "naturalized" by usage. Many teachers, at one time or another, have been given the opportunity to develop a course out of the raw materials of scholarship and professional experience; such a course can be as respectable as another long sanctified by tradition.

Viewed in this light a course assumes certain obligations of functional rather than formal propriety. In the first place, the design of a course should be suited to its avowed purpose. Lecture, discussion, reading, laboratory, or practicum courses are not interchangeable at the curriculum maker's will; nor can the optimum range or depth of a course be determined to serve as a standard for others. A course which aims to provide an overview of a field of learning, let us say An Introduction to Anthropology, is necessarily of broader framework and looser internal construction than an intensified specialized offering in the same field. A course which seeks to develop proficiency in an art, the use of an intellectual method, or a group of skills must emphasize opportunity for individual student performance, perhaps at the expense of subject-matter coverage. Performance courses and those more purely conceptual have different criteria of organization, and inasmuch as differences between such courses are often a matter of degree an almost endless variety in course design is possible.

Secondly, whatever its external form the course should meet the specifications of a good "learning experience for students." The subject matter must not only conform to the requisites of scholarship and be relevant to the purposes of instruction, but should also challenge the students' interest and be suited to their level of competence. The course should be "full" but not so overloaded in content that the task of completing it in the specified time of study is hopeless. Topics of study should be related to each other and arranged in an orderly progression of learning, from the easier to the more difficult, the simpler to the more complex, or from less to greater student self-dependence. The adaptability of the course to newer and more promising teaching methods should be surveyed, since much can be done to suggest effective methods of instruction while the proposal is under consideration. Without changing its substance or emphasis, provision can be made for greater reliance on laboratory or field work, audio-visual instruction, case study, individual student research, or other types of suitable procedure, thus facilitating if not ensuring better instruction. Finally, the course should be adaptable to the use of reliable methods of evaluating students' learning.

5. *Evaluating curriculum innovation.* The subject of evaluation in its general application to the educative process will be discussed in a subsequent chapter; at this point the reference is specifically to evaluating the results of curriculum change. No curriculum project can be so carefully prepared and instituted that its success is assured in advance. There is an element of risk in every curriculum undertaking, and the bolder its reach the greater is the risk involved.

A curriculum planner's task is not done until he has arranged for suitable evaluation of the projected program or offering. In fact, it would be well for him not to consider a plan as ever "completed" or "finished," but to accept continuing responsibility for assessment of its effectiveness. Every curriculum innovation should be viewed as experimental, not only in the sense of its being subjected to the test of performance but also in its susceptibility to continued adaptation or change.

The manner of evaluation depends upon the nature and scope of the curriculum activity. A single new course offering can be evaluated fairly simply. An instructional "log" recording the teacher's day-to-day impressions of the course—accomplishments, problems encountered, difficulties unresolved—can form the basis of conferences with curriculum planners out of which will develop suggestions for further improvement. A survey of students' reactions, preferably conducted and reported by the teacher, can furnish important supplementary information. A formal inventory of student achievement through examinations, problems, and work exercises can at least partially reveal the extent to which the avowed objectives are being met. The students' performance in related or advanced courses contributes further evidence.

Evaluation of a comprehensive curriculum undertaking is more complicated. It may be necessary to prepare a formal plan of evaluation assaying approaches from different directions. A new program of general education, for example, may in part be evaluated experimentally by comparing the performance of matched groups of students in "new" and "old" offerings: this is a laborious procedure which is, however, useful in furnishing objective evidence. Along with this, comprehensive examinations may be administered measuring proficiency in subject matter and growth in power. Questionnaires, survey inventories, or check lists may be employed to take soundings of students' attitudes toward the new courses, the nature and extent of their participation in assigned study, their interest in independent activity, and the carry-over into other kinds of learning. Analysis of students' programs of study and transcripts of their academic records may show whether satisfactory articulation, orderly progression, and creditable accomplishment are being maintained. An important index of evaluation is, of course, the continuous estimate by teachers participating in the program, their evident interest and enthusiasm. A practical plan of evaluation containing several of these features may be fashioned according to the available time and resources of the institution concerned.

SELECTED BIBLIOGRAPHY

A College Program in Action, A Review of the Working Principles at Columbia College, by the Committee on Plans. New York: Columbia University Press, 1946. 175 pp.

Association for Higher Education, *Current Issues in Higher Education, 1953,* Proceedings of the Eighth Annual National Conference on Higher Education. Washington: National Education Association, 1953. 292 pp.

Butts, R. Freeman, *The College Charts Its Course.* New York: McGraw-Hill Book Company, 1939. 464 pp.

Carmichael, Oliver C., "Contemporary Trends in the American Colleges," *Association of American Colleges Bulletin,* 36:488–93, December 1950.

Cohen, I. B., and Watson, F. G., *General Education in Science.* Cambridge: Harvard University Press, 1952. 217 pp.

Eisenhart, Luther P., *The Educational Process,* Chapter II, "The Curriculum" and Chapter III, "Programs of Concentration." Princeton: Princeton University Press, 1945. 87 pp.

French, Sidney J., ed., *Accent on Teaching.* New York: Harper & Brothers, 1954. 334 pp.

General Education in a Free Society, Report of the Harvard Committee. Cambridge: Harvard University Press, 1945. 267 pp.

General Education in School and College, A Committee Report by Members of Faculties of Andover, Exeter, Lawrenceville, Harvard, Princeton, and Yale. Cambridge: Harvard University Press, 1952. 142 pp.

Graeffe, Arnold D., *Creative Education in the Humanities.* New York: Harper & Brothers, 1951. 199 pp.

Hofstadter, Richard and Hardy, C. Dewitt, *The Development and Scope of Higher Education in the U.S.* New York: Columbia University Press, 1952. 254 pp.

Jordan, David Starr, *The Trend of the American University,* Chapter I, "The Evolution of the College Curriculum." Stanford University, Calif.: Stanford University Press, 1929. 126 pp.

McGrath, Earl J., *The Humanities in General Education.* Dubuque, Iowa: Wm C. Brown Co., 1949. 308 pp.

Millett, Fred B., *The Rebirth of Liberal Education,* Chapter II, "Experimental Programs and Courses." New York: Harcourt, Brace and Company, 1945. 179 pp.

Morse, H. T., ed., *General Education in Transition.* Minneapolis: University of Minnesota Press, 1951. 310 pp.

National Society for the Study of Education, *General Education,* Fifty-First Yearbook of the Society, Part I. Chicago: University of Chicago Press, 1952. 377 pp.

Severinghaus, A. E., Carman, H. J., and Cadbury, W. E., Jr., eds. *Preparation for Medical Education in the Liberal Arts College,* Chapter 8, "Some Ventures in College Education." New York: McGraw-Hill Book Company, 1953. 400 pp.

Stevens, David H., *The Changing Humanities.* New York: Harper & Brothers, 1953. 272 pp.

Stickler, W. Hugh, ed., *Organization and Administration of General Education.* Dubuque, Iowa: Wm C. Brown Co., 1951. 431 pp.

Stickler, W. Hugh, Stoakes, J. P., and Shores, L., eds., *General Education: A University Program in Action.* Dubuque, Iowa: Wm C. Brown Co., 1950. 280 pp.

The Idea and Practice of General Education, An Account of the College of the University of Chicago, by Present and Former Members of the Faculty (F. C. Ward *et al.*). Chicago: The University of Chicago Press, 1950. 333 pp.

Valentine, P. F., ed., *The American College,* Chapter 6, "General Education Programs." New York: Philosophical Library, 1949. 575 pp.

VIII. *Principles of Teaching Method*

Teaching as Craftsmanship. There are few teachers who do not take pride in a well-taught lesson, a skilfully-developed lecture, or a course which is challenging to students. Colleges rate "exceptional skill in teaching" high among the criteria determining faculty promotion.[1] Students prefer a well-taught course to an easy one. Craftsmanship in teaching is highly valued by all concerned in education. There is no scarcity of good teaching in the colleges, although from the nature of the commodity supply can never equal demand. Yet college teachers are strangely reluctant to submit their instruction to critical examination; indeed, they tend to be suspicious, if not disdainful, of all talk of teaching "methods."

To an extent this attitude is understandable. By frequently overstating their case, proponents of instructional method in and out of schools of education have not endeared themselves to their academic colleagues. In the preparation of teachers for the lower schools, emphasis on pedagogical technique has tended to detract from mastery of sturdier subject-matter disciplines. Furthermore, methodology does not occupy the same position of importance in higher education as on lower levels: college students are more mature, and more independently competent in learning. It would be a mistake for college teachers to expend their energies more on procedure than on substance of instruction, yet the two are so closely allied that to neglect the former is to hurt the latter.

[1] "Instructional Staff Practices and Policies in Degree-Granting Institutions, 1953–54," National Education Association *Research Bulletin,* Vol. XXXII, No. 4 (December 1954), p. 172.

The college teacher will admit that technical skill in teaching makes a difference in students' learning, and that in actuality wide variations exist in quality of teaching performance. He will also admit that his own teaching has improved with experience, in part "naturally" but more largely as a result of deliberate painstaking effort. This is tantamount to admitting that craftsmanship in teaching is necessary and can be developed. All that systematic attention to method can hope to accomplish is to expedite and reinforce the process of self-improvement.

There is more concerning method of college teaching than the profession has thus far been able to determine. Of the many good college teachers, few have reached the limit of their potential skill; the lack is not in motivation but in definite knowledge of what constitutes instructional excellence and how to achieve it. Successful teaching is too often a fortuitous occurrence; *why* a class period or an entire course turns out exceptionally good we may not always know. Not until an art or science can be reduced to some basic components separable for investigation and controlled use will its mastery be pursued with assured hope of success. In the case of college teaching this is easier said than done.

At this stage of development in the art or science of college teaching, a formal course in "methods" can serve no more than a rudimentary purpose—to acquaint beginners with a few of the essentials. Much beyond this we cannot go. Even gifted teachers have found difficulty in disclosing the secret of their accomplishment; translated into words, the magic of their performance disappears. This much we can say: craftsmanship in teaching is a difficult and elusive art, compounded of moral, intellectual, and esthetic ingredients, and of many technical skills involving operation with ideas and with people.[2] The difference between a novice and an expert teacher is similar to that between an unskilled and a master workman. The sooner a teacher sets out to master the challenges of his craft, the more valuable will be his service to his profession.

What Is Teaching? In essence teaching is stimulating and directing learning by students. Contingent upon the subject of instruction, learning may be stimulated and guided in different ways toward dif-

---

[2] See Joseph Justman, "What Makes the Good College Teacher?," *School and Society,* 70:417–21 (December 24, 1949).

ferent ends; but whether the subject is comparative anatomy, Latin philology, or music, teaching is no more than helping the student to acquire knowledge, skills, ideals, attitudes, and appreciations leading to his changed behavior and growth as a person. Giving a lecture, leading a discussion, demonstrating an experiment, preparing a good examination, and other procedures in teaching are instrumental to this principal function. In the main good teaching takes its cue from the requirements for good learning.

It is impossible to encompass within one definition the meaning of good teaching. Certainly one criterion relates to ascertainable achievement in learning, that is, to the extent to which students learn what they are supposed to learn. Many of the desired outcomes of instruction can be formulated in advance; a teacher of organic chemistry may want his students to learn the structure, properties, and uses of certain organic compounds and, in the process of learning them, to acquire scientific interest and understanding. The greater the student's success in attaining these outcomes, the better has been the teaching. Not all the outcomes of instruction, however, can be preconstituted; in every case there are collateral products deriving more from the human contact than from the nature of the subject. Two teachers offering the same course may achieve different results in the ideals, attitudes, habits, and human values they help to foster. To the extent that they contribute to the educational development of students, these incidental learnings must also be considered in estimating instructional effectiveness.

Students are not taught separately but in classes containing from ten or fifteen to as many as several hundred. Although instruction is imparted to a group it must necessarily aim at individuals. The end result of learning is individual: from the same instruction students will learn different things and progress in different directions. A further measure of teaching effectiveness, therefore, is in the ability to strike the right chord of common learning need in a group of students, yet remain sensitive to the many deviations from the common need and provide for them in instruction. What is realistically possible depends of course upon the size of the group, but the need for attending to the individual is never absent. Even in a large lecture class the skilful teacher can make most students feel that he is speaking to each of them personally, both by the substance of his message and the manner of its communication. In smaller recitation, discussion, or laboratory sections a requisite of good teaching is to complement common group learning with the development of each student's special aims, capabilities, and interests.

By definition a teacher is a specialist in working with people; the specialty becomes an art as the teacher becomes more skilful in helping people to educate themselves and each other. This holds true for individual students as well as for groups. It is the mark of the beginner in teaching that he tells the student what the latter wants or needs to know; the more experienced teacher will help the student to learn for himself; the accomplished teacher will design his instruction from the outset with the aim of developing the student's resources and motivation for intellectual self-dependence.

The advantages of group instruction do not lie only in making possible a more economical management of the school or the college. Although in some respects group instruction may restrict maximum individual accomplishment, it has compensations in learning. Some things students can learn better from each other than from the teacher, and others they can gain *only* through group participation. Ideals, attitudes, and modes of desirable social behavior can be learned more effectively through such activity than in individual sessions with a teacher. In many courses—particularly in the humanities and social sciences—even the substantive content of learning may be deepened and enriched by sharing ideas in group discussion.

Skill in teaching is reflected in the ability to utilize the resources of a group to promote the greatest possible interchange of learning. The good teacher works through the medium of the group, liberating and directing its energies; he plays upon the capacities of students to stimulate each other, to set examples in the exercise of initiative and provocative thought, and to add to the substance of instruction. Often he encourages the students to take a leading role, being himself content to provide support and guidance. There are instances in almost every course when students' contributions excel anything the teacher himself could have initiated, and as a teacher gains in skill he learns to formulate his teaching plans so as to avail himself of such occurrences.

There is a quality of good teaching which may be termed aes-

thetic. In every field of work the artist is distinguished by his quest
for perfection and his pride in quality of production; he may not
always succeed in his purpose but his performance is rarely ordinary.
Whatever his objective he does not neglect the rules of good workmanship or fail to invest his work with distinction. Artistry in teaching adds another dimension of value to its other contributions
toward students' accomplishment in learning: long after the subject
matter of a course is forgotten, the teacher as a craftsman may be
remembered. As for the teacher himself, no small portion of his professional reward is the satisfaction derived from the sense of a job
tastefully done.

There are many styles of teaching, and each teacher's should be
suited to his own person and circumstances. Possibilities of distinction are inherent in whatever accomplishments the teacher possesses
in marked degree—broad erudition, specialized mastery of his field,
competence in research, ability to organize information, skill in exposition, effective individual approach to students, talented group
leadership, and even personal qualities of poise and affability.
Around one or more of these a characteristic style of teaching may
be built; but good style cannot be maintained without attention to
fundamental conventions. Regardless of how superior a teacher's
scholarship, he still requires almost daily preparation for instruction;
no matter how friendly a teacher's relation with students, he cannot
surrender his objectivity of professional judgment.

Certain "ground rules" of teaching need in particular to be respected. Of small nature, they are occasionally disparaged as symp-
tomatic of the "pedagogical mind," but actually are a token of more
solid virtue and distinction. The teacher, for example, has an obligation to observe the same proprieties of conduct that he expects of
students. Punctuality in reporting to class, in keeping appointments
with students, in reading and returning written assignments, in grading examination papers, and any other commitments the teacher
makes to students may not be cheaply regarded. The student likes
to know his standing in a course, as does the teacher in his own
professional affairs: after the student has had a chance to demonstrate performance he should be apprised of its worth. Students, like
teachers, may carry too heavy a work-load: without compromising
his standards, a teacher can be considerate in estimating and timing

his assignments. Ordinary academic housekeeping chores—maintenance of attendance records, preparation of grade reports, requisition of materials and equipment—relished by none, should nevertheless be accomplished with promptness and orderly economy. It is unseemly for a teacher to spend ten minutes of a class period at midterm in taking attendance—as if he were meeting the students for the first time. Teachers are deceived if they regard such minor considerations beneath their concern. Though not the basic measure of good teaching, they cannot be neglected with impunity.

Creative Use of Teaching Method. Essentially every teacher creates his own teaching method. In terms of his personality and experience, the purposes and subject matter of instruction, and the students he teaches, each follows the procedures he judges suitable, choosing and adapting available techniques or devising, when necessary, new ones. One cannot teach well by copying a method which proved effective for some one else. The distaste with which reference to "method" is commonly received would be lessened were this recognized.

The distinction between method and technique is worth emphasizing. A technique is the procedure or device through which a teacher seeks to accomplish wholly or in part a specific instructional purpose. There are many techniques—in lecture, discussion, questioning, experimental demonstration, laboratory work, audio-visual presentation, independent study and research, testing, and others— each subject to flexible rules of operation. The number of possible techniques is not unlimited, although new ones are constantly being developed and familiar techniques modified. Every teacher necessarily employs a number of techniques, serially or in combination, their choice and manner of use depending upon his general method of instruction. The latter is a composite style or quality of teaching, a characteristic mode of instructional behavior reflecting one's own values and educational philosophy. One's teaching method influences not only the choice of techniques and the manner of their use but also goals of instruction, selection and emphasis of subject matter, and relationship with students. The variety of possible teaching methods is unlimited, there being as many variations as there are teachers.

The choice of techniques is influenced by the method which the teacher elects or is impelled to follow. There are those, for example, who lecture as little as possible, preferring less formal processes of group learning. Others rely upon the Socratic manner of questioning because they feel it suits their intellectual temperament. A devotee of audio-visual aids will find occasion to present instructional films, film-strips, and recordings, whereas a colleague in the same course will manage well without them. Mimicry and dramatic representation are sometimes effective devices, but not for the teacher with limited acting talents. One teacher will conduct a course in Shakespearean drama mainly through interpretative reading, another will prefer group discussion of character, plot, philosophical sense, and literary style. The scholar will create opportunities to direct his students toward individual research, the bibliophile to books, and the scientist to the laboratory.

We tend to adopt a method of instruction consistent with our capabilities and the subject of instruction, but usually do not go far enough in systematic self-analysis to enable us to develop a mode of instruction indicative of our best efforts. The choice of method is apt to be too casual, and we are often content to use the approach and techniques which most readily suggest themselves. As a rule we do not expend on method a sizable fraction of the intellectual energy we devote to scholarship. The creative use of method does not presume preoccupation with process to the neglect of substance. But it does presume a conscious attempt to develop a style and manner of instruction well-fitted to the personal and professional resources of the teacher and the possibilities and requirements of the teaching situation. It implies a willingness to experiment with new forms of teaching in an effort to find those which serve best a given purpose.

Factors Influencing Method. Some of these factors have been mentioned in the foregoing discussion. Without attempting a detailed exposition it may be useful to summarize the most important of them.

1. *Method should conform to the objectives of liberal study.* In almost every field of learning there is a difference between teaching the dedicated specialist and the interested generalist. The difference is especially apparent in music and the fine arts where specialization presumes not only a compatible interest but also a degree of aptitude granted to a comparative few. The number of people with a lay-

man's interest in music or art is legion. Teachers in these fields have adjusted successfully to their separate constituencies of learners; it would not occur to a teacher, for example, to treat in the same way students in a course in music appreciation and those in an elective in Advanced Harmony. Emphasis in instructional method would be, on producing on the one hand an informed and critical music-loving audience, and on the other skilled and sensitive musical specialists.

A similar distinction should exist in teaching history, mathematics, science, and other college disciplines. Most students in these fields do not seek to become specialists but to gain values useful in personal development. It is wrong to assume that this purpose can be served by the same methods of instruction employed with specialists: the same methods *may* be appropriate, or they may be inappropriate altogether. A safer course of action is to start by keeping in mind the goals of liberal learning, then to select or design methods which promise to be suitable. We have mistakenly tended to assume that imparting the liberal values inherent in the disciplines of science or history is the same as training for a career as scientist or historian. Excellent training in historical method and independent historical research may be quite unrewarding to the student interested in enlarging his knowledge of past events in order to gain in understanding of the present.

Progress has been made in accommodating teaching method to the needs of liberal learning. Coincident with changes in the content of general education have been changes in instructional approach, emphasis, and technique. In many places science instruction for the general learner has come to rely more on the lecture-demonstration and less on individual laboratory work; the use of mathematics to explain principles and scientific relationships is kept to a minimum; exercises in problem solving are subordinated to an understanding of the problem and the factors entering into its solution; the applications of science are directed toward illuminating the larger world of experience rather than the inner recesses of science itself; there is a more conscious effort to relate the subject matter of science to other fields of learning. Much as the specialized scientist may deplore some of these developments, they are necessary for the education of many students. Rigorous, intensive training in science is better reserved for science "majors."

In its own way mathematics instruction has attempted a comparable modification of some of its general offerings.

There is little use in grumbling about the average student's lack of skill in mechanical routines or in rushing him into further ill-understood techniques. Instead, we accept the student and his preparation as incontrovertible data and begin by discussing the reasonable character of the elementary mathematics which he formerly knew largely by rote. After a brief introduction to the essential logical ideas which are fundamental to any appreciation of mathematics, the evolution of the number system and the essentials of elementary algebra are discussed from a mature and reasonable point of view. After this foundation is laid, the book provides an elementary but critical introduction to several of the most important branches of modern mathematics, without, however, pushing any chapter so far as to strain the student's technical equipment. Applications are discussed throughout, but the discussion is restricted to applications which are within the student's grasp rather than to allow it to degenerate into a Sunday Supplement article on the Wonders of Science.[3]

For some time modern language instruction for the nonspecialist has sought to subordinate mastery of grammar and linguistic structure to fluency in conversation, ease of reading, and appreciation of literature and culture. Indeed in most subjects instruction has been adapted to the purposes of the general learner as distinct from the incipient specialist. But much remains to be done.

2. *Method should be adapted to the capacity of the learner.* No honest teacher is willing to give his subject less than its due in instruction: no teacher wants to cheapen his subject by offering it at low cost in output of study or by simplifying teaching in a manner unbecoming its dignity. We tend to believe that a student who undertakes to learn mathematics or philosophy should learn it in the way it is presented by the mathematician or philosopher. We dislike to compromise our ideals by accommodating instruction to the inadequacies of some students.

Yet common sense suggests that there is no point in teaching a

[3] From the Introduction to Moses Richardson's *Fundamentals of Mathematics* (New York: The Macmillan Company, 1941).

subject unless the student is prepared to learn it. It does little good to give the most beautifully organized lecture if the students are unable to follow intelligently and take notes discriminatingly. At the expense of some disfigurement of his lecture an experienced teacher will take steps to insure that students comprehend its substance. Techniques of instruction can be changed more readily than the student's capacity to learn, and the teacher who would teach must take realistic cognizance of this fact.

Adapting instructional method to the capacity of the learner involves first of all determining the right level of instruction. A discipline can be taught on several levels depending upon the intellectual maturity and receptiveness of the students. Elementary Greek will be taught differently to students with previous training in Latin and to a class of foreign-language beginners. General physics can be offered on a higher level to learners with a background of college science and mathematics. Second, it involves formulating or choosing proper instructional media. In teaching freshmen, for example, it is necessary to realize that they may be insufficiently trained in listening to prolonged discourse, in extended writing, in the use of library resources, reading lists, or even a textbook. These considerations should not deter the teacher from attempting to use more advanced media of instruction than those to which the student has become accustomed, but they should alert him to the necessity of concomitantly preparing and training the student for their use. Third, adaptive instruction involves continuous flexibility in the planning and conduct of teaching. A course outline judged suitable in the planning stage may in practice prove too inclusive; it is more advisable to adjust the outline than to insist on "covering" the planned subject matter at the expense of sound learning. An exercise assigned for study may contain difficulties or hazards in learning unanticipated by the teacher; it is better to alter the assignment *in cursu* than to invite a confused or slovenly performance.

Shaping instruction to the capacity of the learner involves the teacher in the problem of individual differences. Whatever the nature of the course and the size of the class a few basic principles of method cannot be neglected. One is to attempt to know the students as far as possible as individuals. Even in a large lecture group the teacher may obtain pertinent information regarding the composition of the class by a survey of college records and a preinstruction inventory of the students' background of achievement and readiness for learning. In a smaller recitation section, a little time devoted to identifying students as individuals will facilitate adaptation of instruction. Devices such as self-introduction by students, brief individual interviews with the teacher, preparation of class "registers" listing a few pertinent facts about each person, and short, frequent work assignments and test exercises in the early weeks of instruction will help the teacher to learn Who's Who academically. The effort to know the students should persist throughout instruction, with the object of distinguishing abler students who can profit from enriched study, poorer students who require special assistance, and those with special goals and interests in study.

A second principle relates to the desirability of long-term planning of instruction. Even when a comprehensive course syllabus is available, instruction formulated on a day-to-day basis is not readily adaptable to individual needs. The teacher requires the advantage of longer perspective and greater time for preparation to avail himself of possible opportunities for adjustment of subject matter, methods, and materials of study. When instruction is viewed at longer range, it is also easier to detect and minimize difficulties awaiting learners, and to effect by preventive measures what might otherwise require correction and reteaching. A related third principle concerns the superiority of large topical arrangement of study over small-unit organization. The former facilitates advanced planning, makes possible greater variety and flexibility in method, and affords more room for differentiation.

A fourth principle of teaching method pertains to the advisability of experimenting with procedures in teaching individual students and small groups. The tendency is too often to fall into the pattern of the lecture, lecture-discussion, or common assignment of study when more individualized instruction is feasible. Although the lecture and discussion form the backbone of instruction, their use can often be supplemented by individual and small-group conferences, and differentiated reading, study, research, and laboratory assignments. Some courses are more successful if conducted *principally* on this basis. The values are not only in the greater adaptability of instruction but also in added student interest and the probability of more thorough learning. The development of special "honors" work with abler students has been in this direction, and the same principle should be extended as far as possible to all students.

3. *Method should be in accord with sound psychology of learning.* Even on the college-level the significance of motivation as a factor in learning may not be ignored. Intuitively many teachers have sought to make instruction interesting, to foster in students a pleasurable feeling toward the study in which they are engaged. But the importance of motivation transcends the elements of immediate interest and satisfaction: self-identification with an activity is a necessary condition for learning. Some talented writers admit that they find writing arduous, but so thoroughly identified are they with a self-imposed mission that to discontinue writing would be unthinkable.

To help students identify themselves with the subject of study is inherent in the task of instruction. Conscious striving to make a course interesting is only a small portion of this task. Looming larger is the obligation to convey a sense of purpose and personal meaning: "What is this course to me? Why am I studying it?" A student can plunge into the study of a science, become involved in factual memorization, laboratory work, the solution of numerous problems, and even complete the course with a satisfactory grade without ever discovering what he was supposed to obtain from the course. This is not learning, and directing such experience is not teaching.

There are various ways of motivating instruction, and the most effective are those which succeed in developing a lasting sense of purpose. To motivate teaching is not to cheapen or popularize it. The precise, even-toned scholar who can relate his discipline to the meaningful experience of students does more to motivate instruction than the exhibitionist who indulges in theatrics. Growth in teaching skill involves, among other things, progression from extrinsic modes of fostering interest to deeper, more genuine, and intrinsic ways of bringing the student into intellectual communion with a subject. At its best motivation is gradual, unobtrusive, continuous, and cumulative in its effect.

The foregoing is illustrative of one principle of sound psychological doctrine. There are many others,[4] and while the teacher

4 *Cf.* Chapter V, pp. 109–120.

cannot be expected to deal with all psychological *minutiae,* he should be guided in instruction by an awareness of some of the paramount facts and principles of learning. The importance of proper emotional conditioning, the law of readiness, configurational or "whole" (as against piecemeal) learning, appeal to understanding rather than rote memory, multisensory impression, spaced repetition or practice, and the need for expression of what has been learned bear particular examination. There is no reason to fear that adherence to these principles will cramp the teacher's personal style in teaching or conflict with any beliefs and convictions he may have concerning the goals of instruction.

College teaching is apt to be negligent in two respects: in its use of spaced repetition and of direct experience. In some subjects of instruction—for example, mathematics and foreign language—learning is cumulative and repetition inherent in the organization of the subject matter; in such cases, the "law of exercise" tends to take care of itself. In other subjects, such as the social sciences, repetition must be more deliberately provided if retentive learning is to be assured. The tendency in college teaching is to assume that, once understood, a fact or idea will be "learned" or retained. This assumption is not tenable even with able students, and partly accounts for the fact that college seniors may know less of the salient content of a subject than they did as freshmen. Opportunity for repetition at spaced intervals should be forthcoming, not only by straightforward recitation but also through interesting study exercises and problems.

Much of instruction is verbal and conceptual where it could be more concretely based in reality. There is nothing wrong with concepts except the danger of their being misunderstood. Words are often imperfect carriers of meaning, and the teacher who stakes his entire outcome in teaching on the efficacy of language communication takes an excessive risk. Experiential learning is not possible in all courses of instruction, nor is it desirable in any course to keep instruction too long on a perceptual, personal-experience level. But in many subjects opportunities exist to strengthen instruction by grounding it in real experience, and to elevate and refine concepts by relating them to the world of sensory fact. Demonstration and laboratory exercises in science are an effort to do essentially this. Field and workshop activity can be utilized more extensively in foreign-language study, the fine arts, psychology, practically all the social sciences with the partial exception of history, philosophy, and most of the professionally oriented disciplines.

4. *Method should be suited to subject matter.* The subject-matter factor in method helps to explain why teaching procedures cannot be pitted against one another, nor evaluated without reference to their instructional setting. It helps also to explain why teaching techniques cannot be prescribed in a general way: what is valid in one case may be invalid in another. It is impossible to decide, for example, whether lecture instruction is in itself good or bad: in the "right" subject a gifted teacher can, with appropriate technical aids and some marginal differentiation in study, accomplish much by lecturing to a large class.

What constitutes appropriate teaching technique will vary from course to course and among elements of study within a course. Administratively a course may be labeled lecture or laboratory or recitation or workshop: this tends to identify the principal manner of instruction and perhaps determine the size of the class. But within each course different types of teaching procedures will inevitably be employed. However individualized a course of instruction, it may be desirable occasionally to recall students from their separate tasks in order to clarify a common problem by a brief lecture. In a lecture course it is frequently useful to interject short question-and-answer and discussion periods. In so-called recitation or discussion courses teaching techniques need particularly to be varied so as to conform to the requirements of different elements of study. The criterion in shaping method to subject matter is not so much the general category of the course as the precise type of learning inherent in a particular situation. For purposes of method it is superficial merely to identify a course as one of the humanities, fine arts, or physical sciences. A single course in any field may involve visualization of simple and complicated objects of sensory experience, concept formation and relationships, acquisition of skills, development of attitudes and appreciation, problem solving, changes in personal behavior, and the like. Each type of constituent learning may make its own demands in suitable teaching procedure.

5. *A teacher's method should suit him personally and capitalize*

on his special assets. It would be most unfortunate if all teachers tried to be equally witty or solemn, outspoken or reserved, pliant or uncompromising, or followed standard teaching practices. It is a good thing for students that teachers differ in personality and temperament, in conception of their instructional obligation and in their method of fulfilling it; it is good also for the teachers. Common values and ideals such as integrity, kindliness, love of learning, and respect for students may be variously expressed, and for every teacher that form of expression is best which is most consistent with his nature.

Studied unorthodoxy can be as bad as undeviating conformity. Excessive individualism among teachers is distracting and confusing to students, and inimical to the fundamental purposes of education. For a student to work with one or a few teachers markedly unorthodox in their professional ways is probably a salutary experience; to deal with none but professional eccentrics may be good clinical training but is not education. A teacher should not strain to be different: healthy individuality develops naturally from self-awareness and a conscious endeavor to use one's potentialities to advantage without violating the canons of good teaching and sound learning.

Whichever method a teacher uses should show that teacher at his best. We are not all of the same stripe, nor equally gifted in all the capacities useful in instruction. Some of us are humorous, others merely tell jokes; some lecture effectively, others talk at great length. Fortunately teaching is broad enough to accommodate many aptitudes and to afford expression for different talents. It devolves upon us to discover in what ways we can be most useful, to perfect ourselves in these respects, and to make them the personal hallmark of our teaching.

Usually the teacher has latitude in the choice of his instructional procedures. The quick-witted person with self-assured mastery of his subject may elect to engage in a running "give-and-take" discussion with students, developing the course structure as he proceeds; another with less poise or experience or who on principle rejects this procedure may choose a more orderly presentation and sequence of instruction. There is room for the "permissive" teacher and one who prefers stricter class regulation, for the "artist" and the "scientist," for the practical man and the theorist. Students appreciate a teacher not for everything he does but for the things he does well; and in fact this is where his greatest professional contribution lies.

LEVELS OF TEACHING

Mention has been made of a "college level" of teaching; actually there exists not *a* level, but levels. Levels of instruction differ with courses, classes of students, and individual learners. Even the term "levels" is inaccurate, suggesting a succession of plateaus rather than a continuous progression. Students' growth in learning power is steady, gradual, at a given time perhaps imperceptible. To parallel such growth, instruction must also be elevated continuously.

A distinguishing factor among levels of teaching is in the degree of responsibility for learning assumed by students; or, stated differently, in the measure of self-dependence which students exercise. Growth in intellectual self-dependence is manifested by increasing mastery of the tools and resources of learning, ability to acquire, relate, and organize information, reliance upon one's own judgment as against that expressed by others, and ability to formulate means leading toward self-conceived ends. To elevate instruction means to make use of these developing powers of the students in progressively greater measure.

Growth in intellectual independence, though to some extent a function of maturation, may be greatly aided by instruction. Contrarily, using infantile teaching methods may serve to keep students longer on infantile levels of learning. A good teacher is not content merely to keep pace with the students' natural development, accommodating his instruction to what they can comfortably do. Students respond to teaching which aims at higher levels of performance than they can reach unaided. There is pedagogical wisdom in the remark attributed to the late Professor Morris R. Cohen, "I aim not at their heads but where their heads should be."

Determining Levels of Instruction. To determine the extent of students' reach, one must know where it begins. Unless the teacher can estimate their competence in learning he will be working in the dark. Students' academic status as freshmen or juniors offers a clue toward developing an appropriate mode of instruction but is in itself not a sufficiently definite and reliable indication. Before an appropriate course of instruction can be charted a more precise estimate of students' abilities as learners needs to be obtained.

In trying to take the intellectual measure of a class the teacher may have to be content with something short of perfection: particularly in basic or general courses students are apt to be distributed over a wide range of competence. It helps if, at the outset of instruction, the teacher undertakes to learn what he can of the students' previous preparation and present readiness, and if, in the early weeks of a course, he continues to temper his teaching to their revealed capabilities and needs. A teacher can sensitize himself so that he realizes almost instantly whether he is operating above or below the students' reach, and can then raise or "tone down" his instruction accordingly.

To plunge immediately into the new subject matter of a course is neither wise nor economical teaching practice. It is better first to "get the feel" of a class—become acquainted with students, ascertain what they bring to the course, how well they are qualified to proceed, and in what manner they operate. This may be done in part by informal discussion, and when feasible by more formal "pretests" of learning. In the first weeks of the term it is helpful to make frequent short assignments of study tasks, grade them promptly, and be guided by the results. Successive weekly quizzes near the beginning of a course may be more informative in this respect than those given later. Effort to gauge the appropriate level of instruction should be continuous, and instruction continuously adjusted as students develop in intellectual power. To discover that students are below normal academic expectation is not to abandon hope of teaching a course as it should be taught; it is a greater challenge to find suitable means of bringing the students up to a desired standard of performance and to help them improve further.

Finding a common level of instruction for a class of students is at best a compromise, a matter of striking a common mean which may fit no one precisely. As instruction proceeds, however, it should be possible to determine individual deviations and introduce appropriate variations in instruction as circumstances permit. A common level of instruction should not be geared to the brightest nor to the dullest but seek to maintain a proper balance among all students. The difficulty of doing this with a lecture class of a hundred or more students has been acknowledged: it is the principal drawback of the lecture method. Yet teaching wholly by lecture is not typical of American colleges, and more usual-sized class sections permit greater deviation from the common mode.

Appropriateness of Teaching Procedures. Some teachers do exceptionally well with advanced students in specialized study but have no comparable success with beginning students in general courses; others show the reverse capacity. The explanation is not in any inherent peculiarity of the teacher or in the caliber of the students; the reason is often in the instructional method the teacher is impelled to follow whether by intuitive preference or deliberate choice. More skillful selection from a wider range of teaching procedures, and more flexible use of them can promote better results on any teaching level. The validity of a teaching procedure is a function of the instructional level for which it is intended.

A discussional type of procedure for example may be appropriate for students in introductory social science, but uneconomical and even tiresome in an advanced course with students capable of self-directed learning. A lecture course, often used to introduce students to a field of study, is better adapted to students with greater demonstrated interest, scholarship, and capacity for independent work. Intensive laboratory training is needed in preparing science specialists, but may be less fitting for students interested in acquiring a layman's view of science. A common textbook may help to fix the structure and substance of a course, or it may hobble learning. A routine of frequent quizzes may be serviceable on one teaching level, puerile and unbecoming on another.

Progression in teaching can be gauged by yardsticks conforming to students' growth toward independence. One is the role of the teacher himself: as instruction advances the teacher becomes less of an expositor, discussion leader, lesson "hearer," and prime mover of learning and more of an adviser, guide, critic, and study supervisor. Except in lecture courses and in some subjects where teacher dominance may be unavoidable, instruction should become progressively less teacher-controlled and more student-centered.

A second yardstick is the relative emphasis on common and differentiated tasks of learning. Advanced instruction should provide a greater opportunity for students to conceive, plan, and execute differentiated tasks according to their individual purposes, interests, and aptitudes. A third criterion is the quality of students' learning, that is, whether learning is primarily assimilative and reproductive or original and creative. Good teaching on any level affords students some opportunity for an original contribution, but advanced instruction should extend this opportunity. Learning should proceed less by recitation and more by preparation of research papers, original experimentation, literary or artistic production, problem solving, or the application of knowledge to the conduct of real experience.

Progression Within a Course. Whatever the starting level of instruction the teacher should attempt to raise it during the course. Such advance becomes more likely when it is translated into conscious purpose. Thus at the beginning of a course in political science students may be unable to write a satisfactory paper of reasonable length; instead of circumventing this weakness the teacher can set out systematically to improve the students' writing performance. Following a half-dozen carefully prepared, short papers students may be able to show substantial improvement. Those who at the beginning do not know "how to read a book" (meaning the textbook) can be taught to do so before the course is completed. To commence on a simplified level does not imply that it is necessary to continue and terminate instruction on the same level. Correspondingly, if a teacher can begin instruction at an advanced stage it should be his satisfying obligation to carry it even higher.

At times one must exercise great forbearance with students who *should* be ready for advanced instruction but patently are not. At such times it is necessary to reflect that the blame may not rest entirely with the students, that teachers in schools and colleges are not always mindful of the importance of graduating instruction, and that somewhere along the line the students' training has been neglected. The teacher may recall his own experience as a beginner in independent scholarship or teaching when he became aware of limitations not previously recognized which he later successfully overcame.

LARGE AND SMALL-GROUP INSTRUCTION

A point frequently at issue is the extent to which teaching efficiency is influenced by class size. Earlier experimental studies [5] con-

[5] See Earl Hudelson, *Class Size at the College Level* (Minneapolis: Univer-

cluded that under typical instruction measurable achievement of subject matter is not adversely affected by large classes, certainly not to the extent commonly assumed. What these studies could not show is the effect of failing to meet individual needs and foster specialized aptitudes and interests. A teacher cannot get to know each student as well in a class of forty as in a class of fifteen, although he may present his subject as effectively and the resulting average achievement in subject matter may be as high. If to educate is to help each student learn not only common subject matter but also subject matter to some extent differentiated by his interests, then teaching a large group imposes a handicap on teacher and students.

To a degree the argument as between large- and small-group instruction is theoretical. The typical college is apt to have both, not from professional choice but from financial and administrative necessity. The best that can be said for having some oversized classes is that within budgetary limitations the resulting economy makes possible the staffing of important courses with inherently limited enrollment, and the allocation of manpower to essential educational services. It would not be sensible to insist on a maximum class size, let us say, of twenty-five students if in doing so we were prevented by insufficiency of manpower from offering seminars in Greek literature or philosophy to five or six students. Under prevailing circumstances a teacher should be prepared to teach large as well as small sections, adapting his teaching method to the opportunities and limitations of class size.

Fitting Group Size to Subject Matter. A prior obligation, however, is to fit the size of the group to the nature and demands of the subject. Granting the pressure of budgetary necessity, all courses do not lend themselves to large-group instruction. The more personal a subject, the more it affects the student's individual purposes and interests, the greater the need for small-group instruction. The problem may be stated in this way: "In which subjects of study will small-group organization offer the greatest benefit to instruction and in which others can large classes be formed with the least possible loss in instructional effectiveness?"

---

sity of Minnesota Press, 1928) ; also the article "Class Size" in the *Encyclopedia of Educational Research* (Revised ed.; New York: The Macmillan Company, 1950).

A course in art history can be taught by a competent art historian making effective use of visual resources to a class of a hundred or more students, particularly if common lecture instruction is supplemented by small-group discussion; a studio or workshop course in art cannot effectively be taught except to a small class. General psychology on a descriptive level, combining lecture, demonstration, and some discussion can be offered in large-group instruction, but an advanced experimental course for psychology majors may require a small study group. In all fields of study some courses are less suitable than others for large-group teaching, the measure of their unfitness being in the degree to which instruction involves attention to individual needs, adaptation to differences, and mastery of complex skills or techniques.

Adapting Instruction to Class Size. Once a class has been formed its instruction is the teacher's province. Unfortunately at times class size has made little difference either in method or quality of instruction: some teachers do not get to know students in a class of fifteen much better than in a class of fifty. Yet more than any other consideration the desirability of knowing the individual student justifies small-group instruction.

In a small group students can learn more from the teacher, from each other, and by themselves, and to a greater extent fulfil their needs. It falls to the teacher to take advantage of these possibilities in his choice and use of teaching method. Lecturing from a platform to a class of six students would not appear in most instances a sensible procedure, yet unvarying daily discussion does not seem imaginative either. The teacher has many techniques to choose from: he can combine occasional brief lecture with more frequent discussion and, where possible, learning by firsthand experience; partition the group into smaller teams for purposes of research, experimentation, and reporting; individualize instruction by separate assignment of each student to projects, problems, and creative tasks. He is, in short, free to depart completely from the usual routines of instruction. Though normal complaint concerns the work "load" imposed by large classes, the small class with its vast possibilities of instructional accomplishment imposes the greater burden.

Large classes, on the other hand, considerably restrict the teacher's freedom in use of method. Unless he has assistants to guide and supervise individual student activity, he must rely mostly upon his skill in presenting subject matter, devising suitable study exercises which can be checked and graded, and preparing good examinations. He is more or less committed to the lecture as the principal technique of instruction, punctuated by such intervals of discussion as he can manage. The practice of dividing a large lecture class into smaller discussion and study groups, each with its own student-chairman, has been employed in some instances with notable success but its general feasibility may be questioned. Nevertheless it is helpful to approach large-group instruction with awareness of how its more limited opportunities can be exploited. If the lecture method is used it ought to be as skilfully as possible, with safeguards for securing and holding attention, satisfying a range of interests, and anticipating difficulties in comprehension. Audio-visual teaching resources should be canvassed, and reading lists, study references, and exercises prepared for those who need reinforcement in learning. Appraisal of student achievement should be frequent and the results analyzed for elements which may require reteaching. Even with a large class the lecture need not be the sole technique of instruction. Every lesson may point up activities that students can pursue leading off into special side roads of interest. It is surprising how well one can keep track of individual students in even a large class when he puts his mind to it.

Planning Instruction

The need for preparing for instruction is too evident to warrant justification. The self-respecting teacher will not meet a class without having reflected in advance on the substance of the lesson, checked on elusive details of fact, and assembled accessory materials. Most likely he will have proceeded further, shaping in his mind specific procedure, salient points of discussion, and supplemental student activity. All this is performed as a matter of professional routine. In some cases preparation is necessarily more thorough: a lecture in Constitutional Law may require extended research and precise documentation; an experimental demonstration may involve setting up complicated apparatus and a preliminary trial-run; the simplest field trip usually demands detailed preparatory arrangements.

Were the teacher the only factor in the situation, preparation for teaching could be essentially a matter of refreshing one's scholarship with only casual reference to the mode of instruction. But there are students to be considered, and they complicate the picture. Each situation involving learners is different from every other, and the fact that a course has been taught successfully in the past does not assure that it is being taught successfully now. The experience a teacher has gained improves his prospects for success in future instruction. But like the experienced general who must plan each campaign differently, the teacher needs to approach each new term as a separate challenge. The values of experience are dissipated if the teacher merely stirs up memories of past performance, resuscitates old notes, and relies on further improvisation to see him through. Planning instructional method is no more fundamental than preparation in scholarship, but it is a second requisite for effective teaching.

Planning of instructional method involves deliberate selection among the possible techniques of teaching. Laxity in this respect helps to explain why teaching so often falls into conventional molds of the lecture, discussion, or recitation: these are most "natural" and easiest. Referring to the lecture as "the characteristic method of higher education" Schueler thus explains its frequency of use:

It is easier to lecture, not to lecture well but just to lecture, than to engage in almost any other kind of teaching activity. The professor faced with the necessity of teaching the effect on world trade of currency devaluation, or the influence of Freud on the novel of the twentieth century, finds it simplest to prepare a lecture which, once delivered, can be assumed to have 'covered' the subject. The problem of considering the relationship of his students, as individuals and as a group, to the subject, the ways in which they may react to it, and the ways which may be used by the teacher to bring them closer to it and to stimulate and guide the working of their minds, introduces into the professor's preparation and into his classroom procedures that most complex of all variables, a consideration of the student and how he can best learn.[6]

It is precisely this variable which creates the necessity for systematic planning of teaching procedure.

To plan methodically is not to plot in detail every aspect of in-

[6] "The Madness of Method in Higher Education," *Journal of Higher Education,* 22:90–97 (February 1951).

struction but to concentrate on a few basic questions. Which of the possible ways of teaching this topic are most promising and feasible? What kinds of teaching aids would be helpful and are attainable? What sorts of study or learning experiences would be beneficial to students? What special assistance are students apt to need and how can it be provided? In what ways can instructional outcomes be evaluated? Involvement in such planning imposes no commitment to inflexible procedure but makes possible a more conscious design for instruction. It does not inhibit desirable spontaneity, since the latter is sparked more by self-assurance than by temporizing uncertainty.

To an extent instructional planning has to be conducted at long range. Few teachers would commence instruction without envisioning the course in its entirety, outlining a tentative course of study, assembling a bibliography, selecting subjects for special investigation, determining a general mode of procedure, and programing course highlights. As an over-view of instruction this is sufficient, but as each major topic of study is approached more detailed planning —at closer range—is necessary. If a course in Economics includes a unit on the "rise and development of corporations" encompassing several weeks of study, the teacher will find it advantageous to have the unit planned as a whole, centering on such questions as previously suggested. This will not only afford him sufficient time to formulate desired techniques and secure such teaching aids as may not be close at hand but also enable him to determine more specifically the learning potentialities of the entire unit, the progression from lesson to lesson, and the opportunities for individualizing instruction.

Long-range planning helps the teacher to organize instruction on the basis of large units of subject matter. A single class period is seldom in itself a complete instructional unit: more often it is part of a larger whole, the composition of which is more apparent to the teacher than to the students. Conducting instruction in terms of large subdivisions of subject matter enables the student to operate more intelligently through awareness of the interrelationships of constituent parts, and greatly facilitates diversification of instructional procedure. The teacher can better determine when to use lecture, discussion, formal recitation, small-group study, individual library or laboratory work, field trips, and at which points to pause for testing achievement and possible remedial teaching.

Some planning on a day-to-day basis is desirable. Plans do not develop exactly as conceived, and modifications may be necessary. It is well, therefore, to review the plan of the next day's work—how the juncture with the preceding lesson is to be made, the extent of the new lesson, and some of the details of content and technique. Few things are as exasperating to students as unneeded repetition of earlier instruction or unexplainable gaps in subject matter resulting from hazy recollection of what was previously treated. It is especially advantageous to make a last minute check of factual details, reference materials, technical aids or equipment, and instructional notes. Fifteen minutes devoted to such preparation may make the difference between impressive, workmanlike teaching and fumbling, apparently extemporaneous performance.

Instructional planning takes place in advance of, immediately prior to, and during instruction. Plans should not be so fixed that they cannot be modified or even altered in the course of teaching. An unexpected occurrence—a significant event, an emergent problem in learning, a change in students' attitudes or interests—may affect the value of a prepared plan, making it less promising than a revised mode of operation which suggests itself on the spot. A teacher should take advantage of "targets of opportunity" as they arise, and not feel bound to the restrictions of the original plan. The purpose of planning is to promote the best use of the teacher's resources in instruction, not to hinder or confine him.

(For bibliography see the end of Chapter IX.)

IX. *Techniques of Instruction*

It is proposed to review in greater detail some techniques of instruction mentioned in the preceding chapter. The goal is as before: not to reduce fine teaching to a technical operation but to feature technical workmanship as one of the qualities of superior instruction. If attention to technique has any value in college teaching it lies in the varied and imaginative uses which may result, not in the pursuit of any prescribed routine. Every teacher has the right to do things differently.

The subject of teaching technique has lately been receiving attention in college circles and in the last few years a considerable literature has accumulated. The signs point to an intensification of interest. Systematic information on college teaching practices is more available than formerly, but is not yet adequate. The ensuing discussion is bound to reflect limitations, other than those attributable to confinement of space, which the authors are frank to acknowledge.

There are those who belittle technique, insisting that apart from the requisites of scholarship good teaching is largely a matter of following common sense. The position has some merit. Not all teaching problems derive from shortcomings of technique or require technical expertness for their resolution. Personal failings may create difficulties in teaching: remove the cause and you eliminate the difficulty. The lazy teacher who "ad libs" his way through a course needs conscience more than pedagogy. A teacher's voice can intimidate students, make them nervous or fidgety, or put them to sleep. Distemper or arrogance will breed hostility in return, and excessive joviality may produce disrespect. These are not aspects of technique but qualities of behavior governable by common sense. They influence instruction, as—conversely—engaging personal qualities may go a long way toward compensating for technical shortcomings.

On the other hand, technical considerations contribute much to quality of teaching, sometimes accounting for the difference between success and near-failure. Most difficulties in college instruction arise not from personal failings of teachers but from the peculiar demands of teaching and learning on college levels. Such problems cannot ordinarily be resolved by attention to duty and the precepts of common sense: they require specialized knowledge and technical skill. To help the teacher impart his instruction with better effect is all that technique aspires to do.

The number of available techniques in teaching precludes any attempt at comprehensiveness in review. We propose to deal with relatively few—those which are common and by this token important: lecture, discussion, laboratory or workshop procedure, small-group and individual instruction, remedial teaching, and some specific devices associated with their use.

LECTURE [1]

The lecture is so common in college teaching that we forget it is a procedure uncharacteristic of pre-college instruction. Modern secondary education avoids the pure lecture form, preferring techniques which involve students more actively in the learning process. On college and adult levels of learning the lecture is appropriate, particularly after students have been trained in its use. Despite distinctive limitations it is economical of time at a stage in learning when time is of the essence. Its advantages in making accessible to large groups of students the instructional services of an incomparable scholar or teacher and in the economical deployment of manpower have been mentioned earlier. Despite some question as to its popularity the lecture system is securely established, and sooner or later most teachers become initiated into its use. For that matter every

---

[1] For varied but helpful discussion of this subject see Bernice B. Cronkhite, ed., *A Handbook for College Teachers* (Cambridge: Harvard University Press, 1950), pp. 64–71, 89–96; Gilbert Highet, *The Art of Teaching* (New York: Alfred A. Knopf, 1951), pp. 97–121; and Max S. Marshall, *Two Sides to a Teacher's Desk* (New York: The Macmillan Company, 1953), pp. 14–20.

teacher at times employs the lecture in some form, whatever the structure of his course.

The use of the lecture does not require apology. In many circumstances it is the most appropriate form of instruction, and occasionally the *only* appropriate form. It is not feasible to compare the lecture with another mode of instruction as if the two were interchangeable: in the right course and with the right person a single semester of lectures can be more instructive than several years of independent reading and unlimited group discussion. To open up a field of study, draw attention to its vital elements, distil the essence of many years of productive scholarship, bring students abreast of developments in the forefront of research—for these purposes the lecture is invaluable. To listen to a lecture can be a thrilling experience from which the student may gain ideas obtainable in no other way. But, possibly to a greater degree than other forms of instruction, lecturing presumes a high order of intellectual competence on the part of learners.

Conduct of the Lecture. Lecturing to a group of several hundred students in a large hall with the aid of a public address system involves a considerable feat of teaching, if the lecture is viewed not only as a means of presenting information but also of effecting learning. A course of instruction may be defined as "students and teacher working *together* in a sustained way in a common field of study." It is with respect to the italicized word in this definition that difficulty with the lecture technique usually occurs. For a poised, articulate, well-prepared person to "deliver" a lecture, once he has become accustomed to the presence of a "mike," is not hard; what is more difficult is to keep working with the students—to establish contact quickly, pace one's delivery to their capacity to follow, make proper allowance for note-taking, anticipate difficulty or slowness in comprehension, round up mental stragglers, clinch an important point before advancing to the next, relieve fatigue, boredom, or the strain of listening, and at intervals provide opportunity for audience participation.

To achieve a good lecture one must be sure to remain in continuous contact with the audience or learning group. Some audience participation is indispensable, the difference between this and other forms of instruction being in this respect more in degree than in kind. In a lecture, opportunity for student participation is not as frequent, prolonged, or widely distributed, but there must be regard for the principle that learning through listening needs reinforcement in self-activity. To compensate for the restriction of students' verbal expression, the lecturer must learn to *sense* how students are responding in thought to what is said. Like other modes of instruction, the lecture should provide intervals for clarification of thought, assimilation of ideas, and respite from close concentration.

Naturally and informally a mood may be created at the outset which is favorable to the establishment of rapport with students. One device is, before beginning the lecture, to exchange a few words with students within conversational reach on almost any subject that comes to mind—a topic of world news, an item of college interest, an afterthought on the last lecture, or how they fare in the course. Engaging in this friendly gossip will help foster a sense of ease and remind students that the person before them is *their* teacher, and not a stranger addressing them from a platform. Instruction may begin with a few questions providing a brief flashback to the preceding lecture or relating to the day's work; directed to students in various quarters of the room and enlisting the attention of all, the questions will help the audience to merge as a learning group. After a few minutes of such discussion the lecture itself may get under way, starting slowly and gaining in tempo as students become absorbed in listening, but not exceeding the rate at which they can reasonably follow.

A lecture should seldom be presented in one unbroken discourse. Unless exceptionally interesting, a long lecture strains the capacity for concentrated listening, causing intermittent wandering of attention and loss of continuity in thought. In preparing the lecture it may be well to organize it in several blocks or units, each presentable in not more than fifteen minutes of continuous exposition; as each unit is completed, it may be punctuated by a questioning or discussion period of two or three minutes. This should suffice not only to close ranks among the listeners but also to reveal points of difficulty in comprehension which merit further explanation or reteaching. Little is gained by advancing when a breach in understanding has developed. The lecturer should school himself to stay in front of his audience but not to run away from it. By being sensitive to symptoms of audience reaction, even those represented by listening posture, he can estimate how his instruction is registering.

As a rule the exposition should be concluded before the end of the class period so as to allow some time for general discussion. This is the time to gauge audience response, tie up loose threads of thought, and review salient points. Students should be trained to recognize the importance of this interval for summing-up so that there will be no gathering of books and coats and scraping of furniture to distract attention. It is worth explaining at the beginning of the course, the proposed organization of the lecture period and emphasizing the function of the summary discussion. Students need training in the technique of large-group participation: some who would not hesitate to speak out in a smaller-group setting are diffident about asking a question or offering an answer before a large audience; they should be encouraged and helped to do so. Where the lecture-hall is so large as to make it difficult for the student to be heard, the lecturer may have to assist by restating the question or answer.

In holding audience attention throughout the lecture pace of delivery is important. There are times when the atmosphere of a lecture, particularly one dealing with an abstruse or technical subject, may become uncomfortably close. It is then that a sudden change of pace is helpful in reviving the listeners' attention: a brief interruption, a glance around the room, and an interpolated remark by the lecturer may have the effect of breaking audience tension. Observing his audience as he speaks, the lecturer notices that students are becoming listless, that there is shifting in the seats and some inattentiveness; instead of digging harder into the subject, the lecturer would do better to pause, smile, and suggest that this may be a good time to take a "breather," answer questions, or clear up any matter of difficulty. Or the lecturer may say nothing, merely halting momentarily to let the audience settle down and resuming when attention has been restored.

In sum, what are some of the mechanics of good lecture performance? Assuming that the lecture has been well prepared in substance —first, making contact with the audience at the outset and fusing it into a learning group; second, maintaining this contact throughout the lecture through quality of substance, manner of presentation, and intermittent involvement of the group in active participation;

third, providing a discussion period at the conclusion of the lecture
to elicit audience response and for summary purposes; fourth, adjusting the tempo of the lecture so as to gain and hold maximum
attention.

Lecture Outline. A useful guide to instruction and serviceable
also in directing study is the course outline arranged topically in an
order conforming to the lecture sequence and including lists of readings and recommended study activities. Such an outline facilitates
good lecture organization, saves time in daily preparation, and provides advance notice to the student of whatever is forthcoming. Last-
minute determination of lecture content—of items to be emphasized
and others to be touched in passing—can be troublesome. Some
teachers solve the problem of coverage by endeavoring to include
within the allotted time everything of possible value, drowning the
subject in a flood of detail; others ramble as the spirit moves them.
The outline embodies a systematic effort to define the scope of instruction with regard to order and emphasis. It serves as a standard
of relevance binding the lecturer to the subject, but not so tightly
that he is prevented from making necessary adjustments.

An outline presented on the blackboard immediately before the
start of each lecture is not a substitute for a course syllabus issued
earlier to students, since it fails to provide a needed overview of the
course and an opportunity for specific pre-lecture preparation. Although a course outline is necessarily less comprehensive in detail
than one prepared for each lecture it has greater instructional value,
especially if it can be supplemented by a brief blackboard synopsis
developed during the lecture.

Lecture Assignment. For students to obtain maximum benefit
from a lecture, individual participation in study should both precede
and follow it. On their own initiative most students would not engage in preparatory study, hence formal assignments may be necessary. The lecture should be conducted on the assumption that the
assignment has been fulfilled (even if an occasional quiz is required
to enforce compliance), and that students are prepared to receive
a higher order of instruction than would be possible without such
preparation. Unless the lecturer proceeds on this basis, students will
not pay much heed to the assignment and lecture time will be expended injudiciously in attempted "full" coverage, or the lecture

will be in part repetitious of what students have already acquired. The lecturer has enough to do in dealing with essentials, supplementing common information sources, clarifying meanings and relationships, and investing the subject with added educational dimension without traversing ground which students are competent to explore for themselves.

The post-lecture assignment of study furnishes needed opportunity to differentiate instruction. This is something for which the lecture proper is not well adapted: occasionally the lecturer may relate a comment or question to particular students with special interests, but for the most part he cannot deviate from a common direction. The study assignment can be organized so as to afford latitude for special capabilities and interests. Readings and learning exercises can be differentiated in quality and extent. Beyond a common minimal level compatible with respectable achievement each student is free to proceed as far as his educational resources permit. The extent to which the lecturer is able to pursue differentiated instruction depends upon the size of the class, the availability of professional assistance, and his own resourcefulness in assigning and evaluating learning. Where the lecture is coupled with smaller-group conference or recitation, more can be accomplished in this respect.

The post-lecture assignment should not recapitulate knowledge already canvassed by the lecture. Repeating the same information without lapse of time detracts from interest and attention; rather, the study assignment should seek to extend and enrich the substance of learning. A lecture dealing substantially with an explanation of principles may be followed by study problems involving applications; one opening up a subject to general view may be followed by an assignment leading more intensively into special aspects. Assigned study can fortify instruction more effectively through enrichment than repetition.

Audio-Visual Aids. The effectiveness of a lecture, as of other modes of instruction, may be enhanced through the use of audiovisual devices.[2] Not all teachers respond to such devices with equal enthusiasm: the addicts "overdo it," whereas others forego opportunities for their profitable use because of lack of familiarity, or

[2] For helpful reference see Edgar Dale, *Audio-Visual Methods in Teaching* (Revised ed.; New York: Dryden Press, 1954).

timely preparation, or indifference. It pays to explore the aids available for teaching a course particularly through lectures, since verbal exposition alone, however lucid, has its shortcomings. Long ago science teachers discovered the value of demonstrational aids and some have since raised skill in demonstration to a high art. Aural representation has become common in music, as has visual representation in the fine arts; courses in appreciation could hardly be conducted without recordings, slides, or films. Similar accessories are widely used in the social sciences, and lately the value of recordings has become apparent to teachers of language and literature. The use of audio-visual aids in instruction is increasing, although inconvenience in securing them has been a limiting factor. Colleges have begun to develop film and record libraries as adjuncts to their extensive book collections, and teachers have become more systematic in tracking down available materials.

The justification for their use is their anticipated contribution to instructional effectiveness. Unless the teacher is persuaded that such contribution may be forthcoming, there is no point in resorting to them; the elements of novelty and extrinsic interest which they add to a course are not in themselves sufficiently important. Granting their potential worth, the question is "How are they to be used?" As a rule it is better that they be introduced within the instructional context than detached from it. The demonstration of an experiment should be made at the point where it is needed to clarify or establish a scientific principle rather than reserved for the end of the lecture; a film should be presented when it is timely to the subject under discussion. Film showings occupying a full class period should be bracketed by discussion in adjoining class periods in order to tie them closely to instruction. It goes without saying that audio-visual aids should not be so spectacular as to focus attention upon themselves and detract from the substance of learning.

A teacher should be familiar with the aids he plans to use. Many a science teacher has come a cropper through failure to rehearse an experiment or check apparatus in advance. Films should be previewed, and recordings pre-played. Where "live" radio and television programs are to be related to instruction, it is well to learn as much as possible concerning their substance, technique of presentation, and points of relevancy to the course, so as to guide students' listening or viewing. Technical equipment should be checked by the teacher or a qualified operator: it is discomfiting to have a defective projector break down in the middle of a film showing, leaving the students bemused and the teacher to extemporize as best he can. Such minor mishaps have a way of inhibiting further reliance on technical aids, with possible disadvantage to instruction.

Appraising the Lecture. Evaluating one's own lecture performance is not easy, yet an occasional systematic effort may be rewarding. No one technique is sufficient, but several techniques used conjointly can reveal to the teacher a clearer picture of himself. A direct method is to reproduce the lecture on a recorder and listen to it afterward. Recovering from the first mild shock of hearing what sounds like an unfamiliar voice, the teacher can proceed to analyze his performance, noting diction, style of delivery, mannerisms of voice and speech, lucidity of thought and expression, and quality of organization. It pays to be more critical than tolerant, cataloguing faults for future correction. The obvious limitation of this technique is that the teacher may not always be able to recognize his merits and shortcomings.

Students' reactions, direct or indirect, may be of assistance in self-appraisal.[3] It is a wholesome and sometimes chastening experience to gather a sampling of students' lecture notes and look them over; although ordinarily more indicative of the students' than of the teacher's failings, they can furnish leads for the improvement of instruction. A student questionnaire is a tricky device, but prepared strictly as a diagnostic instrument and not as a popularity poll, it may be helpful in pinpointing unsuspected strength or weakness. Experienced teachers are more apt to resort to indirect estimates of student reaction than to solicit direct comment: while justified in principle, this practice is less likely to furnish the specific diagnostic clues a teacher requires in order to perfect his performance.

An exchange of visits with a colleague, if possible one lecturing in the same course, is always helpful. Participating at the audience level, the visitor is better able to analyze students' reactions and judge instruction objectively, noting similarities and differences with respect to his own and gaining ideas for his own as well as his col-

[3] This topic is further discussed in the next chapter.

league's improvement. Allowance should be made for individuality in teaching, and no attempt should be made to promote imitation or large-scale borrowing. An informal conference following the exchange of visits will be beneficial to both teachers.

Related Conference or Recitation. Customarily the large-group lecture is paired with the smaller-group conference or recitation. Theoretically the two techniques complement each other, combining to form a balanced learning experience. A weakness in the arrangement grows out of the need for assigning different teachers to the several conference groups, with the result that coordination between lecture and conference becomes difficult to maintain. Conference teachers have been known to run ahead of the lecture, to lag behind, and in some cases to plot an independent course. These instances may be atypical, but they dramatize the difficulty and also suggest how it may be obviated.

The lecturer and the conference teachers constitute a team, performing their separate roles in relation to a common task. It is desirable, first, that they plan the course together: a teacher cannot teach effectively unless he is in accord with the way a course has been designed; each colleague's ideas should be weighed, and a consensus reached which is reasonably acceptable to all. Second, it is necessary that conference teachers maintain contact with the lectures, if possible through personal attendance, otherwise by frequent joint meetings of teachers. Liaison through a common course outline is effective only when the outline is sufficiently detailed and the lecturer is careful to follow it or consult with his colleagues on any major deviation. Third, lecturer and conference teachers should remain in instructional harness, treating not the same specific items but the same general topics. The proceedings of the conference need not invariably follow the lecture: on occasions, by agreement, the conference may be used to introduce a subject rather than develop it. But, whatever the plan, instructional activities should always be correlated.

The purpose of the conference is to offer types of instruction which the lecture itself is not able to effect. In part it supplements the lecture by elaborating content, digging into details, clarifying explanations, and providing exercises in application; but mostly it is follow-up of individual learning. This is the time to direct individual study, measure progress, assist the slow or temporarily disabled, and work with the superior or those with specialized interests. The conference also gives students a chance to *respond* to learning to a much greater degree than is possible at a lecture.

For the conference teacher to employ the lecture technique is as inadvisable as repeating the lecture content. His instruction should be more informal and intimate, following the student's leads in questioning and discussion and being responsive to his needs. Discussion should not be aimless, yet move freely within the limits of the subject and occasionally beyond them. Contrasted with the necessarily controlled conduct of the lecture, "permissive" instruction is all the more welcome. Though group discussion may predominate, a definite portion of time should be allotted to meeting with students individually for consultation on their problems.

Some teachers utilize the conference hour primarily for recitation, that is, for hearing lessons and rating student performance. As an evaluation procedure this is costly in time: there are more economical ways of assessing achievement, some by the lecturer himself. As a method of teaching it is uninspired. Some questioning by the teacher is profitable as a means of fixing essential information or dispelling common misunderstanding. But an entire session devoted to quizzing students becomes either a tense ordeal or a boring routine. The first few minutes of the hour may be devoted to an oral or written quiz, after which instruction should become more nourishing. Once or twice in the course the full period may be used for an extended evaluation exercise.

DISCUSSION [4]

The teaching procedure most frequently employed is the discussion. It blends with other modes of instruction such as the lecture, recitation, or student report into various patterns the common fea-

[4] See also "The Discussion Method in Teaching: a Symposium," *Journal of General Education,* Vol. 8, No. 1 (October 1954); "The Thought Process of Students in Discussion," Chapter I in *Accent on Teaching,* S. B. French, ed. (New York: Harper & Brothers, 1954); Harry Ruja, "Experimenting with Discussion in College Teaching: A Survey of Recent Research," *Educational Administration and Supervision,* 39:321–42 (October 1953); and Joseph Axelrod *et al., Teaching by Discussion in the College Program* (Chicago: University of Chicago Press, 1949).

ture of which is shared colloquy. Essentially it may be defined as an effort to have students learn by thinking and talking together as a group, and developing through the group process a shared appreciation of subject-matter. This mode of instruction suggests itself whenever the important outcomes of a course are derivable from common deliberation and exchange of thought following from and leading to individual reading and study. It is the method likely to appeal to the teacher who subscribes to "no method." It holds its popularity deservedly, but is by no means as casual and artless a technique as its practice sometimes implies.

Like the lecture, the discussion offers special learning opportunities not equally realizable through alternative techniques. It enables students to advance in creative thought by their own efforts, to make progress as a result of their own and others' response to the stimulus of questioning and volunteered expression. It enables students to enrich their own conceptions by reacting to those of others. If the level of discussion is high enough, even the teacher learns by being involved in such a process. A second great benefit is found in the opportunity it provides for training in collaborative effort. Discussion is not the only form of group learning, but like others it makes possible the development of attitudes and skills which contribute to collective accomplishment without which academic training, however intensive, is one-sided. Not alone in exchange of thought but in solving problems and carrying out missions or assignments in study, members of a discussion group can be taught to work together in small or large combinations.

A good talk is not necessarily good teaching. Some fine discussions take place in anterooms, cocktail lounges, and midnight soirees in girls' dormitories, but their educative quality is not always assured. The animated tone of a discussion, the extent to which it elicits participation, and even the worthiness of the subject are not alone the test of good instruction. At times we all find ourselves entering a classroom not as well prepared as we should like: yet we can meet the class, engage in a "stimulating" discussion, and terminate the session with most of our self-respect intact. Therein lies the danger in teaching by discussion: in the comforting delusion that if a teacher is sufficiently master of his subject, the need for careful preparation is not so compelling. "I do not find in my teaching any correlation between the way I prepare and the success of the subsequent discussion," a young instructor stated recently. By a superficial criterion of "success" the statement may be judged true: as an exercise in teaching, an unprepared discussion which turns out effective is an accident. The sin is not in the occasional unavoidable failure to prepare; it is in the specious generalization that lively conversation is good teaching.

The test of instructive discussion lies in a few commonplace questions. "Through this discussion what have students learned that they could not otherwise have known?" "How far has this learning advanced them toward mastery of the subject?" "In the time spent in discussion, was maximum use made of opportunities to learn?" "Could learning have been better effected through different instructional means?" Focusing attention on considerations of learning effectiveness as distinct from external stimulation reveals some of the greater challenges facing the teacher.

Teacher's Role in Discussion. This must vary with the teacher's personality and the philosophy of teaching to which he subscribes. A forceful person becomes a strong discussion leader unless he is careful to exercise restraint. The proponent of the "nondirective" method necessarily subordinates himself to the group, using his authority as teacher sparingly. The Socratic teacher remains in the center of discussion, directing thought through his line of questioning. It is difficult to define the teacher's role other than by suggesting that, insofar as he may lean toward one extreme or the other, he runs the risk of either suppressing group thinking or dissipating its values through aimless drifting.

From the standpoint of learning, a satisfactory role is that which fosters the students' initiative and gives free rein to their ideas without surrendering the teacher's responsibility for keeping the discussion within the bounds of relevance, impelling deeper and more incisive thought, and at critical points contributing information which the group itself cannot produce. Speaking to their fellows and not to the teacher alone, students should carry the burden of discussion, their remarks reflecting responsible and cohesive thought. An idea once given currency should be pursued until its inherent contribution has been realized. Students should feel free to differ with one another and with the teacher, provided they speak responsibly.

The teacher may participate on an equal basis but is further obligated to help students perceive deeper meanings and relationships, to insist on probing ideas fully, to evaluate, criticize, and even on occasion to take up the reins of a discussion and alter its course.

Make an effort to study your own role the next time you lead a discussion. Do you literally or figuratively confront the student when he speaks so that he feels bound to address himself to you, or by your attitude do you encourage him to share his ideas with the class? Do you remain in the background of a discussion permitting students to assume control, or do you unobtrusively exert your influence to raise the quality and level of group discussion and incline it toward more productive effort? In short, what is the substance of your contribution? Whatever your chosen role, improvement in its performance presumes awareness and disciplined control of what you are doing.

Planning the Discussion. As in other forms of instruction, planning a discussion involves attention to technique as well as subject matter: how to select and arrange subject matter for clear and orderly development, how to begin the discussion, what sort of questions to ask, what instructional aids to prepare, what supplemental learning activities to introduce, and how to terminate the lesson—this last being based on the proposition that a good discussion should be effectively concluded and not simply allowed to expire.

Preparing the lesson need not be expensive in time if the daily plan is part of a longer-term arrangement: for certain of the activities the stage will have been set in advance; others will require last-minute attention. The practiced teacher knows how to telescope his planning procedure, designing the main outlines of the lesson in a few strokes. Reviewing the subject matter, he can simultaneously cast it in a form suitable for presentation; from the many questions which suggest themselves, he will select the few most interesting, thought-provoking, and pivotal; supplemental learning exercises— study assignments, student reports, panel discussion, demonstration, a film showing—will most likely have been arranged in advance and can now be worked into the plan; for an appropriate lesson ending he may propose a problem, exercise in application, creative project, summary or critical evaluation. Over a period of years a teacher will accumulate a store of teaching materials, illustrative aids, and study activities from which he can quickly select those suitable for the immediate purpose. The daily plan need not be written out, although it is helpful to append notes to such subject-matter, as one may require a memorandum of procedural items which may otherwise escape the memory.

Common Teaching Aids. Like the actor in the theater, the teacher is provided with props designed to assist him toward more telling performance. The most commonplace are blackboard and chalk. Judged by the use to which these accessories are sometimes put, one of their common functions seems to be to let the teacher work off accumulated nervous energy. The stick of chalk is mistreated—now broken in two, juggled, dropped, picked up, juggled again—to the evident amusement of the class. The blackboard is also misused—to pound home a point (literally), scribble and quickly erase a word, or draw a cabalistic design; without pause in speech a teacher will whirl to the blackboard, write and noisily dot a word, and whirl back to face the class, seemingly pleased by this gymnastic performance.

The blackboard is made to be used in less dramatic and more controlled fashion. Except when blackboard exercises are customarily part of instruction (as in some mathematics courses), it should not be utilized for extended writing; a lengthy lesson outline, assignment, or series of examination questions are better presented through the medium of the individual copy. When representation to scale or precision in diagraming is desired, free-hand blackboard drawing should not be attempted; carefully prepared charts, large enough to be viewed by the class, can do the job better. The blackboard may be used for a brief lesson outline to guide instruction; for a terminal summary outline of discussion; to develop a problem or exercise illustrative of a principle or point of instruction; for rapid free-hand drawing of sketches or diagrams not requiring precision; and for deliberate accentuation of key items in instruction.

The mimeograph or duplicating machine is another serviceable instrument, utilized by some teachers to excess, by others hardly at all. It is well to remember that prior issuance of instructional materials to students is conducive to a more intelligent approach to learning and independent study. On the other hand, materials should not be issued unless they are germane to instruction, and never so freely that they cannot be assimilated; students learn to discount quantities of mimeographed materials to which little reference is made later. A practical suggestion relative to the physical preparation of mimeographed materials may not be out of place: such preparation should be handled by a skilled professional typist. Some "home-made" productions we have seen belie the worth of their content and offer a poor example of workmanship for students to emulate.

Questioning. Much of the real success of teaching by discussion hinges on the quality of the questioning, that is, the intellectual substance of the questions and the manner in which they are presented. Unless the discussion is completely spontaneous and "nondirected," its path will be controlled by the kinds of questions propounded; even a student-centered discussion presumes a line of inquiry initiated by someone. Class sessions that should have been taut with interest have been known to languish for lack of skilled exercise of the questioning technique.

Not all important questions projected during a discussion can or should be prepared in advance: such a practice might result in holding the group too rigidly to a fixed path of learning and inhibiting spontaneity of expression. The wiser course is to formulate key questions, insert them at appropriate points in the discussion, and have others in readiness to submit as necessary. A discussion which "takes hold" generates its own questions, emanating more often from students than from the teacher. The greater the teacher's mastery of the subject, the more significant his questions; the more accomplished the group, the more challenging the questions it will set for itself. The substantive quality of questioning is a function of thinking, and as such is impossible to achieve by prescription.

Questions vary according to the function they serve. There are teaching questions which elicit from students information tributary to learning; thought-provoking questions which generate ideas radiating in many directions; drill questions which prompt repetition of learning for the sake of better retention; test questions which seek to assess the amount and quality of learning; problem questions which challenge power in application and use of knowledge; attention-getting questions aimed at reviving the drowsy or recalling the inattentive; and rhetorical questions which the teacher asks without expectation of an answer, as a way of varying his form of utterance by breaking the monotony of the declarative sentence. The various types are generally not interchangeable, although a question may serve more than one purpose.

Within limits the form of a question follows its function. A thought question may be short or long, but as a rule will not be in "Yes-No" form, call for a cryptic reply, or by its wording suggest the answer. On the other hand, drill questions may be of a brief, rapid-fire order, evoking responses correspondingly short; the premium is not so much on determining the correct response as on issuing it promptly. A "why" question presumes more considered reflection in responding than does the usual "when" or "what" question. There is an element of skill in fashioning the form of a question to the nature of the response sought; a disappointing answer is often traceable to an ill-adapted form of question.

Variety in function and form of questioning lends interest to instruction and increases its effectiveness. No discipline consists wholly of facts to be assimilated, or ideas to be reflected upon, or problems to be solved; each is a synthesis of mental operations requiring for their sustenance different kinds of stimuli and instructive aids. We fall too readily into a characteristic pattern of questioning which may not do justice to the variety possible or necessary. A lesson pivoting on a few general thought questions may be slow-footed and somnolent unless the subject itself is exceptionally evocative; it can be enlivened by introducing a change in the character and pace of questioning. A recitation progressing by a succession of brief, pointed questions may become disjointed and tiresome for lack of a substantial theme; it can be improved by pursuit of more thoughtful inquiry.

The manner of stating the question influences the quality of response. A question is a directive to thought: it should be clear in intent and precise in expression. Whatever difficulty it possesses should be inherent in its thought, not in its wording: many questions one hears in a college classroom are not intrinsically challenging once their language has been decoded. Directive terms such as "discuss," "indicate," "describe," "explain" lack sufficient definiteness to be of good service. A question should be a single, compelling invitation to response, not a cumulative spray or shower of invitations. Center your attention on questioning technique the next time you observe a colleague in action. Does he state the question, stop, and await the answer, or does he follow it in quick succession with another, and another—each succeeding question designed to clarify the original but serving only to blur its memory? A sensible question, clearly worded, does not need to be paraphrased or embroidered. And how often do you encounter the teacher who does not wait for the student to answer but supplies the answer himself? Conversation is disconcerting when the questioner insists on answering his own questions, and gradually the other participant subsides into the role of listener. Students may not be quick to answer a question but they should have the opportunity of coming to grips with it. Be patient in hearing out a student.

Questions should be adapted to the level of instruction; as a course progresses the character of the questioning should be elevated. It is by asking himself questions that a student learns to master a subject. The questions addressed to him in instruction should increasingly challenge his understanding, insight, grasp of relationships, appreciation, and critical evaluation of the content of study. It is evidence of growth when at the end of a term of instruction a group can engage in spirited deliberation of questions of much higher content value than those characteristically introduced at the beginning.

Some Specialized Techniques

Laboratory and Workshop. Laboratory work has long been a feature of instruction in the natural sciences, and under one or another designation the workshop principle has similarly been applied in teaching the fine arts and music, creative writing and dramatics, and numerous technical and applied studies. Recently the terms "laboratory" and "workshop" have been generalized and expanded in use, and in various forms are associated with courses in psychology, the social sciences, foreign language, home economics, health education, and preparation for teaching. The essential principle involved is learning by doing, with the burden of course activity placed upon the student working under the teacher's direction. Although not identical, the two techniques have features in common, and for the sake of brevity in this discussion will be treated together as "laboratory instruction."

The values of laboratory instruction for the student lie in the opportunity to experience a learning situation at first hand, to translate theory into practice, to develop, test, and apply principles, and to learn methods of procedure—with greater reliance on his own power and with greater freedom from the restrictions which group work often imposes on the individual. For the teacher it is a chance to observe the student in action, assess his worth, correct his mistakes, and guide him in a promising direction. An incisive question or two may reveal whether the student appreciates what he is doing or is trying to follow instructions without comprehending them; a little encouragement or special help may kindle or intensify interest in learning and provide the basis for independent accomplishment in the future. In some subjects laboratory instruction is a necessary complement to lecture, discussion, and other verbal media of teaching; in special experimental or technical courses it may serve as the basic procedure. Although laboratory work does not preclude organized large-group effort, it is more often conducted as individualized or small-team activity.

A danger in laboratory instruction stems from the normal temptation to which a busy or preoccupied teacher is subject, namely, to conduct his own work while leaving students to do theirs. Teachers have been known to absent themselves for portions of a laboratory period in order to carry on other pressing work or to remain seated at their desks, accepting interruptions from such students as apply for help. Even good students need supervision, and poor students may fail to recognize their mistakes or be unwilling to admit them. Unsupervised activity may nullify the benefits which the laboratory is supposed to afford and instead promote poor work habits. A mediocre student is more likely to solicit help from another student than from the teacher, and come away with faulty or incomplete information or with correct "answers" which are not fundamentally understood.

Laboratory instruction presumes skill in teaching different from that involved in the conduct of lecture or discussion. The premium is not on a careful exposition or development of course content but on the ability to guide the student in the creative accomplishment of tasks without depriving him of the chance to do his own work and, at the same time, without allowing him to commit serious mistakes. Just the right proportion of reserve and readiness in advancing suggestions is necessary; the teacher must "size up" the student to know at which point to offer help, when to withhold it. Preparation for laboratory instruction is essential, but the preparation consists in thinking over what the *students* will be doing, the preliminary verbal instruction they will require, the difficulties they are likely to encounter, and some of the questions by which the quality of their performance can be appraised and their learning experience improved. Preparation should also concern itself with ensuring accessibility to needed equipment and materials and arrangement of proper conditions for work.

A science student, for example, pursuing a laboratory investigation has an opportunity to relive the experience of the pioneer research worker who originated the hypothesis, developed the experiment, and confirmed his discovery. A laboratory manual which outlines in detail the experimental procedure to be followed and requires the student merely to furnish answers deprives him of intellectual challenge and potential profit; the teacher who stands at the student's elbow and prompts him at every step achieves the same effect. To be instructive, the laboratory manual should be so prepared as to state the problem to be investigated, fill in the necessary background, suggest a general mode of procedure, and leave to the student the task of formulating a precise plan of investigation, setting up the experiment, and reaching significant conclusions. The teacher can make a personal contribution by observing the student at work, occasionally helping him over a hurdle, and leading him by question or quiet suggestion to realize greater learning possibilities in what he is doing.

Speaking generally, sufficient use is not being made of the opportunity to train students in the technique of team and paired investigation. Much of the current research in science is conducted on an organized team basis, and while each member of the team needs to be a skilled research man, he must also know how to work in concert with others. Students need practice in the joint planning of an investigation, in fairly apportioning the work, in coordinating experimentation, in checking one another's results. Particularly is this true in workshop activities where the pooling of effort by several students makes possible an attack on problems of greater magnitude or significance than could be entrusted to a single person. The recent development of the workshop as a technique of in-service training in several professions has underlined the value of such collective effort. It is surprising how unprepared students are to engage in shared undertaking at the beginning, and how rewarding can be the results in learning once they have been trained to overcome this handicap.

Small-Group and Individual Instruction. To teach a seminar or direct a small number of gifted students in advanced study is for many teachers a prized objective—a respite from the struggle with oversized classes and their component of indifferent students, and a chance to apply their scholarship in the interests of those who can and will learn. Even apart from higher-level work with "honor" students, tutorial or small-group instruction is often preferred to the more conventional class arrangement. Yet teachers engaged in such instruction will testify that few tasks can be more exacting of energy and skill, though the experience itself is stimulating.

Some individual or small-group work is indispensable in a college program. However attentive to individual needs a teacher may be in ordinary class instruction, there are practical limits: somewhere and at some time—particularly in pursuit of his chosen field of concentration—a student deserves to have the teacher's attention focused solely on himself. Second, in order to make the most of their talents, superior students need at times to be liberated from working in group harness. Third, some of the most valuable courses attract few students, and if they are to be offered at all, must be conducted for a small constituency. Finally, many teachers are of the opinion that tutorial instruction is an invaluable aspect of formal educational experience or at least that, without the values gained from persistent individual contact with a teacher, a student's education is impoverished.

Teaching a few students could be a lazy man's pastime. What makes such teaching arduous is trying to use it as an opportunity for a new and different kind of instruction. To conduct a lecture or discussion with a small group of students is simple, but what a wasteful method of teaching them! On the other hand, if the teacher resolves to help the students make the most of their capabilities, there follows an almost endless process of getting to know them, encouraging and guiding their special endeavors, thinking with them, patiently correcting their faults, and seeing them through the accomplishment of their purposes. Every thesis adviser knows the extent of the discipline involved in supervising a student's research project while trying to understand and strengthen it in terms of the student's own ideas. It is easier for the teacher to try to fashion the student in his own intellectual image than to penetrate the student's mind and work with what is there. Yet the latter is more in the nature of what is required if the student's potential is to be fulfilled.

With respect to technique of small-group instruction an almost endless variety presents itself. The teacher may use to advantage every common technique and add others of his own invention. The group may work as a unit, as individuals, or in combination. A brief assignment directing students to authenticate an historical date or event can lead to fascinating investigation, discussion, individual reports, analysis of documents, and side-trips in research. The class can meet in the library and conduct an intensive examination of source materials. Microfilmed documents can be brought into the classroom and viewed there. Other classes may be visited, teachers invited in for consultation, or a correspondence initiated with scholars outside the college looking toward an exchange of information. More work can probably be done outside the classroom than within it, and the teacher must be thoroughly prepared to use to maximum advantage discussion and conference time.

In tutorial or individual instruction emphasis is on the special purposes and needs of the student in relation to the realizable opportunities of the course. It is unseemly to proceed as if the student were an audience to be addressed; or to map out the course as for a large group whose individual capabilities and goals are not readily ascertainable. The individual student is not there primarily as a listener, and his needs in instruction can be identified. Planning should be cooperative with respect to content and method of learning. The student should be invited to formulate his purposes in study, develop a method of attack, and outline a suitable program; the teacher should consider these proposals and improve them through ideas drawn from his greater knowledge and experience. The contract made, the burden of activity should then be on the student, with the teacher assessing and guiding progress, opening up new avenues of exploration, refueling the student's interest and ambition. Individual instruction can be an exciting interplay of minds or a deadly sequence of stilted recitation, depending upon how the teacher interprets the two roles in the partnership.

Remedial Teaching. However skilled the instruction and diligent the student, there will be occasions when remedial teaching is necessary. No matter how carefully students are selected for admission to college, there will be some with special disabilities in learning which require correction through clinical methods. There are able students who for some reason have not learned to spell correctly, punctuate a sentence, or perform basic arithmetical operations; intelligent young people who have never learned how to study; otherwise fair students with pronounced difficulty in mastering a foreign language, mathematics, or science. Though it may be intermittent, remedial teaching is an inherent feature of classroom instruction. On an institutional basis most colleges find it desirable to operate with organized facilities for systematic correction of special disabilities, such as speech, reading, and study "clinics" and remedial workshops.

Whether remedial teaching is conducted by the teacher in the ordinary course of instruction or by a specialist working from a central college facility, the underlying principles of successful remedial treatment are the same: to identify the disability, ascertain—if possible—its cause, and develop suitable corrective measures. Remedial instruction is essentially individual: occasionally it may be possible to group students with common disabilities, but even in such cases, though the symptoms are similar, the causes and needed remedies may be different. A student's failure which on the surface seems attributable to laziness, indifference, or neglect of study may turn out to be rooted in psychological factors, or traceable to some serious fault in earlier training. The causes of persistent disabilities are not easily identifiable; and though the teacher should not be quick to speculate on possible hidden origins, it would be a mistake to accept the obvious surface explanation that the student has failed to apply himself industriously, and that a compensatory period of study will correct the condition. Where long-standing disability exists, it is untenable to assume that reteaching alone will supply the corrective.

The teacher is not omniscient concerning the students he teaches.

The best he can do is to try to determine from available evidence the possible cause of a student's difficulty, and devise an appropriate way of dealing with it. If the evidence points to a physical or psychological cause the problem should be referred to a physician or psychologist; the teacher should not attempt to fulfill the role of psychologist any more than he would that of medical practicioner. In most cases the causes will be less complicated and more amenable to instructional treatment; in such instances it should be possible to plan with the student a program of remedial teaching designed for his special needs. A student may be deficient in compositional skill simply because he has never mastered the mechanics of sentence structure. In a college student such ignorance may be deplorable, but good sense suggests that it is better to spend less time in shedding tears and more in developing with the student a graded sequence of writing exercises aimed at helping him unravel the mystery of the sentence. So also in the treatment of difficulties in foreign language, mathematics, science, music, or anything else. Do not generalize too much, try to determine the specific cause of the problem, try to find or invent a suitable remedy, and patiently teach.

SELECTED BIBLIOGRAPHY

Axelrod, Joseph *et al., Teaching by Discussion in the College Program.* Chicago: University of Chicago Press, 1949. 68 pp.

Cantor, Nathaniel F., *The Teaching-Learning Process.* New York: Dryden Press, 1953. 350 pp.

———, *Dynamics of Learning,* Second edition. Buffalo, N.Y.: Foster and Steward, 1950. 296 pp.

Cronkhite, Bernice B., ed., *A Handbook for College Teachers,* Chapters V–VII, "Varieties of Teaching Method." Cambridge: Harvard University Press, 1950. 272 pp.

Dale, Edgar, *Audio-Visual Methods in Teaching,* Revised edition. New York: Dryden Press, 1954. 534 pp.

de Kiefer, Robert and Cochran, L. W., *Manual of Audio-Visual Techniques.* New York: Prentice-Hall, Inc., 1955. 220 pp.

Eisenhart, Luther P., *The Educational Process,* Chapter IV, "Methods of Instruction." Princeton: University of Princeton Press, 1945. 87 pp.

French, Sidney B., ed., *Accent on Teaching.* New York: Harper & Brothers, 1954. 334 pp.

Haas, Kenneth B. and Packer, Harry Q., *Preparation and Use of*

Audio-Visual Aids. New York: Prentice-Hall, Inc., Second edition, 1950. 327 pp.

Highet, Gilbert, *The Art of Teaching.* New York: Alfred A. Knopf, 1951. 291 pp.

Lynd, Helen M., *Field Work in College Education,* Sarah Lawrence College Publications, No. 5. New York: Columbia University Press, 1945. 302 pp.

Marshall, Max S., *Two Sides to a Teacher's Desk,* pp. 13–143. New York: The Macmillan Company, 1953. 284 pp.

Millett, Fred B., *The Rebirth of Liberal Education,* Chapter III, "Experimentation in Techniques of Teaching." New York: Harcourt, Brace and Company, 1945. 179 pp.

National Society of College Teachers of Education, Twenty-Seventh Yearbook, *The Study of College Instruction.* Chicago: University of Chicago Press, 1939. 314 pp.

Peterson, Houston, ed., *Great Teachers.* New Brunswick, N.J.: Rutgers University Press, 1946. 351 pp.

Reed, Anna Y. *et al., The Effective and the Ineffective College Teacher.* New York: American Book Company, 1935. 344 pp.

Russell, John Dale, ed., *New Frontiers in Collegiate Instruction,* Volume 13 of the Proceedings of the Institute of Administrative Officers of Higher Institutions. (Specifically Chapter VII, "Techniques of Handling Large Classes;" Chapter XI, "Audio-Visual Materials;" and Chapter XII, "Laboratory Demonstration Methods.") Chicago: University of Chicago Press, 1931. 248 pp.

Schueler, Herbert, "The Madness of Method in Higher Education," *Journal of Higher Education,* 22: 90–97, February 1951.

Severinghaus, A. E., Carman, H. J., and Cadbury, W. E., Jr., editors, *Preparation for Medical Education in the Liberal Arts College,* Chapter 9, "The Teacher and His Methods." New York: McGraw-Hill Book Company, 1953. 400 pp.

"The Discussion Method in Teaching: A Symposium," *Journal of General Education,* Vol. 8, No. 1, October 1954.

Valentine, P. F., ed., *The American College,* Chapter 7, "Experimenting in College Instruction." New York: Philosophical Library, 1949. 575 pp.

Ward, F. Champion *et al., The Idea and Practice of General Education,* Chapter 10, "Teaching." Chicago: University of Chicago Press, 1950. 333 pp.

Weaver, Gilbert C. and Bollinger, Elroy W., *Visual Aids, Their Construction and Use.* New York: D. Van Nostrand Company, Inc., 1949. 388 pp.

X. *Evaluating Learning and Teaching*

Past Practice and Current Conceptions. An enterprise is judged not only by the effort and skill which enter into its performance but also, as far as possible, by results. Educational evelution has been thorough and precise in some respects, lax or inadequate in others. Practically since the formation of the school students have been subjected to examinations in subject matter of learning, and with respect to such examinations education has done its consistently best job of evaluation. Much care has gone into preparing and improving them, and although students continue to complain about examinations—sometimes with cause—on the whole their effect is beneficent. Not only do they provide an indication of results in learning, but the discipline of taking them contributes a forceful incentive to study.

It is undeniable that much can be ascertained concerning the quality of students' learning through a good conventional examination. But even a good examination may leave untouched outcomes of instruction which do not readily lend themselves to tangible appraisal—ideals, attitudes, intellectual powers and habits. In the schools of ancient Athens music and gymnastics were taught not as builders of melody and muscle but as molders of disciplined mind and body; but how was such accomplishment judged? In our days we teach the sciences not as systems of fixed knowledge but as ways of thinking and gaining knowledge in the realm of nature. Yet how is learning customarily evaluated in biology, chemistry, geology, or physics?

Instruction also has long been subject to evaluation, though not as rigorously as students' achievement in subject matter. We choose college teachers carefully, hoping thereby to secure good instruction, and in a crude sort of way continue to assess their teaching effectiveness throughout their professional career. But while this evaluation may be roughly adequate for purposes of determining appointment, retention, and promotion, it is insufficiently diagnostic for purposes of supervision and self-improvement in instruction. The teaching process has not been analyzed with enough precision to ensure discriminating evaluation. Supervision has been intermittent and directed more toward administrative than intrinsic uses. Self-improvement in instruction has been left mainly to the conscience and insight of the individual teacher.

With respect to programs and courses of instruction evaluation has been weakest. Surely there must often be doubts concerning the efficiency of a course with reference to its imputed objectives, or the soundness of the objectives themselves; yet how are these doubts resolved? More often by controversial discussion and ultimately by decisive pressure of events than by dispassionate consideration of evidence. Properly conducted debate is itself a means of evaluation and there are occasions when no alternative exists to subjective judgment. But the resolution of an argument can also be influenced by authority or vested interest. "Evaluation" of the latter sort is not in the best interest of education yet in the history of the college vital decisions affecting subjects of instruction have often been made in this manner. The end is not yet. Most courses today are conducted with no more reliable evidence of the suitability of their content and form than is afforded by plausible assumption. In fairness it should be added that teachers try to be guided by an honest estimate of their experience, and that the alternative to trial-and-error procedure is in many instances unfeasible or difficult.

Current conceptions of evaluation hold, first of all, that so far as possible education should be subjected to processes of appraisal emphasizing the orderly array and review of evidence in contrast to forensic or arbitrary judgment. It is admitted that much which is central in education, particularly in the realm of disputable values, is unsuited to "scientific" or "objective" evaluation. Nevertheless, once educational goals have been posited progress toward them should be ascertainable in a trustworthy way. Where findings are obtainable by strict attention to objective evidence, educators are not justified in resorting to less convincing means of arriving at conclusions.[1]

There is also insistence that evaluation canvass more widely the outcomes of instruction transcending the learning of subject matter. This serves to explain the current preoccupation of evaluation specialists with defining instructional objectives and tracking down elusive "values." While assessment of achievement in subject matter is important, it may not in itself disclose the "hidden," ulterior outcomes of learning. Ability to identify authors and substance of literary works is not, for example, an indication of how the student has been moved to expand his literary interests and deepen his appreciations. The test of education is in immediate and later living; since the feasibility of such direct evaluation is limited, the nearest clues are in the attitudes, ideals, interests, and changed modes of behavior the student derives from his studies. With increasing persistence evaluation has been probing the contributions of specific disciplines to these ends, while making occasional attempts to survey the estimated effect of college education on later adult living.

It is much easier to prepare a good factual test in science or literature than one of critical thinking, appreciation, or attitudinal and behavioral change. Many of the new instruments of evaluation are so far from perfect as to draw criticism from college teachers and even uninitiated laymen. Yet in their refusal to be deterred from investigation of these fundamental but less accessible outcomes, the evaluationists are often more soundly motivated than their critics.

Evaluation of the conventionally-sought outcomes and of the instrumental teaching-learning process has not slackened but has been intensified. Forms of achievement testing have been improved, and new devices added to facilitate appraisal of growth in aspects of personality, interests, and skill in work and study. The scope of evaluation has been extended by renewal of confidence in the validity

[1] No attempt is being made to document the interpretative statements in these paragraphs. They are drawn from current theory and practice in evaluation as understood by the authors. For a good overview of the subject, the reader is referred to J. Wayne Wrightstone's article on Evaluation in the *Encyclopedia of Educational Research,* W. S. Monroe, ed. (Revised ed.; 1950), pp. 403–7.

of subjective insight and judgment, and by marshaling the resources of clinical psychologists and trained personnel workers. Diagnostic appraisal of teaching performance has been stimulated by increasing recognition of the importance of sustained supervision and the growing practice of teacher rating. But considering its earlier neglect, the greatest strides are being made in evaluation of courses of study—prior to, during, and subsequent to instruction.

Lacking an assured direct approach, curriculum evaluation often covers a wide front, proceeding by flank as well as straightforwardly. What sort of evidence can be gathered bearing directly on the goals of instruction? To what extent can incidental or intermediary learnings be taken into account? In what ways can unforeseeable outcomes be discovered in the course of evaluation? What are the attitudes of the students involved in the course—the satisfactions, annoyances, or difficulties they experienced? What are the teacher's reactions? The reactions of counselors who worked with students? The work that students produced, the books they have read, the number of hours spent in the library, the time consumed in off-campus study, even offhand comments about the course to parents and friends are surveyed, sorted, and included in the final accounting. By no means all or most of the techniques are statistical: there are observations of classes, conferences with teachers and counselors, interviews with students, consultations with "outside" colleagues, visits to other institutions and comparative studies of similar undertakings. The task is burdensome, many of the findings are of marginal value, and some must simply be winnowed out. Regrettably, if evaluators are not careful, there may be some disruption of teaching. Yet in the final analysis creditable progress has been made in facing up to a professional responsibility heretofore sidestepped.[2]

Another conception of evaluation relates to purpose. Evaluation is not viewed as an end in itself nor as the servant of administration: it is meant to serve the educational process in its various aspects. An institutional self-study, however critical in its findings, never results in mass resignation or dismissal of faculty and rarely in complete

[2] See, for example, Paul L. Dressel and Lewis B. Mayhew, *General Education, Explorations in Evaluation* (Washington: American Council on Education, 1954); and Paul L. Dressel, *Evaluation in General Education* (Dubuque, Iowa: Wm C. Brown Co., 1954).

scrapping of the curriculum. Most often it produces an accelerated effort to find and correct weaknesses, improve the program of studies, and step up instruction; it may result in development of new courses and new appointments to the teaching staff. Evaluation of a specific course is seldom made in order to decide whether the course should be kept or dropped: usually it seeks to stimulate improvement. While earlier in a teacher's career evaluation of his teaching performance may be associated with administrative decisions affecting retention or promotion, for the larger portion of his professional life it is meant to serve his needs in self-improvement.

The function of evaluation is to assist in the improvement of teaching and learning, and those associated with evaluation are in a true sense partners in instruction. Indeed, the teacher is himself the chief evaluator—of what he teaches, how he teaches, how well the students learn. It is a mistake to regard evaluation as a large-scale operation involving a full-dress review, the use of elaborate testing or survey apparatus, and the services of special technicians. Periodically such an operation may be necessary, as in institutional accreditation or when there is reason to believe that formal inventory-taking is desirable. But the more common and significant kind of evaluation is that conducted unobtrusively from day to day under the instigation of the teacher working alone or with aid from others. Results of such evaluation are most useful when plowed back into instruction.

Evaluation and Measurement. It is of practical importance to distinguish between evaluation and measurement.[3] A mistaken identification of the two threatened for a time to retard progress and divide the profession within itself. The effect of mistaken identity is still felt in some quarters: it accounts for the persistence of strong feelings for or against objective examinations; for the naive faith with which IQ scores are accepted as a definitive measure of intelligence; for excessive reliance on examinations in estimating educational accomplishment; and for other unjustified evaluation practices. Generally a more balanced view has come to prevail: it finds room both for measurement and for the more qualitative kind of evaluation based on personal judgment. The skilled evaluator

[3] See also H. H. Remmers and N. L. Gage, *Educational Measurement and Evaluation* (New York: Harper & Brothers, 1943), pp. 29–30.

makes use of both in such a manner as to realize their complementary values.

The measurement idea extends far back into school history, but the modern "movement" dates from early in this century when, under the leadership of E. L. Thorndike, J. McKeen Cattell, and others, a "science" of education emerged; the movement reached its peak in the 1920's and since then has leveled off. Its purpose was simple and creditable: using the techniques of science and a maximum degree of objectivity, to assess human behavior in precise, quantitative terms, and in this way to minimize the error of unwarranted dogma, bias, or accidental misjudgment. Distrustful of verbal definition, it tried to express itself in sharper mathematical language. Intelligence is admittedly a quality of behavior, not a numerical value; yet in the view of measurement experts progress toward understanding intelligence was expedited by the development of an instrument capable of defining intellectual capacity in measurable units. Similarly ideals, attitudes, knowledge, skills, and other characteristic outcomes of instruction could be weighed on a quantitative scale.

In the span of a generation this dedication to the pursuit of objective evaluation brought striking results. It produced scores of measuring instruments—intelligence, achievement and aptitude tests, interest, attitude, and personality inventories, and the like—which despite their shortcomings are yet of practical utility; it focused attention on the range of individual differences and stimulated efforts to adapt instruction to the needs of the individual and the homogeneous group; it fostered curriculum reorganization in the lower schools and purged courses of study of inert and useless elements; it contributed to the improvement of instruction, guidance, supervision, and administration.

With added maturity the science of education came to realize the extent to which it was being hampered by its own restrictions. There is much in education which cannot be studied objectively and precisely, which cannot in fact *be measured;* to ignore this in evaluation may be to overlook what is most significant in human behavior. People are commensurable only in specific and relatively superficial aspects: to be understood, each should be viewed in his own terms, as a complete person. The factor of motivation can hardly be measured at all: it may be discerned through perceptive study of an individual and by establishing the right kind of rapport. In short, objective measurement is a partial and incomplete way of learning about people.

Such considerations induced changes in thinking about evaluation. Subjective judgment is no longer regarded as reprehensible but as something to be relied upon—to be trained, controlled, and responsibly exercised. Objective measurement has not been abandoned, but its role in evaluation has been redefined.[4] Efforts to extend and improve testing have been coupled with the development of new evaluation processes which stress the use of trained personal judgment—processes utilizing observation, interview, appraisal of performance, study of educational records, behavioral history, projective testing, results of clinical research, as well as data of standardized testing. Indeed it has now become clear that the latter are more meaningful when interpreted within the larger context of evaluation derived from a many-sided study of the individual.

How Much of Learning Can Be Evaluated? Despite considerable progress in evaluation, much of the end-product of learning cannot be reliably ascertained by any means at the teacher's disposal. Most of the evaluation instruments developed so far are more helpful in studying the individual as the total product of heredity, maturation, and learning [5] than in separating out the results of instruction in a particular course. From the teacher's point of view it is useful to know, through the specialist's interpretation of the Thematic Apperception Test or the Rorschach, what sort of person the student is, but the results do not indicate how much his own instruction has contributed to making this person. Even power tests of logical and critical reasoning are more serviceable as a general index of mental competence than as a measure of growth through a set sequence of learning experiences. Yet the teacher is as much concerned with

[4] Walter S. Monroe, "Educational Measurement in 1920 and in 1945," *Journal of Educational Research,* 38:334–40 (January 1945).
[5] A valuable source of information concerning such tests is the series of Mental Measurement Yearbooks edited by Oscar Krisen Buros, the most recent —at the time of writing—being *The Fourth Mental Measurements Yearbook* (Highland Park, N.J.: Gryphon Press, 1953). Tests are listed under each of the several categories and carefully reviewed so as to identify their uses and limitations.

fostering character development and general intellectual power as he is with subject-matter proficiency, and in knowing how well he succeeds.

Lacking convenient ways of approaching some of the less accessible outcomes of instruction, the teacher tends to center evaluation on what is most evident— mastery of the subject. In itself this aspect of evaluation is important and worthy of the teacher's best effort. Course examinations should be given, and so constructed as to test the variety of learnings inherent in the subject—not only the facts of knowledge but also the ability to use knowledge, recognize or establish relationships, derive or validate principles, solve problems, and in general move with competence within the scholarly province of the subject. Formal testing can go further than it customarily does in estimating extent and quality of independent learning, growth in generalized powers of thinking, and progress toward differentiated personal objectives. There is no disposition here to belittle the usefulness of formal testing: what is needed are better tests.

At the same time the teacher should also be involved in other types of evaluation activity shared with colleagues or designed and initiated on his own responsibility. In some he may be assisted by objective devices, in others subjective judgment alone must serve. It is important to evaluate students as people, both as a necessary condition for teaching them and as a means of assessing their total progress toward educational objectives. Since it is unlikely that the teacher will be furnished a prepared personality inventory of each of his students, he must take the time (if class size permits) to know them, and to continue studying and evaluating them as instruction proceeds. Although the focus of attention is on intellectual quality and achievement, traits of character and personality should not go unnoticed: emotional maturity, behavior in a group, sense of moral and social responsibility, initiative, leadership, attributes of democratic living. Properly recorded, such evaluation is useful also to counselors and succeeding teachers.

It is not expected that evaluation of a student will ever be "complete." The best a teacher can do is to take account of the factors in personal development to which he is sensitive and which he trusts himself to judge. Without overdoing the judicial role a teacher can sharpen his senses by becoming a little more evaluation-minded.

Evaluation is a state of mind as much as it is a process. The instructor who critically regards his practices each day, who seeks to find in his students evidence of the effect of his instruction and of their own endeavors in terms of progress toward accepted educational goals, will find that evaluation-centered thinking is a continuing, rewarding, and integral part of his teaching. On the contrary, evaluation which is periodic or spasmodic is usually not well conceived and has very little effect other than the development of a distaste in both teacher and student for such ventures.[6]

The Teacher and the Evaluation Specialist. Teachers may be diffident in their approach to evaluation (by other than the conventional methods), viewing it as a special province of the trained technician. On the whole this attitude of caution is justified and salutary: there are limitations to the competence of otherwise well-trained teachers in the use of specialized evaluation instruments, and for that matter even evaluation specialists must exercise care in entering the field of psychometrics. The amateur psychologist, whether teacher or layman, is capable of inflicting much damage; to interpret a Rorschach requires considerable specialized skill, and even the administration of an individual test of intelligence such as the Binet demands some training. Educational evaluation even apart from psychometry often requires the technical assistance of an expert. A true-false examination apparently so easy to construct can produce havoc among students; a short fact-finding questionnaire may turn out to contain embarrassing ambiguities; and the attempt to appraise an experimental course of study will certainly exhaust the resources of teachers unless a specialist is at hand to advise them. Evaluation processes have developed to the stage where the services of trained technicians are indispensable. But these services are almost always paired with the teacher's own efforts and made subservient to them; very rarely does the specialist "come in and take over" even when the teacher has reached the limit of his evaluation competence.

What does the evaluation specialist do? His primary duty is to serve in a consultative capacity to teachers, advising on evaluation problems and assisting with evaluation tasks. Particularly when new or unfamiliar practices are involved, such technical assistance is

6 Dressel and Mayhew, *op. cit.*, p. 24.

needed: in offering professional judgment on new proposals, formulating technique, constructing or previewing a new type of examination, preparing a check list or questionnaire, passing on the merits of a standardized test, locating reference or research material, or advising on management of data. The presence in a college of an able technician who makes himself acceptable to his teaching colleagues is enough to stimulate desirable ventures in evaluation.

A second function is to serve the institution in its collective aspect, guiding evaluation policy, coordinating the preparation of comprehensive examinations, administering testing programs, conducting research and development of new evaluation instruments, compiling evaluation data and presenting them in a way most useful to his colleagues. How integral a role such "examiners" can play in the educational conduct of an institution has for years been demonstrated at the University of Chicago; more recently a published study by the University of Minnesota has revealed the variety of useful information a concerted program of institutional evaluation can bring to light.[7]

What is the teacher's role in evaluation? Mostly he is responsible for the continuous appraisal of students' efforts in learning and his own in teaching. Were there no grading systems whatever, the teacher would still be bound to engage in evaluation. Occasionally these efforts will go beyond the immediate tasks of teaching and learning into a fuller investigation of backgrounds of students, values of the subject, and his own professional attributes. A second function is to prepare and submit such evaluation data on students as the institution may periodically require—grades, personality ratings, summary reports for inclusion in cumulative personnel records, and the like. The two functions are not identical, but there is no clear demarcation between them. Most teachers have felt at one time or another that they could dispense with the semiannual rite of holding final examinations and assigning course grades. Yet the orderly conduct of study in institutions serving hundreds of students requires some sensible system of grading, and this is reason enough for the teacher to accept seriously what may be an uncongenial chore. A

[7] Ruth E. Eckert and Robert J. Keller, *A University Looks at Its Program,* Report of the University of Minnesota, Bureau of Institutional Research, 1942–52 (Minneapolis: University of Minnesota Press, 1954).

third function is to cooperate with colleagues in the evaluation of interdisciplinary programs, experimental courses, and such other projects as may be under way. The execution of this task involves sound educational judgment as much as technical knowledge of evaluation.

TECHNIQUES OF EVALUATION

Examinations and Their Uses. In their variety and function examinations have almost as wide a scope as education. There are scales of general intelligence and specific aptitude, tests of sensory and motor abilities and physical skills, examinations of academic achievement, tests of power in performance, projective tests of character and personality, and a large array of inventories of traits, interests, and special proficiencies. Examinations are utilized not only in teaching but also in determining qualification for admission and for graduation, in educational prognosis, placement, counseling, and other educational services. Along with the usual teacher-prepared examinations there are standardized tests of wider applicability, possessing established validity and reliability, and norms for easier comparison. There are standardized tests usable only by specialists, others which are self-administering or administrable with utmost ease. Not all such tests are of equal merit or comparable utility, but once their special features are known most can be of service in evaluation.

There are more functions and forms of examinations than the teacher may expect or need to know. Of available standardized tests it is sufficient that he be acquainted with those applicable to his field of teaching [8] and with others of institutional utility (i.e., entrance, placement, or comprehensive senior examinations) which students commonly take. More important than possessing descriptive information about existing tests is knowing how to use testing as a tool in fostering and evaluating learning in one's own courses. This ability involves an understanding of test uses, some skill in test preparation, and proper application of test results.

As in this instance, the subject of examinations is often discussed within the context of evaluation; this suggests a narrower function of testing than is warranted. A test is more than a tool for ascertaining how well students have learned in order that one may rate them

[8] For listed tests see Buros, *op. cit.*

properly. It is a multiple-purpose instrument useful also in planning instruction, motivating study, diagnosing difficulties in learning, conducting remedial instruction, offering opportunity for review and application of learning, and discovering one's faults in teaching. This is not to minimize the serviceability of tests for grading purposes but to suggest that the teacher who customarily administers only an end-of-course examination is making partial and inadequate use of testing.

As a matter of fact tests in themselves seldom provide a sufficient basis for comprehensive evaluation of student achievement. In most courses there are attendant learnings not measurable by tests but appraisable by other means—talking to the student, noting or recalling his daily performance, observing changes in attitudes and interests, estimating his accomplishment in collateral activities. A test can never capture or reproduce an entire learning experience; at best it affords a fair but limited sampling.

Function and Form of Examinations. It should not be inferred that there is perfect correspondence between the functions and forms of examinations. Test construction has not progressed to this stage of refinement, and practical considerations intervene to make the possibility little more than visionary. A teacher has limited time to devote to the preparation and conduct of tests, and no single examination can embody the varied learnings inherent in any course or large topic of study—the facts, skills, principles, relationships, critical judgments, or creative possibilities in the use of knowledge. At best the teacher can focus on one or two predominant instructional objectives and choose the form of examination most nearly appropriate for their assessment. Thus discussional questions on an essay examination can reveal a student's broad grasp of knowledge, his method of intellectual attack, ability to relate ideas and bring them to bear upon a given situation, and to express himself effectively; they are not likely to reveal his point-by-point mastery of the subject or accurately chart deficiencies in understanding, judgment, or power of application. The student writes about what he knows; what he does not know can only be indirectly deduced. To obtain a better measure of range and penetration of knowledge and a more precise analysis of strength and weakness, a series of graded exercises or limited-essay type questions or a comprehensive objective-type examination would be more serviceable.

Despite lack of perfect correspondence there is a relationship between examination function and form; in any event some types of tests serve a given purpose better than do others. A true-false quiz of a hundred items can measure retention or recall of factual information, takes a short time to administer, is easily scored, and may furnish a reliable representation of comparative achievement. Although it has become popular to discredit knowledge of discrete facts and the use of true-false tests in this connection, no course of study is so constituted that it has no need of essential facts to cement larger understandings; and occasionally it may be desirable to test knowledge of facts alone. Exclusive use of true-false quizzes would be poor testing practice, but evaluation which disdains pointed assessment of factual knowledge is also inadequate. The true-false examination cannot measure as well the ability to use knowledge in the context of experience, and for this purpose other forms of testing are available. Multiple-choice test items are difficult to construct, but may be rewarding in the opportunities they offer students for the exercise of discriminating judgment. The use of "situation" items makes it possible to center a series of thought-provoking questions around a single sizeable problem, and to test both knowledge and power in an objective way.[9] The written essay examination remains a good medium for testing quality of sustained thought and expression, while for deeper and persistent inquiry into ranging mastery of a field of scholarship the individual oral examination is without peer.

A teacher cannot afford to commit himself to a specific form of examination. "I do not believe in objective tests" or "I use only objective tests" are both admissions of error. Test forms are not so fixed that the teacher is dependent upon those in conventional use if they appear unsuitable: he is free to experiment with others of his own design. But the effort should be guided by consideration of purpose—"What am I trying to evaluate through this examination?" Several types of exercises may suggest themselves which in combination promise greater return than any one; or no test exer-

[9] See E. F. Lindquist, ed., *Educational Measurement* (Washington: American Council on Education, 1951), pp. 241–48, "The Interpretive Test Exercise."

cise may suggest itself as appropriate, in which case the teacher should turn to some method of evaluation other than testing. Practical factors cannot be omitted from consideration: class size may dictate against use of the essay test, or insufficient time for test preparation against a comprehensive objective form. In other than predominantly skill or performance courses it is well to employ varied forms of testing. The time factor in test preparation can be reduced by compiling a store of test materials and using them, with appropriate revision, with successive classes.

Essay Examinations. The return to prestige of the essay examination has been mentioned. Its earlier disparagement by measurement specialists was occasioned by the frequency of ill-conceived and carelessly worded test questions producing aimless performance and unreliable evaluation. Items such as "Discuss the growth of the Industrial Revolution" or "Write a 1000-word essay on Chaucer" could not be justified either as incentives to thought or trustworthy measures of performance. The fault was not with the test but with its makers: subsequent experience with objective examinations proved them equally vulnerable to the effects of poor construction. The worth of a test is determined not by its form but by the quality of effort entering into its preparation. Good teachers know this, and in using the essay test try to invest it with challenge and clear direction.

An essay examination can provide an instructive experience in exploration and organization of thought, and lucid and cogent expression. It is a useful measure of ability to reproduce knowledge, of creative power, critical and interpretative insight, and expository skill. It is a flexible instrument, permitting adaptation to different kinds of subject matter and varying abilities and interests of students. In modified "short" form, it may range over an area of scholarship, yielding limited responses relatively easy to grade. There is no denying, however, that the essay examination offers special problems in preparation. It appears so easy to construct that the temptation is to spend less time in this task than is essential. There is a tendency to skirt consideration of course objectives and scope and to proceed to the formulation of thought-provoking test items: the result may be an attractive, self-contained examination unrepresentative of what the teacher has undertaken to do in instruction. The small number of test questions places a premium on the measuring capacity of each, and operates against comprehensive sampling. Words such as "discuss," "explain," "indicate," "describe" are overworked, and usage has blunted whatever specific directive quality they once had. The more ambitious the sweep of a question, the more difficult to find words which portray the teacher's meaning but do not restrict the student's thought.

A good examination should be clear in language and definite in the tasks it sets for the student. These tasks should be selected not only for their intrinsic worth but in relation to the outcomes of instruction to be evaluated. Whatever else it may do, the examination should be an instructive experience enabling the student to learn something new. Questions should be provocative in thought content and interesting in form. It is well for the teacher occasionally to experiment with a variety of question forms including analysis of a given problem situation, evaluation of stated evidence, or criticism of a cited portion of text. Departing also from the traditional form of answer, the teacher may call for a variety of responses including preparation of an outline, developing a given topic sentence, formulating a list of significant questions, or proposing a method of study for a given problem. When sustained thinking is less of an objective of evaluation than grasp of a salient idea, the short or "controlled" answer form may be used, limiting students' responses to a sentence, paragraph, or enumeration of several items.

Customarily essay examinations are conducted as timed exercises. Whether a time limitation should be imposed depends upon the purpose and nature of the examination. When creative power is under evaluation, the student should not be penalized for the creative method he employs to secure best results, even if expensive in time. If practical considerations demand the imposition of a time limit, the allowance should be sufficient to enable the student to perform in workmanlike fashion the task before him. Hurrying students through an examination impairs its value as a learning experience and may compromise its effectiveness in evaluation. On the other hand, when speed of operation is itself an element in comparative evaluation—as in testing knowledge of fact, skill, or problem-solving—a common time limit is warranted.

To be useful in measurement an examination should produce a spread in scores indicative of real or probable differences among students. It should be pitched on a sufficiently high level of ability to challenge the efforts of the superior, yet not so high that it discourages the others. A test which few succeed in passing is as faulty a measure of evaluation as one yielding only high scores. Test scores should be accepted realistically for what they are—imperfect indices of achievement in learning. A "zero" score on a test does not indicate that a student knows nothing about the course, only that the test exercises were beyond his reach. If the test is valid, such a student is certainly failing in his work, but the extent of his failure is not indicated.

Much attention has been devoted to improving the reliability of scoring essay examinations. In the opinion of experts:

by observing certain procedures the reader-reliability of essay examinations could be materially increased . . . In general essay examinations appear to be somewhat less reliable than objective examinations, but in the case of an essay examination which is wisely formulated and marked with approved procedures, the reliability is likely to be not materially less than that of the typical teacher-made objective test.[10]

It is well to be forewarned and to make allowance for natural limitations in rating essay examinations. Answers can be easily differentiated as good, bad, or in between; they can be more precisely graded in broad categories of merit such as *A, B, C,* and *D* or by numerical values. Such grading affords a trustworthy basis for comparative ranking of students, for pass or failure, and other gross uses of evaluation.

But except after refined analysis to which they are seldom subjected, answers cannot be rated 69, 78, or 87 in the ordinary sense of these number values. It is a mistake to assume that a teacher, however experienced, can attain this degree of precision in subjective appraisal of a complex product. Number values may be used as grades, but with the understanding that such values are arbitrary representations of assumed categories of merit, and not exact quantities obtainable by counting, measurement, or arithmetical processes. Recognizing the limited significance of such numbers the teacher will be less tempted to employ them in statistical operations, as for

[10] Walter S. Monroe, "Educational Measurement in 1920 and in 1945," *Journal of Educational Research,* 38:338 (January 1945).

example finding the exact average of four essay test scores and using that average as the final course grade. A final course rating of 79 or 81 computed by this method suggests a precise evaluation but is in fact spurious.

The teacher may use any reasonable method of scoring which serves his purpose. Some teachers are satisfied to sort answers into three or four groupings according to merit, later assigning an approximate letter or number grade to each answer. A more careful approach is to break down each answer into its major elements and to rate these elements separately, or to read each answer several times, applying each time a different evaluative criterion, as for example quality of thought, organization, expression. The most conscientious teachers prepare model answers and try to determine the degree to which they are matched by students' responses; it is questionable, however, whether this laborious procedure is justified by the results obtained. The nature of the test influences the manner of scoring: the more general the questions the broader will be the grade categories, whereas more pointed, specific questions and those limiting the range of response will lend themselves to closer scoring.

Objective Examinations.[11] The term "objective" relates primarily to a manner of scoring rather than to a specific type of examination. Objective tests differ not only in form or structure but also in evaluative function, adaptability to subject matter of instruction, and ease or difficulty of construction. The uses of the different forms tend to complement each other as do, in a more general way, essay and objective tests. Unless their function is understood, comparison of the several forms of objective tests is not apt to be meaningful. Objectivity in scoring is itself a matter of degree: in some cases the completion form of objective test may approach the controlled or limited essay in subjectiveness of judging response.

It may be helpful to summarize the uses of objective tests with reference to the different forms. One use is in *taking inventory of achievement over a wide range of learning,* that is, in testing mastery of facts, skills, principles, and their application, separately or in simple association with one another rather than as part of a large con-

---

[11] For the teacher concerned to improve his skill in objective-test preparation, a helpful guide is available in Robert M. W. Travers' *How to Make Achievement Tests* (New York: The Odyssey Press, 1950).

figuration of ideas. Assume that, either for the purpose of grading students or planning instruction, the teacher is desirous of determining how well students have fared in learning the basic elements of a course. For this purpose the essay examination would not be most serviceable: it could not control the kind and amount of specific information which would be forthcoming. The objective test places directly before the student the items to which he must address himself and impels commitment to an answer; the items are obtained as a result of deliberate selection and not by chance; the sampling is larger and distributed over a greater range of learning than in the essay test.

The choice of test form is influenced by the nature of the subject, the scope of learning encompassed, the degree of penetration sought, the amount of time at the teacher's disposal, and his personal preference. Of the common types of objective tests each has qualifications. The true-false test is a broad-range instrument, relatively easy to construct, and economical to administer and to score; it measures recognition and recall of knowledge better than higher or more penetrative forms of learning; when trying to be subtle or discriminating in assessment, it often becomes confusing. The multiple-choice test is a more flexible and appropriate measure of comprehension of principle, relationship of ideas, analysis and interpretation of data, and skill in problem solving, but it is harder to construct and necessarily more limited in range of sampling. The completion test is distinctive in requiring the student to furnish the answer (rather than to react to a statement which may or may not embody the answer) but is more controlled and specific than the essay. It is useful in testing definition of terms and concepts, knowledge of key words and ideas associated with a given context, and ability to share in developing a train of thought. Responses in completion tests may range from one word to several sentences, making the completion test a flexible medium but tricky to construct and sometimes hard to score. Subjects such as mathematics and laboratory science have their own forms of test exercises appropriate for measuring achievement. Whichever type the teacher decides to use, he should be certain that the test content is representative of the major elements of instruction, that items are well-distributed, that each item is significant, that each is clear in meaning, and that answers assumed correct are indisputable.

A more specific use of objective testing, related to the first though not identical, is for *diagnostic work in instruction*. For this purpose the essay examination is in most instances too general and the objective survey test too scattered. The need is for test exercises systematically built around those learnings which the teacher regards as fundamental or critical for continued progress in study, organized if possible in related sequence and graded order of difficulty. Analysis of the results of such testing should disclose common and individual impediments to learning to which reteaching will be directed. Diagnostic testing is not of the same crucial importance in loosely-organized content subjects as in highly-integrated tool, operational, or conceptual studies such as mathematics, language, and the sciences. But they can be used in all subjects with profit to instruction.

Compared with objective tests of general achievement, diagnostic tests are deeper, more intensive, and more finely graduated in difficulty. A true-false test is not as serviceable in this connection as the multiple-choice type, since a diagnostic test must take several soundings of the same or related subject matter at different levels of learning. Variations of the multiple-choice form, especially the "situation analysis" or "case study" type of question are well-adapted to this purpose, and the problem exercise is ideal provided it suits the subject matter. Diagnostic test construction is slow and detailed work, presuming not only the scholar's mastery of the subject but also the sensitive teacher's knowledge of the learning experience of students.

Two additional uses of objective testing may be briefly noted— for *comparative evaluation* and as a *periodic spur to continued effort in learning*. For determining the relative rank of students or measuring the progress of an individual from a given starting point of instruction, the objective test is a more precise tool than the essay. Standardized tests are well suited for the purpose, their established norms or percentile rankings affording easier comparison and their several equivalent forms making possible retesting at intervals. Available standardized tests may not, however, correspond with the teacher's emphasis in instruction and the subject matter included in the course; in which case the teacher must prepare his own objective achievement test. Such a test should be broad in scope and inclusive in sampling, making provision for differences in students' interests and special attainments. It should attempt to measure both what the student can learn in class by being attentive to instruction and what he can learn for himself.

Frequent quizzes foster sustained application to study and intensify effort in learning. With the ordinary-sized class this purpose may be served by a sequence of short objective tests in true-false or completion form which can be administered in a few minutes and scored in half an hour. Such tests need not evoke great power or concentration, nor need the teacher be concerned about niceties of sampling provided the items are fair, clear in meaning, and unequivocal in answer. Preparation of these tests may take a little time, but with slight adaptation they can be used again. Final course evaluation should not be based chiefly on the aggregate scores of such tests but, along with evidences of more substantial achievement, they should be included in the total assessment.

Preparing Objective Test Items. "Those who have not tried to write objective test items to meet exacting standards of quality sometimes fail to appreciate how difficult it is to write such items. . . . Experienced professional item writers regard an output of five to fifteen good achievement test items per day as a satisfactory performance. This contrasts sharply with the widely held notion that any good instructor can produce an acceptable test in an evening or two. . . . The cost of a finally reviewed and approved test item may run from perhaps $3.00 to $10.00, depending on the content involved and the care exercised." [12] Although not presenting the same kind of challenge or difficulty, each test form has its own requirements.

The true-false test has its special snares in items which are significant and clear but the response to which is almost self-evident; in items technically correct but essentially trivial; or in couplings of ideas which through excessive generality and vagueness lead to confusion ("Plato's theory of the state was aristocratic in that it held men to be of unequal intellectual quality and intrinsic worth.").

Those with experience in writing multiple-choice items will testify how often they bog down in the search for suitable alternatives to the correct response. A perfect multiple-choice question is an artistic

[12] Robert L. Ebel in *Educational Measurement, op. cit.,* pp. 185–86.

achievement: it centers on an idea or problem related to an important outcome of instruction; stated alternatives are relevant to the central idea, apparently reasonable, and graduated in proximity to the correct response; the latter is of indisputable authority; the language of the exercise is clear, without word-traps; and the whole is so conceived as to compel discriminating selection of the right answer through use of informed thought, not guesswork, memory, or sheer intelligence.

Completion exercises have been produced by copying a page from a textbook leaving proper-sized gaps at frequent intervals, but this practice leads only to poor testing. The right kind of completion item is either a problem for which the answer is to be supplied; or a statement organically complete except for the words to be inserted ("Archimedes' Principle states that the buoyant force exerted on a body submerged in a fluid is equal to ————"); or a passage so constituted as to orient the student to its background and train of thought, and to require him to furnish missing key words and phrases essential to the context but not betrayed by it. The ratio of *given* to *omitted* words must be high, and possible words to be inserted must not admit of too many variations. The best way to obtain such a passage is to write it. Matching questions have their own subtleties of construction, but their limited usefulness does not warrant investment of great effort in mastering them.

Despite their demands in preparation objective test forms are worth experimenting with. The several basic types which have evolved are not fixed, and in each case variations are possible which may lend themselves satisfactorily to a given purpose. Thus true-false statements may be grouped around a sizeable unit of thought and aimed so as to penetrate that thought with sharp questioning; for example, evidence may be cited relating to an experiment or research and a series of true-false statements drawn requiring the student to identify warrantable conclusions.[13] Ebel lists eight varieties of the multiple-choice form.[14] The problem or situation exercise is adaptable to various kinds of subject matter and forms of question-

[13] See Robert M. W. Travers, *op. cit.*, pp. 46–49. Also specimen items from comprehensive examinations at the University of Chicago, Benjamin Bloom *et al.*, in *The Idea and Practice of General Education*, pp. 303–24.

[14] *Educational Measurement* (E. F. Lindquist, ed.), *op. cit.*, pp. 195–200.

ing. In developing test forms the teacher undertakes an interesting task, and has the opportunity not only to serve better his own purposes in evaluation but also to make a wider professional contribution.

Informal Means of Evaluating Learning. In every course there are outcomes of instruction not measurable by examination which it may be important to assess. A student's acquired interest in the subject, the habits of study he has formed, his attitudes toward his teacher and associates are part of the sum of educational experience not ordinarily revealed by testing; nor are some other intellectual, moral, or esthetic attainments which may be more enduring than the subject matter. It helps the teacher to know what the student is thinking *about* the course as well as *in* the course. For these reasons informal means of evaluation are a necessary complement to the formal testing exercise. Among them are activities which are part of the routine of instruction not consciously identified with evaluation, but their usefulness is enhanced by recognition of their evaluative possibilities.

1. *Observation of students.* No better way exists of obtaining a life portrait of the student than by observing him in action every day. The impression is sustained, cumulative, and often more trustworthy than that gained through intermittent appraisal. Even in large classes exceptionally good and poor students are noticed quickly, and the teacher can help to expedite a clearer perception of each student through a gradual, continuous sorting-out process— making a tentative estimate of each student's worth and correcting the estimate on the basis of further observation. With classes of normal size meeting two or three times weekly, it should be possible by midterm to identify each student personally, thereafter according closer attention to his individual progress and extending, deepening, and refining the formed impression.

It is well to learn students' names quickly, and to approach students as if one meant to know them. To fortify the memory, notes of their performance should be kept, though not to the extent of recording a grade each time the student recites or making a daily memorandum of his activities. Several times during the term each student can be brought under particular scrutiny, and a summary notation made of his accomplishments with special reference to such items as are not indicated by grades. By the end of the term the teacher should have for each student a brief written record supplementing the testimony of test scores and grades. Such a record is usable long after personal recollection of the student has faded and the course grade has lost its meaning.

2. *Teacher's own estimate.* The personal element is seldom absent from evaluation, no matter how impersonal the instruments employed. Even objective tests have to be prepared by someone and test scores require interpretation. The role of judgment is not to displace objective methods but to combine with them in lending significance to the raw data of evaluation. In many instances the teacher's subjective estimate of the student is itself an important datum of evaluation, to be considered along with the more specific results of testing. In all courses outcomes not otherwise measurable can to some extent be estimated subjectively. How well does the student personify in his behavior some of the purposes of the course? To what extent can he be expected to advance these purposes in the future? These are proper considerations to be included in gross accounting of student achievement.

Looking at the record of grades and test scores, we are inclined to defer in our judgment to this more "concrete" evidence, not pausing to question what these scores specifically indicate, how adequate were the exercises on which the scores are based, what sort of learnings are not reflected in the record, or how well the record squares with what we have learned about the student in other ways. Reliance on the impersonal record sometimes results in an unjust evaluation of the student. The teacher's deeply-felt "intuition" about a student may be trusted more confidently, particularly since in evaluation it is better to err on the side of generosity than parsimony.

One learns to judge students as he learns to teach. The good teacher's estimates can be relied upon, the poor teacher's evaluations are worth no more than his instruction. With increasing understanding of students and their needs comes greater competence to teach them properly and to judge them fairly and sympathetically.

3. *Students' reactions to learning.* The judgment of students may be enlisted in evaluating their learning. Although their relative lack of maturity, personal stake in the course, and less certain perception of ulterior goals of instruction may militate against a reliable com-

prehensive evaluation, in some specific respects they are the best judges of what they achieve or fail to achieve through study. Supplementing other evaluative data, information furnished by students may assist in diagnosis of strength and weakness in learning, and the practice of self-evaluation is itself salutary in promoting better learning.

Do students perceive the need for learning the subject and the importance of the major topics of study? Are they satisfied with their progress? How much independent work of voluntary nature do they do? What sort of work? Do they find opportunity to apply their knowledge to life experience? If so, are they successful in making the application? What are their personal potentialities and limitations with regard to the subject? What specific difficulties do they encounter in learning? How could their learning experience be made more effective? These and related questions students are able to answer with some degree of reliability.

One way to obtain this information is by talking to students, informally and—on occasion—formally in a group. It is worth "stealing" a little class time from the pursuit of subject matter to gauge the students' own reactions to learning. In such discussion it is important to avoid being inquisitorial or, on the other hand, too submissive. Students should feel free to speak frankly without fear of reprisal, and the teacher to follow his own judgment in deciding what is acceptable and how much is to be discounted.

A second means of securing this information is through a questionnaire, more impersonal and systematic than the other but less advantageous in other respects. A good questionnaire is hard to produce, it necessarily defines and limits the nature of the response, and does not provide for collective exchange and clarification of comment. Moreover, unless preceded and followed by discussion explaining its purpose and analyzing its results, it constitutes a stilted exercise. If the teacher can find and assemble a questionnaire to fit his purpose, its use will be worthwhile provided students understand and accept it as a feature of a larger process of self-examination.

4. *Students' performance in subsequent pursuits.* Judging the efficacy of learning by its contribution to advanced study or related professional activity is a legitimate enterprise in evaluation, and though findings may come too late to benefit the students originally

involved they can be applied toward improving results in succeeding classes. Few courses of instruction are wholly a preparation for other courses; almost every course has some purpose or claim to students' attention which makes it distinctive. But courses, whether in the same field or a common curriculum, should be so articulated that each contributes to the student's readiness to engage successfully in related higher pursuits. Some courses are more directly preparatory than others, but in all courses success in learning may *in part* be gauged by what the student does or fails to do in more challenging related activity. What the student learns in "freshman composition" should serve all courses involving written expression, and the study of foreign language, mathematics, science, history, and literature should prepare the student to deal more effectively not only with advanced courses in the same fields but with all courses to which their learnings are applicable.

Without sense of inferiority or self-debasement a teacher should invite criticism of students' learning accomplishment from colleagues teaching advanced or related courses. The criticism should be hospitably received and fairly appraised, and if judged sound its implications should be followed. Sometimes an additional emphasis in in instruction, a change in the relative allotment of time to certain topics of study or in the substance of study assignments will effect the desired improvement without need for major revision. Occasionally the criticism will be judged groundless and allowed to go unheeded.

The teacher should be alert to other evidences of student accomplishment in related areas of activity: grades in advanced courses, admission to seminar and "honors" study, achievement in comprehensive examinations, eligibility for awards, and performance in graduate or professional study. Although deductions concerning the direct relationship between such accomplishment and earlier experience in a specific course must be made cautiously, significant evidence will sometimes present itself. An unexpectedly large incidence of failure among one's former students in the next higher course calls for a conference with the teacher and perhaps a review of instructional and learning activities in both courses. Consistent inability to spot students in one's classes who earn later distinction in other special fields of activity is perhaps an indication that the teacher is not getting to know the students as well as he should or looking after their special needs.

5. *Reactions of others.* Judgment of success in learning is made by persons who, through their association with students, have an opportunity to observe their reactions to and use of course experience. In this category are counseling and administrative colleagues, teachers, parents, and among the public particularly those in an employment relationship with former students. There is a tendency for teachers to avoid involving "outsiders" in evaluational activity for fear of prompting undue interference in instruction, and this fear is understandable. Yet by tapping these "outside" sources of information the teacher can obtain additional insights as to how students learn, how well they retain and use their knowledge, what they are satisfied with, and what they complain about.

The teacher need not canvass such information with methodical regularity. Some of it will reach him by chance through a social meeting with parents or alumni, a conference with an administrative or placement officer, and the like. Some contacts should be developed more systematically. The teacher should arrange to meet with students' counselors for an exchange of information regarding their achievements and needs, and whenever necessary to consult medical, psychological, and other specialized advisers. He should also take pains to keep informed of changing processes and requirements in those areas of industry, business, government, or the professions which afford a practical outlet for the product of his instruction.

Evaluation of Teaching. In a book seeking to be of professional assistance to the college teacher, no subject is of greater consequence than evaluation of teaching. In various contexts in these pages references have been made to the objectives and methods of such evaluation. No comprehensive restatement is attempted here, only a short summarization which seems appropriate in concluding the discussion.

The objectives of instructional evaluation are twofold: to provide a progressively better and more satisfying learning experience for students and to promote the personal and professional growth of the teacher. Important and helpful as supervisory evaluation may be, the teacher's own efforts to appraise and improve his performance are more essential. Self-evaluation is more continuous, inclusive, deeper, more directly contributive to the good of students and teacher, and an indispensable condition for achieving instructional mastery.

Requisite to self-evaluation is a clear realization of the goals of instruction in one's courses, formulated primarily as outcomes in behavior—changes in ideals, attitudes, ways of thinking, doing, and living—secondarily as acquisitions of subject matter. Another requirement is some understanding of the teaching process: how students' learning may be guided and fostered through appropriate teaching practice.

The criteria of good teaching are first in the instructional results achieved. Do students learn what they are supposed to learn? How far is their attainment above the normal expectation for such a group? Is the accomplishment of superior students in keeping with their greater potentialities? Do the others rise to the challenge of the subject as far as their capacities permit? A second criterion is in the climate of learning and the attitudes and feelings induced by the learning process. Do the students enjoy their learning experience? Does the climate of instruction recognize and foster intelligence, creativity, and self-expression? Are relations among students and with the teacher friendly, cooperative, and conducive to mutual respect? A third criterion is found in the teacher's reaction to his teaching task. Does he enjoy it? Is he satisfied with his performance? Does teaching this class challenge his interest and abilities?

Self-evaluation is not an episodic occurrence but a steady process conducted without fuss or fanfare and with little or no interference with instruction. It is exemplified by the teacher who quietly goes about the business of preparing his work, teaching his classes, reflecting on results achieved and the manner of their achievement, and resolving in the future to do better. Only occasionally will he interrupt the normal course proceedings by introducing special self-evaluation measures distinguishable as such.

Of the means employable by the teacher to obtain information on which to base self-appraisal, the following may be specifically cited. It will be noted that some have greater utility than others, and that the teacher has a latitude of choice governed by appropriateness to purpose, available time and opportunity, and personal preference.

1. *Demonstrated achievement of students.* A correspondence exists between student achievement in learning and teaching effectiveness. Although the prime responsibility for learning is the student's, the teacher has a share in affecting the outcome. Every measure of student attainment, formal or informal, is to some extent an indirect measure of teaching competence. While in any specific instance quality of learning may not be a true indication of quality of teaching, over a period of time and with different student groups it gains in validity as an index. Unsatisfactory results of even a single examination should prompt the teacher to review the teaching and learning practices which might be responsible.

2. *Students' reactions to learning.* These have a correspondent relationship with instructional effectiveness, being an external and perhaps superficial indication of how well the teacher fares. The fact that students are satisfied with their learning experience does not signify that instruction is intrinsically good or could not be better; it is, however, a favorable sign. On the other hand, student dissatisfaction with learning is a warning signal, and warrants a reappraisal of objectives of instruction, content of study, the learning process itself, and specific instructional procedures through which it is directed.

3. *The human climate of instruction.* As in the previous instance this is more of a general symptom than a specific condition. Instruction may be technically good and productive of satisfactory achievement, yet frigidity or tension between teacher and class may inhibit greater achievement and impair enjoyment of the course. It is the teacher's duty to try to ascertain the cause, analyzing his approach to instruction, attitudes toward students, characteristic methods, routines of class management, as well as the underlying attitudes of students. Apart from what it adds to effectiveness, a congenial relationship with students is one of the compensations of teaching, and should not be lost by default.

4. *Observation and analysis of one's own performance.* The teacher is in the best position to judge his capabilities and accomplishments. He should learn to observe a lesson while teaching it, being conscious of his own performance and the responses of students. Thereafter he should spend some time in reflecting on the lesson, reviewing its events, and trying to decide how it could have

been improved. Especially following a "difficult" period is it desirable to try to pin down the cause of the difficulty and to plan remedial measures for the future. A bad lesson should not be "written off," nor a good one allowed to recede in the memory without reviewing the circumstances which contributed to its success.

5. *Keeping a record or "log" of course events.* In teaching a new course it may be helpful to keep a record of important happenings in instruction. If time permits the record may be in the form of a professional diary; otherwise a weekly log of events. At the end of each month the teacher will have before him sufficient detailed information to check his bearings in the course and plan more intelligently for the future. He will note recurrent problems and possibly decide to discuss them with colleagues. Such a record is also a valuable aid in planning the course for a succeeding term.

6. *Being visited by a colleague and visiting him in turn.* The usefulness of a regular exchange of visits, particularly with experienced colleagues in the same course or teaching department, has been discussed. Such visits should not be approached as formalities or professional good-will calls but as opportunities to gain insight into one's teaching problems by inviting criticism of one's own performance and getting the benefit of observing another's. The exchange of views which follows should be neither so critical as to cause hard feelings nor so insipid as to be worthless. Appreciative of differences in conception of the course and in style of teaching, two colleagues may discuss even sensitive problems of teaching without incurring the risk of offense.

7. *Conference with a supervisor.* On the college level teachers do not ordinarily seek the advice of a professional superior unless they are in difficulty. Yet much can be gained from conferences with senior colleagues on normal or routine problems of instruction. Merely explaining a problem sometimes helps to clarify it, and by virtue of their greater experience supervisors may be helpful with suggestions for instructional improvement. Frequently the teacher will leave with good advice and strengthened confidence in his own accomplishment.

8. *Inviting the judgment of students.* Although the practice of having students engage in evaluation of teaching has become increasingly common, many teachers studiously avoid its use. Except

as institutions occasionally undertake such evaluation on a college-wide basis,[15] there is no compulsion in the matter and the teacher may suit himself. Students inevitably form judgments of their teachers, and knowing them can sometimes be helpful in disclosing unsuspected strength or weakness. Most students are pleased to cooperate and, as a rule, are discriminating, fair, and generous in their estimates.[16]

If a teacher decides to avail himself of this practice it is well to use an anonymously completed questionnaire, constructed in such a way as to direct students' thinking along specific lines of teacher accomplishment. The following items could be listed, using a four-point scale (outstanding, above average, adequate, poor) for intervals in rating:

1. Scholarship
2. Teacher's interest in the subject
3. Clarity of course organization
4. Skill in presentation, explanation, and questioning
5. Stimulation of student interest
6. Opportunity for student participation
7. Relationship with students
8. Quality of assigned work; amount of assigned work
9. Caliber of examinations
10. Fairness in grading

Complex items such as "skill in presentation, explanation, and questioning" could be broken down into lesser components, and provision made for students to insert an independent comment. Use of an explicit questionnaire reduces the chances of resorting to unwarranted flattery or reckless criticism.

[15] See Abraham S. Goodhartz, "Student Attitudes and Opinions relating to Teaching at Brooklyn College," *School and Society,* 68:1–5 (November 20, 1948).

[16] Detailed studies of student surveys of teaching have been carried on at the University of Washington since 1924. Comparison shows student judgment to be consistent and, on the whole, to agree fairly well with ratings of teachers by their colleagues. Undergraduates and graduate students tend strongly to agree in their estimates, and superior students do not rate differently from the others. Students' judgment seems independent of their class standing or grade in the course. The most frequently mentioned fault of teachers is that of "belittling" students. (E. R. Guthrie, *The Evaluation of Teaching,* A Progress Report [The University of Washington, 1954].)

SELECTED BIBLIOGRAPHY

Adkins, Dorothy C. *et al., Construction and Analysis of Achievement Tests.* Washington: Government Printing Office, 1948. 292 pp.

Buros, Oscar K., ed., *The Fourth Mental Measurements Yearbook.* Highland Park, N.J.: The Gryphon Press, 1953. 1163 pp.

Cronkhite, Bernice B., ed., *A Handbook for College Teachers,* Chapter III, "How Shall We Evaluate Teaching?" Cambridge: Harvard University Press, 1950. 267 pp.

Darley, J. G. *et al., The Use of Tests in College.* Washington: American Council on Education, 1947. 82 pp.

Dressel, Paul L., ed., *Evaluation in General Education.* Dubuque, Iowa: Wm C. Brown Co., 1954. 333 pp.

———, and Mayhew, Lewis B., *General Education, Explorations in Evaluation,* Final Report of the Cooperative Study of Evaluation in General Education. Washington: American Council on Education, 1954. 292 pp.

Ebel, Robert L., "Tests and the College Teacher," *Journal of General Education,* 3:157–60, January 1949.

Eckert, Ruth E., *Outcomes of General Education.* Minneapolis: University of Minnesota Press, 1943. 210 pp.

———, "Ways of Evaluating College Teaching," *School and Society,* 71:65–69, February 4, 1950.

———, and Keller, Robert J., *A University Looks at Its Program,* Report of the University of Minnesota, Bureau of Institutional Research, 1942–52. Minneapolis: University of Minnesota Press, 1954. 223 pp.

French, Sidney B., ed., *Accent on Teaching,* Chapter XVIII, "Evaluation as an Aid to Instruction." New York: Harper & Brothers, 1954. 334 pp.

Greene, James E. and Findlay, Warren G., "Evaluation Procedures for the Improvement of Instruction," *Educational Record,* 30:33–44, January 1949.

Guthrie, E. R., "The Evaluation of Teaching," *Educational Record,* 30:109–115, April 1949.

Learned, William S. and Wood, Ben D., *The Student and His Knowledge,* Carnegie Foundation Bulletin No. 29. New York: Carnegie Foundation for the Advancement of Teaching, 1938. 406 pp.

Lindquist, E. F., ed., *Educational Measurement.* Washington: American Council on Education, 1951. 819 pp.

Marshall, Max S., *Two Sides to a Teacher's Desk,* Chapter V, "Evaluation." New York: The Macmillan Company, 1953. 284 pp.

————, "Grading the Teacher," *American Association of University Professors Bulletin*, 38:257–67, May 1952.

Sims, Verner M., "Improving the Measuring Qualities of an Essay Examination," *Journal of Educational Research*, 27:20–31, September 1933.

Smith, Eugene R. and Tyler, Ralph W., *Appraising and Recording Student Progress*. New York: Harper & Brothers, 1942. 550 pp.

Travers, Robert M. W., *How to Make Achievement Tests*. New York: The Odyssey Press, 1950. 180 pp.

University of Chicago Board of Examiners, *Manual of Examination Methods*, Second edition. Chicago: University of Chicago Bookstore, 1937. 177 pp.

Ward, F. Champion *et al.*, *The Idea and Practice of General Education*, Chapter 11, "Examining." Chicago: University of Chicago Press, 1950. 333 pp.

INDEX

A College Program in Action, 147, 166
Abilities of college students, 32–33, 81–82, 87–92, 118–120, 176–179, 183–184, 215
Adkins, Dorothy C., 248
Adolescents, college students as, 120–126; recent studies of, 121; anxiety as a problem of, 122–123; sex adjustment of, 123–124; conflicts with adult society, 124–126
Aesthetic quality in teaching, 171–172
American Association of Collegiate Registrars and Admissions Officers, 80, 83
American Council on Education, 3, 22, 48, 49, 52, 65, 76, 127, 248
American Youth Commission, 64
Aptitude tests and testing, 223, 228
Arbuckle, Dugald S., 48
Ascertaining need for curriculum change, 158–161
Assessing instructional needs of a class, 183–185, 241
Assignment of study, 172–173, 178, 184, 186, 188, 198–199, 206, 214
Association for Higher Education, 64, 76, 166
Audience contact, in the lecture, 195–196, 197
Audio-visual aids, 173, 174, 188, 189, 199–201
Axelrod, Joseph, 203, 216

Barzun, Jacques, 48
Beginning teacher, 24, 56, 59–63
Blackboard, uses of, 207
Blegen, Theodore C., and Cooper, Russell M., 76
Bragdon, Helen D., 48
Buckton, La Verne, 99, 101
Buros, Oscar Krisen, 224, 228, 248

Butler, Judson R., 155
Butts, R. Freeman, 4, 142, 166

Cantor, Nathaniel F., 216
Carman, Harry J., 48, 65, 76
Carmichael, Oliver C., 22, 140, 166
Cattell, J. McKeen, 223
Changes in the college, 5, 9, 28, 45–46, 79–83, 132, 136, 142–145, 158–159
Character formation, as educational goal, 6, 10, 12–14, 21, 117–118; through satisfying experience, 112–113
Citizenship, education for, 7, 12, 17–19, 90, 106–107, 117, 124–126
Class size, 27, 170, 177–178, 186–189, 195, 237, 239
Climate conducive to good teaching, 69–70
Cohen, I. B., and Watson, F. G., 166
Cole, Luella, 126
Cole, Stewart G., 22
Colgate College, program of general education, 154–155
College curriculum, as educational instrument, 3, 30, 129–130, 147; practical elements in, 6–8, 20, 93; scope of, 20, 113, 132; changes in, 80, 132, 146–156; variation in, 105–106, 132, 135, 139; teacher's concern with, 130–131; general attributes of, 131–135; strengths and weaknesses of, 135–141; developments of, 142–145; techniques of revising, 156–165; evaluating the, 219, 220, 221
College enrollments, 10, 11, 32, 64, 79–80, 88
College of General Education, Boston University, 155–156

251

College of the University of Chicago, program of general education, 149–151

College teacher's responsibilities, 24–48; growth of, 27–29; as course instructor, 29–34; as scholar, 34–38; as counselor, 38–42; as faculty member, 42–45; as citizen, 45–48; information concerning, 58; attitude toward, 60–61

Columbia College, program of general education, 147–149

Comprehensive examinations, 141, 149, 165, 227, 228

Comprehensiveness of curriculum offerings, 131–132. *See also* College curriculum

Conant, James B., 22

Concentration of studies, principle of, 133

Corporate nature of the college, 28, 67

Council of State Governments, 79, 84, 96, 126

Counseling, *see* Personnel work in college teaching

Course outline, use of, 198, 202

Cowley, William H., 27, 48, 110

Craftsmanship in teaching, 168–169, 193

Crawford, A. B., and Burnham, P. S., 126

Creative use of teaching method, 173–174

"Credit" system, weakness of, 141

Cronkhite, Bernice B., 3, 48, 56, 194, 216, 248

Cultivation of interests, as a goal of instruction, 16–17, 96–97, 118

Cultural and scholarly interests of college students, 96–97

Curriculum making, teacher's responsibilities for, 24, 28, 44, 59, 130–131; techniques of, 156–165

Dale, Edgar, 199, 216

Darley, J. G., 248

de Kiefer, Robert, and Cochran, L. W., 216

Democracy, as a personal creed, 116

Demonstration technique, 170, 173, 175, 188, 200, 206

Dennison, C. P., 48

Dewey, John, 64, 109

Diagnosis of students' disabilities in learning, *see* Remedial teaching

Discussion technique, 163, 170, 173, 185, 188, 196, 197, 203–210, 213

Disparity among college courses, 133

Donham, Wallace B., 22

Dressel, Paul L., 221, 248

Dressel, Paul L. and Mayhew, Lewis B., 221, 226, 248

Early American college curriculum, 142–145

Ebel, Robert L., 237, 248

Eckert, Ruth E., 76, 248

Eckert, Ruth E. and Keller, Robert J., 227, 248

Economic competence, as an objective of education, 19–21

Economy in teaching, 194, 206

Educated person, conception of, 21

Education, as development of the person, 2, 21, 3, 40, 57, 118; liberal, 3, 6–8, 19–21, 136, 174–176; and traditional values, 4, 8–10; and mental discipline, 5–6, 15–16, 110–112; goals of, 12–22, 138–139, 157–158, 174–176; and health, 13–14, 124; character, 14–15, 125–126; and the cultivation of interests, 16–17; civic, 17–19, 116; as a quantity of behavior, 26–27; opportunities for, 86–87; in the high school, 87–92; and individual differences, 102–109, 135–136, 170, 177–178; interests and effort in, 112; general, 146–156; evaluation in, 218–226

Educational Policies Commission, 65

Eisenhart, Luther P., 166, 216

Election of studies, principle of, 133–134, 136–137, 144–145

Equality of opportunity for higher education, 86–87

Evaluating, curriculum, 164–165, 219, 226; students' achievement, 172, 189, 203, 211, 222–226, 228–243, 245; instruction, 201–202, 205–206, 221–222, 229, 243–247

Evaluation, past practices and current conceptions in, 218–222; and meas-

ical examination of, 18; personal, in teaching, 30; ways of evaluating, 222

Improving instruction, 31–34, 60–63, 63–65, 69–74

Individual differences, among students, 10, 32, 33, 57, 78, 81, 83–84, 87–88, 102–109, 177–178, 184; among teachers, 35–36, 42, 170, 174, 181–183, 185; in professional growth of teachers, 51–52

Individuality and difference, 104–109

Individualizing instruction, 176–179, 183–186, 188, 199, 203, 213, 214

In-service training, 61, 64, 72–74, 213

Institutional self-studies, 28, 221, 227

Instructional "log," use of, 165, 246

Integration of studies, 27, 139, 140, 147, 155

Intellectual independence, as a goal of instruction, 15–16, 111; in learning, 116–118, 210, 211, 214

Intelligence, of college entrants, 87–88; and success in college, 99–100; differences in, 103, 106; higher levels of, 118–120; measurement of, 223, 226

Internal regulation of programs of study, 134–135, 138, 141

Jones, Howard Mumford, 22

Jordan, David Starr, 27, 166

Judd, Charles H., 102, 120, 127

Kallen, Horace M., 22

Katz, D., and Allport, F. H., 93, 127

Kelly, Fred J., 52, 56, 76

Kingsley, Howard L., 127

Klapper, Paul, 52, 54, 76

Kuhlen, Raymond G., 102, 123, 127

Laboratory instruction, 173, 210–213

Laboratory manual, uses of, 212

Landis, Paul H., 127

Large vs. small group instruction, 162, 177–178, 186–189, 211

Learned, Henry S., and Wood, Ben, 141, 248

Learning, conditions of, 30, 69, 176–181; knowledge of learning process,

56–57, 109–110; and mental discipline, 110–112; satisfactions in, 112–114, 122–123; and experience, 114–116, 179, 211; independence in, 116–118, 183, 185; levels of, 118–120, 164, 177; evaluation of, 218, 220, 222, 223, 224–226, 228–243

Lecture, 27, 114, 163, 170, 173, 174, 177, 178, 185, 188, 189, 190, 194–202, 213

Lesson organization, 181, 196–197, 206

Levels of teaching, 118–120, 177, 183–186, 194, 210

Levels of thinking and learning, 118–120, 164, 177, 194

Liberal education, as an aim, 3; and practical values, 6–8; and ethical living, 14–15; as cultivation of interests, 16–17; and economic competence, 19–21; balance in, 138, 140; as a factor in teaching method, 174–176

Lindquist, E. F., 230, 238, 248

Livingstone, Sir Richard W., 22

Lloyd-Jones, Esther, 38, 39

Lorge, Irving, 109

Lynd, Helen M., 217

McGrath, Earl J., 166

Marshall, Max S., 15, 194, 217, 248

Measurement, of intelligence, 103, 222; in education, 222–224. *See also* Evaluation

Meland, Bernard E., 127

Mental discipline, 5–6, 7, 15, 110–112, 132, 144

Methods of teaching, 58, 109, 114–116, 118, 138–139, 163, 164, 168–192

Millett, Fred B., 166, 217

Mimeographed materials, uses of, in instruction, 207–208

Monroe, Walter S., 220, 224, 233

Morse, H. T., 146, 166

Motivation of study, need for, 112–114, 179

Multiplicity of curriculum offerings, 132–133, 137–138, 139

Valentine, P. F., 146, 167, 217
Veterans as students, 85
Visiting classes, *see* Observation of teaching
Vocational, orientation of students, 19–20; choices of students, 95–96

Ward, F. Champion, 23, 167, 217, 249
Warner, W. Lloyd, Havighurst, Robert J., and Loeb, Martin B., 84, 128

Weaver, Gilbert C., and Bollinger, Elroy W., 217
Whitehead, Alfred N., 23, 64, 109
Wilson, Logan, 49, 54, 77
Woodburne, Lloyd S., 77
Woody, Thomas, 23
Work schedules of teachers, 71–72
Workshop techniques, *see* Laboratory work
Wrightstone, J. Wayne, 220